SOCIO-ECONOMIC CONDITIONS IN DROUGHT-PRONE AREAS

By the Same Author

Agricultural Prices and Development with Stability, 1973.

Impact of Drought on Rural Life (Co-author), 1975.

Socialist Agricultural Price Policy, 1979.

Marketable Surplus and Market Dependence in a Mlllet Region, 1980.

Farmers' Movements in India (under publication).

SOCIO-ECONOMIC CONDITIONS IN DROUGHT-PRONE AREAS

A Bench-mark Study of Drought Districts in Andhra Pradesh, Karnataka and Tamil Nadu

M.V. NADKARNI

Assisted by

R.S. DESHPANDE, M. NAGESHWARA RAO AND CHARLES NELSON

Foreword by

G.V.K. RAO

CONCEPT PUBLISHING COMPANY, NEW DELHI

This study was sponsored by the Central Water Commission, Government of India.

First Published 1985

Published by

Naurang Rai
Concept Publishing Company
H-13, Bali Nagar
NEW DELHI-110015 (India)

Printed in India by

Hans Raj Gupta & Sons
Anand Parbat
NEW DELHI-110005

Foreword

DROUGHT-PRONE areas account for about two-thirds of our country, and have a much greater proportion of the poor than other areas. They are relatively backward, and were left out of the benefits of the Green Revolution at least in its initial phases. They used to attract attention only when famines struck, when concessions were extended in terms of remission of revenue, and postponement of loan recoveries. Obviously, they needed far more help on a durable basis. When it was realised that regional disparities widened in the wake of the Green Revolution and the problem of poverty persisted, programmes were launched in the early seventies to enable drought-prone areas to overcome the disadvantages of their environment. Now almost every district in such areas is covered by these programmes which promote irrigation, soil and water conservation, animal husbandry and other activities. HYVs suitable for adoption in such regions have also been introduced, thus diminishing the disparities in agricultural development.

Even before the Drought-prone Area Programmes were launched, planned steps had been taken to extend irrigation to these areas on a massive scale. Irrigation will have to continue to play the role of helping such areas overcoming their problems, since it can stimulate not only agricultural production, but also animal husbandry and industrialisation. There are schemes now, though in a blue print stage, to transfer water on a massive scale to needy areas with the hope that once these areas have adequate irrigation, it will change their face and launch them on a course of prosperity. Though such expectations about irrigation are not baseless, it is nevertheless necessary to have a critical look at what irrigation has already done, what shortcomings have been experienced and compare its impact with other strategies of enabling drought-prone areas to overcome their uncertain dependence on agriculture and their consequent poverty. Though the role of irrigation cannot be denied, the strategy of rural development has to consist of an optimal mix of strategies instead of disproportionately relying only on irrigation.

Professor Nadkarni has done well to exploit the opportunity of making a benchmark study to give a comparative appraisal of three major strategies of rural development in drought-prone areas—irrigation, animal husbandry and rural industry. His findings may not be very palatable to irrigation enthusiasts, but should nevertheless compel their attention. He is not against irrigation as such, but only against ill-managed extension of irrigation, and a disproportionate reliance on it to the exclusion of other strategies like rural industries which seem to have even a better impact on transforming the rural economy. Of the three strategies, animal husbandry by itself had the lowest impact, and had a chance of succeeding well only where irrigation and rural industry were present. Prof. Nadkarni has identified several backlash effects or opportunity costs of irrigation, which bring down the overall impact of irrigation. No irrigation administrator can afford to ignore these negative effects, if irrigation has to make an optimal impact.

But even to make rural industries play their effective role as instruments of rural development, Prof. Nadkarni has made it clear that they have to make inroads into the larger economy. But this is not possible unless they are enabled to overcome the unfair competition from large industries in the monopoly sector.

It is interesting to find that Prof. Nadkarni has ingeniously used the method of cross section comparison of villages at different levels of development and environmental conditions, to probe into the dynamics of the process of overcoming drought-proneness and poverty. He has explained how the phenomenon of poverty and inequality undergoes qualitative changes in this process, and how even when absolute poverty is reduced, inequality increases. He has discussed this process in terms of three different theoretical perspectives on regional underdevelopment, and shows how they become relevant in different situations, though no single theory can be universally valid in all places, situations and stages of development. He shows how commercialisation of agriculture—often decried as exploitative—has nevertheless played a progressive role, associated as it was with increasing the total produce per household and its incomes. But the same process does not solve the problems of poverty fully, and in fact increases inequality, which seems inherent in capitalist and market-based development.

I am happy that Prof. Nadkarni has continued his interest in the problems of drought-prone areas in addition to his other interests. He has already contributed to a better understanding in this field through his earlier work on the impact of droughts and on growth and instability in agriculture. With this study, he has further taken an important stride in this field. I am glad that this was made possible by the sponsorship and encouragement of the Central Water Commission.

Dr. M.V. Nadkarni is one of our competent and perceptive observers of the rural scene. Development is a difficult process, and any study which analyses its various changing facets would be most welcome. I do hope that this productive study would be of use to the CWC and also to planners at the Centre and in the states. I wish this book a good reception which it well deserves.

Bangalore
9th January 1985

G.V.K. RAO

Preface

WHEN the Central Water Commission (CWC) approached our Institute in 1978 with a request to take up a socio-economic survey of drought-prone areas in the three southern states, Professor V.K.R.V. Rao kindly asked me to undertake it. Both Prof. Rao and Mr. K.S.S. Murthy of CWC encouraged me to cover the three states in a single project, which was academically rewarding as it gave a rich kaleidoscope of spatial contrasts in levels of development.

This is more than a mere bench mark study. It is an investigation into how and to what extent drought-proneness affects socio-economic-conditions and levels of development, how they are altered by the introduction of irrigation and other strategies of rural development like introduction of animal husbandry and industry. The study tries to probe into factors that lie behind differential levels of development and into some of the backlash effects of the development process. It attempts an assessment of how conditions of poverty and inequality, rural structures and quality of rural life are altered in the process of development. This is done through the analysis of both secondary data from official sources and primary data collected by us in 15 villages. The reference period for primary data is 1978-79, which was weather-wise a normal year.

The report on this project was cyclostyled and released in two volumes, one in early 1982 and the next in mid-1982. It was circulated by the CWC among several research institutes, the Planning Commission, and several government departments, most of whom kindly sent their critical comments and suggestions. Subsequently some of the important findings of the study were published in the *Economic and Political Weekly*, and the *Business Standard*.

In a meeting of the Advisory Committee of the project in

January 1984, the CWC encouraged me to prepare a press copy for publication of the study, taking into account comments received. Though the revision was expected to be marginal and completed early, regrettably it took longer. Apart from my other preoccupations, I had to have a thorough look at the manuscript before its publication, using updated secondary data, including a few more aspects not properly attended to earlier, and making the study more compact and readable to be of interest to academic colleagues, students and policy makers in general. In the process, detailed tables had to be deleted which would have consumed a lot of space in the book. In any case these were made available to the CWC earlier.

I have benefited from many in preparing this study. A preliminary meeting before starting the project, chaired by Prof. Y.K. Alagh and attended among others by Prof. R. Radhakrishna was helpful in planning the subsequent work. Both Prof. L.S. Venkataramanan and Prof. V.M. Rao were members of the Advisory Committee on behalf of our Institute, whose advice and encouragement were valuable in completing the project. Discussions with Mr. K.S.S. Murthy and Mr. Gokhul Prasad of CWC were also very useful at various stages and improved my understanding of drought-prone areas. Shri A. R.S. Murthy and Shri K.S. Ayodhyanath of CWC took the trouble of accompanying us to several villages during our preliminary visits and helped us in various ways. The District Statistical Offices at Anantapur, Bijapur and Coimbatore, and offices of the Assistant Director of Industries and also of Agriculture, DPAP, and local Co-operative Societies were a great help in collecting data regarding respective districts.

The project involved a good deal of hardwork on the part of several colleagues. The names of those who worked as project staff are presented below separately. The services of Mr. Pralay Kumar Ghosh were available in an early phase of the project, covering a part of the Census Survey of Villages. Mr. R.S. Deshpande helped in collecting detailed secondary data of all the districts in the three states, updating it and processing it even after the project was over. He helped in the regression analysis of some of the primary data as well. Mr. M. Nageshwara Rao and Mr. Charles Nelson helped in supervising the day-to-day field work and subsequent tabulation of the primary data. They also helped in collecting official data of the three selected districts and made field notes, which were useful in preparing district and village profiles. The Field Investigators-cum-Technical Assistants canvassed household schedules and subsequently assisted in tabulation of data. They held postgraduate degrees in economics and sociology—mostly in economics, and did their job competently and conscientiously. The field notes containing their impressions and experiences were also of help, apart from my own, in preparing district and village profiles. Among others, I should particularly mention Messrs P. Thippaiah, K. Muthayan and Appanna Reddy who were keen observers. Some of the remaining tabulations were completed by Mr. N. Narasimha. Messrs G.S. Sastry and Johnson Samuel were of assistance in occasional calculations.

Mr. B.G. Kulkarni prepared the maps and the chart presented here, enhancing the utility of the study. Mrs. Padmasini Sridhar gave ever smiling and prompt service in getting some of the statistical analysis done through the Institute's microprocessor.

Mrs. G.T. Rajeswari typed the manuscript diligently, tolerating my handwriting. Her services were useful both while preparing the earlier version in mimeo form and the press copy.

I am sincerely grateful to all of the above, particularly to the Central Water Commission for the opportunity they gave, and to all the Members of the Advisory Committee and other participants in its meetings who contributed to the success of this project. Neither the Commission nor the Advisory Committee is responsible for the views expressed here, for the analysis and interpretation of the data, and for errors of omission and commission.

I thought of exploiting the goodness of Dr. G.V.K. Rao and also his rich practical experience in agricultural development and planning, by requesting him to write a foreword to this book. I am indebted to him for kindly agreeing to it. I also thank my Publishers for their consent to bring out this book promptly.

Though a critical analysis of the impact of irrigation is made in the study, it is not the intention of the study to deny its role in overcoming drought-proneness. The intention is only to identify shortcomings so that they can be overcome. There is no reason for us to be prejudiced against irrigation.

Institute for Social
and Economic Change
Bangalore 560072

M.V. NADKARNI

2 January 1985

Advisory Committee

At the Preparatory Stage

(For this and a similar other CWC Project, it met at ISEC in April 1978, before the Project was started)

Chairman—Prof Yoginder K Alagh
Other Members, and some of the
Participants : Mr K S S Murthy of CWC
Prof K K Subramaniam
Prof R Radhakrishna
Mr C S Seshadri, then Director, ISEC
Prof V M Rao
Prof M V Nadkarni

Advisory Committee of the Project

(after the project was started)

Chairman : Member, Central Water Commission (WR) Mr M N Venkatesan, during the first meeting in February 1980;
Mr H S Krishnaswamy, during the second meeting in January 1984

Other Members : Joint Advisor (I & CAD) Planning Commission
(Mr K M Maheshwari, during the first meeting)
Director, Institute for Social and Economic Change, Bangalore
(Prof L S Venkataramanan, during both the meetings)

Mr Gokhul Prasad, CWC (during the first meeeting)
Prof V M Rao, ISEC, Bangalore (both meetings)
Prof M V Nadkarni

Some of the other participants : Mr D P Sehgal, CWC (during the second meeting)
Mr K K Kathuria, CWC (during the second meeting)

Project Staff

Hon. Project Director and Principal Investigator :
Dr. M V Nadkarni, Professor, ISEC

Project Appointments

(A) *Research Analysts*

Mr R S Deshpande (now, Assistant Professor, ISEC)
Mr P K Ghosh (for 6 months only)
Mr M Nageshwara Rao
(now, Assistant Professor, ISEC)
Mr Charles Nelson

(B) *Field Investigator-cum-Technical Assistant*

Mr A Mohan Amarnath
Mr C Annadurai
Mr A Devanbu
Mr T Govindaiah
Mr D D Jagannath Rao
Mr S Krishnappa
Mr K Muthayan
Mr K N B Raghavesh
Mr M S Raghukumar
Mr Appanna Reddy
Mr Jagan Mohan Reddy
Mr P Thippaiah

Contents

Foreword v
Preface ix
Advisory Committee xiii
Project Staff xv
List of Tables xviii
List of Maps and Figure xx

1. Introduction 1
2. Dimensions of Drought-prone Environment 23
3. Profiles of the Selected Districts 52
4. Profiles of the Selected Villages 76
5. Structure of Rural Economy and Households 101
6. Quality of Rural Life 129
7. Commercialisation of Agriculture 146
8. Impact of Irrigation on output, Cost and income from Agriculture 170
9. Total Income of Households : Focus on Poverty and Inequality vis-a-vis Levels of Development 197
10. Overcoming Drought-proneness and Poverty: A Conclusion 218

Index 232

List of Tables

1.1 Selected Villages, their Location and Irrigation and Diversification Status **12**

1.2 Total Rural Households as per Census Survey, Sample Size in Number, and Weights Used **15**

2.1 Demographic and Socio-Economic Features of Drought-prone (DP) and non-drought-prone (NDP) districts **26**

2.2 Indicators of Agrarian Structure and Development of DP vis-a-vis NDP Districts **32**

2.3 Distribution of Districts (number) according to Growth Rates per Annum in Production and Yield of Foodgrains during 1956-57 to 1980-81 **39**

2.4 Distribution of Districts (number) according to Instability in Production and Yield of Foodgrains during 1956-57 to 1980-81 **41**

4.1 Village Particulars from Population Census **100**

5.1 Occupational Structure: Village Typewise **105**

5.2 Average Proportions of Peasant Castes, Economically Backward Castes and Scheduled Caste and Tribe Households among Households Categories **112**

5.3 Loans Outstanding and their Sources **114**

5.4 Concentration Ratios (Gini Co-efficients) for Operated Land **119**

5.5 Features of Land Distribution **120**

6.1 A Few Dimensions of Rural Quality of Life across Village Types **134**

7.1 Village Price Level Relative to Corresponding District Averages for farm produce **152**

7.2 Proportion of Sales to Farm Produce and Village Ranking accordingly **15S**

8.1 Features of Land Use **173**

8.2 Output, Cost and Income from Cultivation per Hectare of Gross Sown Area **181**

8.3 Impact at Different Levels of Irrigation **186**
8.4 Output and Income from Agriculture per cultivating household **188**
9.1 Total Income per Household by Main Categories and village Types, and Poverty **202**
9.2 The Poor and the Poorest two Household Categories Relative to the Richest **207**
9.3 Co-efficient of Variation in Income of Households of different Categories within Villages **211**

Appendix Tables

Chapter : 2

I. Socio-Economic and other Indicators—for the selected districts and state averages **44**
II. Growth in Foodgrains Production and Yields : District-wise **46**

Chapter : 5

Regression Equations **126**

Chapter : 6

Regression Equations **142**

Chapter : 7

Gross Value of Agricultural Output and its Sale **164**

Chapter : 8

Cost of Cultivation and Income from Agriculture **190**

Chapter : 9

I. Regression Equations **214**
II. Total Income per Household Villagewise and household Categorywise **215**

List of Maps and Figure

Maps :

1. Drought-prone areas in Karnataka, Andhra Pradesh and Tamil Nadu **22**
2. Anantapur district 49
3. Bijapur district **50**
4. Coimbatore district **51**

Fig :

Response of output and costs per hectare to level of irrigation **196**

1

INTRODUCTION

OBJECTIVES AND SCOPE

An interesting feature of the Indian scene is that in spite of generally low levels of income and quality of life, there are rich contrasts in socio-economic conditions and in levels of development and poverty across regions. Often these contrasts can be as glaring as between developed and under-developed countries. This is so even among drought-prone areas. This study is an investigation into how and to what extent drought-proneness affects socio-economic conditions and levels of development, and how they are altered by the introduction of irrigation, and other strategies of rural development like animal husbandry and rural industry. The study also attempts to probe into the factors that lie behind differential levels of development and see whether higher levels of development have contributed towards lowering poverty and inequality and improving socio-economic conditions of particularly the rural poor.

Irrigation has long been treated as the most important and effective strategy for the development of a region, particularly if it is drought-prone. It enables farmers to raise high value crops, adopt double cropping and achieve higher productivity. As a result, it could increase employment and income in agriculture. By making more water and fodder available, it could stimulate animal husbandry. If irrigation is long established in the region, it could promote diversification of the economy by stimulating industrial development. This is because, as investible surpluses are generated in agriculture, they seek opportunities of making profits outside agriculture also. Production of sugarcane, cotton and so on also make it possible to start industries for processing them. Irrigation in course of time could improve the general quality of rural life and socio-economic conditions in general.

This was intended to be a bench mark study by the Central Water Commission who sponsored it. Their purpose was to see what impact inter-basin transfer of massive amounts of water (if and when it takes place) could make on the regional economy and on rural households, by comparing pre-transfer and post-transfer situations. It is not the objective of this study to examine the case for such a transfer, nor to make any social cost-benefit analysis of the proposed project. This was not the task assigned to us. Water after all is a vital need for human existence and for all economic activity. Even apart from the needs of agriculture, scarcity of drinking water could make regional development an impossible dream. The case for inter-basin transfer of water to promote regional economy could, therefore, be a serious one. Even if irrigation has not achieved expected results, the case for inter-basin transfer of water is not thereby necessarily weakened. Our findings, therefore, should not be taken as reflections on the project.

A bench mark study has certain limitations in being used for making comparisons between 'before' and 'after' project situations. So many other factors may have entered the picture in the meanwhile that all the differences between the two situations cannot be attributed to the project alone. There could be other unforeseen difficulties in comparability. Moreover, the time, effort and resources invested in a bench mark study would not be worthwhile, if its utility were to be seen only after several years when a repeat study is undertaken. Both the sponsor and the author, therefore, thought that this should be more than a bench mark study, since a study of such magnitude has the potential enough to derive insights from variations within the cross section comprising the study area. The impact of irrigation itself could be studied on income and other factors determining levels of development through such a cross section comparison. It also gave an opportunity to study why the impact of irrigation was what it was, and also compare it with other strategies of rural development like animal husbandry and rural industries. After all, it may not be possible to provide irrigation to all regions or all villages, but drought-prone areas could and should have other means of development as well.

But the study is not limited to assessing the impact of some of these strategies of rural development including irrigation. As stated in the opening paragraph, we are interested in understanding regional variations in socio-economic conditions and levels of development. Even the success of irrigation and other strategies of development are conditioned by several factors—environmental, institutional and historical, interacting with each other. To begin with, it would be useful to briefly review a few theoretical perceptions which are meaningful in understanding regional variations.

First of all we have what is often known as the Positivist Theory which regards objective factors outside human institutional framework as determining our well-being, or the development of a region. In fact, even if some factors are exogenous to man, it is the ingenuity with which he adapts himself to them or uses them that determines his well-being. Climate has often been assigned a crucial role in explaining at least regional variations, and also temporal variations within a given region in poverty and levels of development. Ahluwalia has explained variations in the levels of poverty—though not the average level itself—in terms of fluctuations in agricultural production and occurrence of droughts.[1] Similarly the notion that regions having a high frequency of droughts are also the regions which are the most backward and have high concentration of poverty is also quite widely held. Such an approach to studying regional variations often tends to over-emphasise the role of resource potential of regions. Though we cannot altogether rule out the role of climate, rainfall, availability of irrigation, or lack of resources as possible factors behind poverty, it cannot obviously be a general or universal explanation. We intend to test how far this is so, instead of taking it for granted as obvious.

If paucity of natural resources as *the* determinant factor or as a general theory of backwardness were to be obviously correct, we would find it difficult to explain the prosperity of quite a few nations like Japan which are resource-poor and yet have an advanced standard of living. Similarly, it would be difficult to explain why several resource-rich nations in Africa and Latin America are poor. Even within India, we may recall that quite a few of what today are called as backward and drought-prone regions, were seats of prosperous kingdoms and empires only a few centuries ago. Today's backward and drought-prone district of Bijapur in Karnataka once upon a time was the seat of the famous kingdoms of the Badami Chalukyas and later of the Adil-Shahs. Similarly, the prosperous and mighty Vijayanagara empire not only had its capital in today's drought-prone district of Bellary, the bulk of the empire was in what is identified as drought-prone area today. This has been the case in other parts of India too. Bihar, one of the most backward of India's states today had mighty and prosperous empires in the past. Its backwardness even today, cannot be attributed to resource scarcity.

At the other end, we have the Dependency Theory which regards underdevelopment of 'peripheral' regions as a counterpart process of capitalist development of 'metropolitan' or 'centre' regions. What holds in the international economic relations in the capitalist world at large, holds good within a country too, according to this theory.[2] The poverty of peripheral regions is due to their resources being exploited to the advantage of metropolitan or centre regions, rather than due to an underutilisation or lack of resources in the former. Hence, commercialisation of a peripheral region opens it up for exploitation by other regions. This approach is applied to explaining urban-rural differences too, whereby rural underdevelopment is a part of the process of metropolitan or urban development.[3] Commercialisation of agriculture and of rural areas would appear here as an essentially immiserising process, tending to increase rural poverty. While we cannot altogether rule out the validity of this approach in quite a few regions such as in Latin America and Africa, we are hesitant to accept it as general explanation or a grand theory of all regional variations. Perhaps it is futile to search for such a theory. We would rather like to examine empirical evidence and see if indeed commercialisation of agriculture or of villages has indeed been positively associated with lower levels of development and high levels of poverty and if not, why it is so.

In terms of a historical perspective, Krishna Bharadwaj has made an interesting analysis of regional (inter-state) variations in agricultural and industrial development in India.[4] Our colonial past has cast a shadow on the post-Independence development too. She has argued that land settlement patterns had differed from region to region and in regions where Zamindari and subinfeudation dominated, agricultural investment and growth were stunted and, usury and unproductive consumption and equally unproductive commerce dominated. It is well-known that though Zamindari was abolished, landlordism continued in these areas, tenants being converted to the status of labourers without tenancy rights through 'voluntary surrender' by tenants or resumption of land by landlords for 'personal cultivation'. Thus semi-feudalism dominated these areas.

On the other hand, though there was exploitation and subleasing even in Ryotwari areas, there was more direct connection between producers and the state, a better recognition of tenancy rights, and in some of these regions, land transfers from farmers to money lenders and traders were also restricted, as pointed out by Bharadwaj. This made productive investment in agriculture more attractive and ushered in capitalist development in agriculture. These regions also received greater attention even in government investment in agriculture. Public sector irrigation cannot be the only factor behind better agricultural performance, because conditions were favourable for even private investment in irrigation here. On the other hand, the introduction of government irrigation in semi-feudal regions did not produce the desired impact and led to underutilisation of irrigation potential.[5]

Punjab, Haryana, Gujarat and the southern states of Andhra Pradesh, Karnataka and Tamil Nadu—which form the study area here—had a dominantly Ryotwari land settlement. These states fared better in agricultural performance than Bihar, West Bengal, Assam and such other areas where Zamindari and feudalism prevailed. As a result, the extent of poverty was more in the latter states, whereas Ryotwari areas had a *relatively* better well-being in terms of per capita consumption and income. The better agricultural performance and lower poverty also created conditions for the survival of rural and indigenous industries including handlooms under colonial rule, and later supported industrialisation efforts. Though industries were set up in some of the centres within the erstwhile Zamindari areas, industrialisation was confined to metropolitan centres, and did not make an impact in the interior.

Bharadwaj has made a very useful contribution by applying the Marxian historical approach to the understanding of regional differentiation, which seems to be more relevant than the Dependency Theory of capitalist underdevelopment in studying the backwardness of states like Bihar. Her approach can throw insights into situations which differ widely in institutional set-up and are at different historical stages of development. We find, however, that even within areas which by and large were all under Ryotwari settlement, there have been wide variations in the levels of development. This has been so atleast in our study area of the three Southern states. This would suggest that there can be no one theory alone for explaining regional differences. It is not intended here to imply that theorising is futile, but only to suggest that factors of development and underdevelopment could differ from region to region, and different situations may well demand different theories to understand them. The various theoretical perspectives are, however, helpful for the hypotheses they suggest which can be tested in different situations.

In studying what holds back the development of drought-prone areas, it is important to remember that it is not merely the level of rainfall but the impact of uncertainty therein on attitudes and institutional factors and capacity for adjustment to droughts, that are crucial. In a study to assess differences in risk attitudes of different types of farmers in semi-arid tracts, Binswanger found that higher levels of risks in such tracts led to under-investment in agriculture relative to the expected profit maximising levels. He also found 'a slight negative association between risk aversion and land holding size', suggesting that risk aversion would decline with increasing farm size.[6] Had he standardised holdings for irrigation differentials, he would have perhaps found even stronger negative association, and not merely a slight one. Droughts also deplete the resources of farmers involving the sale of even productive assets like bullocks to such an extent that even during a normal year they are short of productive resources, thus affecting their production potential in the long run.[7]

This has naturally a depressing impact and could well be one of the factors behind low productivity and lower levels of investment in drought-prone areas. But it has an impact on institutional setting, in the form of size of holdings being larger in such areas. The larger holdings have a greater capacity to take risks and survive droughts, and can therefore, thrive better. The large holdings need not necessarily have a lack of investible surplus and risk aversion. Since the bulk of land is concentrated in their lands, agricultural growth need not necessarily be inhibited due to risk aversion. But presence of investible surplus need not necessarily lead to investment; it could also lead to unproductive and ostentatious consumption and to socially pernicious investment as in usury. The presence of a large number of farmers without viable holdings and agricultural labour with little opportunity of remunerative employment, creates favourable conditions for usury and unfavourable conditions for rural industries to thrive. Endemic poverty cannot support such industry.

It is, therefore, one of the objectives to see how the institutional structure of agriculture as well as growth performance differs as between drought-prone and nondrought-prone regions. This could indirectly throw some light on whether attitudes to risk play an important role in inhibiting the development of drought-prone areas. We shall also see whether and how far differences between drought-prone and other regions in respect of key socio-economic and agricultural indicators are significant and whether they have narrowed in the course of economic development in general.

Though our study covers three states—Andhra Pradesh, Karnataka and Tamil Nadu, for analytical purposes they are often treated together while analysing both inter-district and the inter-village variations. Pooling the data together for all the three states has given not only more observations for statistically dependable analysis but also wider contrasts for the purpose of our study. Moreover, not only the three states but even the drought-prone zones therein are also contiguous. However, we have not altogether ignored inter-state differences. Wherever necessary, state-wise differences and inter-district differences within the states have been presented. It would however be misleading to assume for policy and planning purposes, that the experience and estimates of respective states alone are relevant for the concerned states. It is our belief that there is more to learn from the analysis of drought-prone areas as a whole, irrespective of whether they are in one's own state or in neighbouring states.

DATA BASE, STUDY AREA AND SURVEY PROCEDURE

Our study is based both on secondary and primary data. In the next chapter, variations in important socio-economic and agricultural indicators are studied taking districts as units of observation. These inter-district differences are studied, particularly to know the impact and features of drought-prone environment, based on secondary data from different official sources. Population Census of India, Livestock Census, Census of Agricultural Holdings, District Census Handbooks, Season and Crop Reports, District Gazetteers, Reports of India Meteorological Department on Rainfall, some of the Drought District Reports prepared by the Central Water Commission, Reports of the Irrigation Commission and National Agricultural Commission etc. have been referred and used as sources of secondary data. Where possible and necessary, gaps in figures were filled and data were updated on the basis of information provided by the respective Directorates of Economics and Statistics, Agriculture and Industry, both from the state level offices and offices of districts selected for collection of primary data.

Though an inter-district analysis of data can yield some interesting insights, a closer view of selected regions and villages would be necessary in the interest of a greater understanding of drought-prone economies. After all, an inter-district analysis presents too aggregative a view to give an idea of how drought-prone conditions operate at the village and household levels.

We made a purposive selection of three districts for an intensive study—Anantapur from Andhra Pradesh, Bijapur from Karnataka and Coimbatore from Tamil Nadu. Though one district from each state has been selected, they are not to be taken as typical or representative of the respective states. There was no such intention in selecting them. We rather considered all the districts of the three states together and based our selection on the criterion that each of the selected districts represents some typical characteristics so that they could help our understanding of different conditions in drought-prone areas. Anantapur was selected because it had the lowest level of normal annual rainfall among all the districts (viz., only 552 mm, being the average during 1925-74 period), unmitigated by irrigation. The district had only 14.7 per cent of irrigated area[8] (average during 1970-71 to 1975-76).[9] Bijapur was selected because it had the lowest yield of foodgrains per hectare, viz., only 407 kgs (average for 1969-70 to 1974-75). Low productivity of land is an important indication of the impact of drought-proneness over the years. It may be noted that Bijapur also has low normal rainfall (viz., 584 mm average during 1925-74), though it is higher than in Anantapur.[10] On the other hand, Bijapur has a higher frequency of failure of rainfall than Anantapur. Bijapur also had one of the lowest levels of irrigation, being only 4.8 per cent during 1970-71 to 1975-76 (averaged for five years).

While Anantapur and Bijapur were selected on the ground of their being typical drought-prone districts, the considerations behind the selection of Coimbatore were a little different. Coimbatore also is drought-prone in the sense of having a low level of normal rainfall (second lowest in Tamil Nadu) viz. 747 mm (average during 1925-74); it also showed the highest frequency of failure in rainfall (below 25 per cent from the normal) among all the districts of the three states. But this district also has a relatively long history of irrigation, affording a scope to study the difference made by irrigation in a typically drought-prone district. Moreover, it is only partially irrigated—39.7 per cent during 1970-71 to 1975-76 (averaged for 5 years). Though irrigation has made certain areas prosperous, other areas are drought-prone and we can see whether differences between dry and irrigated villages in a district with a long history of extensive irrigation are as large as those in other districts. Moreover, the district presents itself as an example of a fairly diversified economy, with a relatively well developed industrial base consisting mainly of agricultural processing industries, textile and engineering units. The development of industries, transport and other infrastructure, has a better regional spread than elsewhere in the country. Even small towns below the level of taluk headquarters are better developed in this district, and the difference between villages and towns appears less marked here than in other districts. Very often diversification of economy is suggested as a solution to the problem of drought-prone areas, and the district provides a scope for an analysis of the impact of this diversification at the household level.

We selected 15 villages for our field investigation, 5 each from Anantapur, Bijapur and Coimbatore, in such a way that there was a sufficient diversity in their characteristics. This diversity was necessary because we could then investigate how village types were associated with different levels of development and also different kinds of structural features. A pure random sampling, we feared, may not throw up this diversity. When the sample is so small as 5 villages from each district, it would not in any case—howsoever selected—be so representative that estimates for the district or the state as a whole can be made with perfect confidence. Within the resources available, it was more meaningful to analyse types of villages and their characteristics, so that emerging relations or associations can be understood. After all, this understanding was more useful for policy formulation than building up estimates for districts or states.

Our sample is such that some villages are highly irrigated, some moderately so, some rainfed and some with a diversified economy having dairy, sheep or goat husbandry, or rural industry. By a diversified village economy, we mean that it is not dependent on cultivation alone but also on other activities. In selecting the villages on the basis of irrigation and diversification, the District Census data proved to be outdated. We had to consult Agriculture, Irrigation and Drought-prone Areas Programme officials, go to several villages to see for ourselves what picture they presented and then select the villages. Our final selection of villages has been presented below in Table 1.1. They have been listed districtwise, with villages in Anantapur first, followed by those in Bijapur and Coimbatore. Within each district they have been arranged in descending order of irrigation as prevailed in 1978-79 as per primary data collected by us from households.

The table also presents the status of the villages in terms of the *relative* presence or absence of irrigation, animal husbandry and rural industry. Presence is indicated as having the value of 1 and absence as zero. In the case of irrigation, only villages having 30 per cent or more of net sown area irrigated in 1978-79 are treated as relatively irrigated or wet villages. In the case of animal husbandry and rural industry no such neat line of demarcation could be defined. Nearly every village may have a few heads of cattle and three or four artisans, but they do not make the village diversified enough. The demarcation has been based on our judgement of the village economic activity, derived from field visits and discussions with village officials and knowledgeable persons in the village. This judgement proved to be correct in the course of the survey undertaken subsequently.

The status of villages in terms of irrigation and diversification has enabled us to develop a village typology based on levels of development. This would be used later while analysing inter-village differences.

Our village types are :

Dry (D)—(a) Least diversified
—(b) With animal husbandry (AH) only
—(c) With industry only
—(d) With both AH and industry
Wet (W)—(a) Least diversified
—(b) With AH only
—(c) With industry only
—(d) With both AH and industry only.

Looking at the values in the table indicating irrigation and diversification status, we can identify the type to which each village belongs. This is indicated in the last column of Table 1.1.

TABLE 1.1 : **Selected villages, their location and, irrigation and diversification status**

Village and district		Taluka	Location code	Per cent area irrigated		Relative presence (1) or absence (0) of			Village type
				1968-79*	1978-79@	Irrigation	Animal husbandry	Rural industry	
1. Rayalacheruvu	(A)	Tadapatri	2	44.4	56.6	1	0	1	Wc
2. Korrapadu	(A)	Anantapur	74	6.0	48.8	1	1	0	Wb
3. Goridindla	(A)	Anantapur	88	8.2	9.9	0	1	0	Db
4. Chinnamushturu	(A)	Uravakonda	31	1.2	7.8	0	0	0	Da
5. Beluguppa	(A)	Kalyandurg	4	2.2	2.6	0	1	1	Dd
6. Mughalkhod	(B)	Mudhol	30	17.1	61.5	1	0	0	Wa
7. Nandyal	(B)	Bijapur	53	4.4	32.6	1	0	0	Wa
8. Mulsavalgi	(B)	Sindgi	98	3.0	17.9	0	1	0	Db
9. Kambagi	(B)	Bijapur	52	2.1	6.9	0	0	0	Da
10. Sulibhavi	(B)	Hungund	168	1.3	2.5	0	0	1	Dc
11. Sholamadevi	(C)	Udumalpet	86	100.0	88.0	1	1	1	Wd
12. Kokkampalayam	(C)	Dharapuram	38	32.0	67.8	1	0	1	Wc
13. Kalangal	(C)	Palladam (Tirupur)	90	NA	44.9	1	1	1	Wd
14. Sirukinar	(C)	Dharapuram	33	3.0	28.3	0	0	1	Dc
15. Vadakalpur	(C)	Avanashi	25	16.0	14.1	0	0	1	Dc

(A) Anantapur (B) Bijapur (C) Coimbatore

*As per District Census Handbook (1971).

@ As per data collected by us.

At one end, we have Chinnamushturu and Kambagi which are Dry and Least diversified (Da), which is the most under-developed type. At the other end, we have Sholamadevi and Kalangal both in Coimbatore—which belong to type Wd, the most developed one.

Coimbatore villages are generally more diversified than those in Anantapur or Bijapur. It is difficult to find a village in Coimbatore depending on cultivation almost exclusively. This cannot be solely attributed to the higher level of irrigation in these villages. The irrigated villages are not necessarily more diversified, though dairy appeared to be better established in villages having a comfortable, if not high, irrigation. The villages with significant rural industry, like Beluguppa, Sulibhavi and Vadakalur, were in fact much less irrigated than others. It may be noted that all the selected villages in Coimbatore had rural industry. It would not have been typical of Coimbatore, even if we found one without.

The selected villages were surveyed twice. First, a census survey covering all the households in the concerned villages was conducted during October and November 1978. The intention of this survey was not only to have a complete listing of households in different strata on the basis of which stratified random sampling can be made for the subsequent sample survey, but also to obtain basic information about rural households, covering land and other important assets held by households, workforce and their occupation, literacy, housing condition etc. This helped in understanding the structure of the rural economy, and the quality of rural life to some extent. During this survey, general particulars about the villages were also collected, such as infrastructure, access to market facilities, type of economic activities in the village, situation regarding drinking water, sanitary conditions and the like. In all, 8959 households were covered by the census survey in all the 15 villages together, with an average of 797 households per village.

The sample survey was started towards the end of May 1979 with 1978-79 as the reference year for information collected. Weather-wise, it was a normal year, particularly in the three districts surveyed. The purpose of this survey was principally to gather data for making a quantitative assessment of income of households from all sources. The details required for this could not have been collected through a census survey, the questionnaire used in which had to be within reasonable limits as it involved all households in the selected villages.

A stratified random sampling procedure was adopted for the intensive survey. The household categories listed in Table 1.2 below were taken as the strata, from each of which a random sample of households was selected. A uniform proportion of sample from each stratum could not be taken, since in some cases the number of households involved was very small and in some cases fairly large. We had to ensure a minimum number from each stratum, resulting in even a hundred per cent or a large portion of sample in a few cases. In other cases where we had a fairly large number, smaller portions were interviewed. Once the number was decided, households were identified, using random number tables, from the complete list of households obtained earlier through the census survey. Table 1.2 here presents details or the sample size in all strata and villages.

When no uniform proportion of sample is taken, proper weights have to be used in making population estimates for the concerned strata and villages for the concerned aspect. A mere addition would not just do. The values derived from the sample, therefore, were multiplied by corresponding weights, that is ratios of the total number of households in the population (as in our census survey) over the sample numbers for each stratum. These strata estimates were in turn added up in making population estimates for concerned villages. These weights have also been presented in Table 1.2.

It may be noted that weights refer only to the basic strata or categories of households and not to sub-totals (cultivating or noncultivating households) and totals (all households). The population estimates for sub-totals and totals are not derived directly by using weights, but only by adding up the population estimates of component strata. As such no weights have been shown for sub-totals and totals in the table. On the whole, taking all the 15 villages together, a sample of 8.2 per cent of cultivating households and 9.1 per cent of noncultivating households was taken. The overall sample for the intensive survey amounted to 775 households, that is 8.65 per cent

TABLE 1.2 : **Total rural households as per census survey (a), sample size in number (b), and weights used (c)**

Household category	R'ruvu			K'padu			G'dla		
	a	b	c	a	b	c	a	b	c
Cultivating Households—									
1) With less than 1 hect.	121	9	13.4	78	5	15.6	30	4	7.5
2) ,, 1.0 to 1.99 ,,	54	4	13.5	50	4	12 5	25	3	8.3
3) ,, 2.0 to 3.99 ,,	55	4	13.7	42	4	10.5	237	5	47.0
4) ,, 4.0 to 5.99 ,,	24	4	6.0	17	3	5.7	92	4	23.0
5) ,, 6.0 to 9.99 ,,	14	5	2.8	18	3	6.0	77	4	19.3
6) ,, 10.0 to 19.99 ,,	5	2	2.5	17	3	5.7	38	4	9.5
7) ,, 20.0 & more	3	2	1.5	10	4	2.5	17	5	3.4
Sub-total	276	30	—	232	26	—	516	29	—
Nonculti. households—									
1) Agri. Labour	213	7	30.4	86	6	14.3	120	7	17.1
2) Dairy, sheep & allied	4	4	1.0	2	1	2.0	1	1	1.0
3) Self-employed artisans	36	5	7.2	15	4	3.7	19	4	4.7
4) Traders	41	4	10.3	10	2	5.0	24	3	8.0
5) White collar	24	2	12.0	3	1	3.0	6	2	3.0
6) Others on salary	61	3	20.2	3	1	3.0	5	2	2.5
7) Casual nonagri. labour	24	3	8.0	11	2	5.5	1	1	1.0
8) Rentiers, pensioners & others	18	4	4.5	4	2	1.5	15	4	3.7
Sub-total	421	32	—	134	19	—	191	24	—
All households	697	62	—	366	45	—	707	53	—

Note : All cultivating households irrespective of their main occupation have been included among cultivating households. Noncultivating households have been categorised on the basis of their main occupation.

TABLE 1.2 : (*Contd.*)

Household category	C'turu			B'ppa			M'khod			N'yal			M'valgi			K'bagi		
	a	b	c	a	b	c	a	b	c	a	b	c	a	b	c	a	b	c
Culti. Hhs																		
1.	27	4	6.8	40	4	10.0	70	5	14.0	8	3	2.7	23	4	5.8	43	4	10.8
2.	7	3	2.3	63	4	15.8	45	6	7.5	25	5	5.0	59	4	14.7	49	4	12.2
3.	19	3	6.3	77	4	19.2	58	4	14.5	22	4	5.5	98	4	24.5	67	4	16.7
4.	14	2	7.0	49	4	12.2	37	4	9.2	14	3	4.7	54	4	13.5	48	4	12.0
5.	14	2	7.0	50	4	12.5	22	3	7.3	15	3	5.0	78	4	19.5	62	4	15.5
6.	10	2	5.0	46	4	11.5	9	3	3.0	2	2	1.0	53	4	13.2	45	4	11.3
7.	6	3	2.0	20	4	5.0	1	1	1.0	nil	—	—	15	3	5.0	8	3	1.0
Sub-total	97	19	—	345	28	—	242	26	—	86	20	—	380	27	—	322	27	—
Non-culti. hhs																		
1.	43	4	10.7	274	6	45.7	100	7	14.1	23	4	5.7	90	6	15.0	40	5	8.0
2.	nil	—	—	nil	—	—	1	1	1.0	nil	—	—	1	1	1.0	nil	—	—
3.	8	4	2.0	64	12	5.3	12	5	2.4	nil	—	—	11	4	2.8	2	2	1.0
4.	11	2	5.5	60	4	15.0	4	2	2.0	2	2	1.0	6	2	3.0	7	3	2.3
5.	3	2	1.5	41	2	20.5	3	1	3.0	nil	—	—	11	2	5.5	4	2	2.0
6.	nil	—	—	33	3	11.0	1	1	1.0	nil	—	—	1	1	1.0	nil	—	—
7.	20	4	5.0	4	2	2.0	nil	—	—	nil	—	—	15	3	5.0	1	1	1.0
8.	8	4	2.0	25	3	8.3	5	2	2.5	nil	—	—	8	3	2.7	2	2	1.0
Sub-total	93	20	—	501	32	—	126	19	—	25	6	—	143	22	—	56	15	—
All hhs	190	39	—	846	60	—	368	45	—	111	26	—	523	49	—	378	42	

TABLE 1.2 : (*Contd.*)

Household category	S'bhavi			S'devi			K'yam			K'gal			S'nar			V'lur		
	a	b	c	a	b	c	a	b	c	a	b	c	a	b	c	a	b	c
Culti. hhs																		
1.	148	5	29.6	127	10	12.7	72	4	18.0	39	3	13.0	42	4	10.5	112	6	18.7
2.	125	4	31.3	22	4	5.5	69	6	11.5	72	4	18.0	79	5	15.8	113	5	22.6
3.	129	4	32.2	11	2	5.5	81	4	20.2	75	5	15.0	24	4	31.0	86	4	21.5
4.	64	4	16.0	4	4	1.1	40	4	10.0	42	4	10.5	67	4	16.7	20	2	10.0
5.	69	4	17.3	nil	—	—	41	7	5.9	24	2	12.0	62	5	12.4	4	2	2.0
6.	32	4	8.0	nil	—	—	23	3	7.7	18	4	4.5	45	4	11.3	nil	—	—
7.	2	1	2.0	nil	—	—	5	2	2.5	4	2	2.0	3	1	3.0	nil	—	—
Sub-total	569	26	—	164	20	—	331	30	—	274	24	—	422	27	—	335	19	—
Non-culti. hhs																		
1.	72	6	12.0	399	14	28.5	219	13	17.0	168	12	14.0	139	8	17.4	279	11	25.4
2.	1	1	1.0	nil	—	—	2	2	1.0	145	10	14.6	4	4	1.0	3	1	2.0
3.	251	20	12.6	57	5	11.4	56	6	9.3	32	5	6.4	57	7	8.1	240	17	14.1
4.	23	4	5.7	62	7	8.9	23	3	7.7	13	2	6.5	34	6	5.7	21	5	4.2
5.	21	2	10.5	14	2	7.0	4	1	4.0	4	1	4.0	16	1	16.0	10	1	10.0
6.	7	2	3.5	16	3	5.3	3	1	3.0	58	2	29.0	5	3	1.7	16	2	8.0
7.	57	3	19.0	35	—	—	2	1	2.0	16	1	2.0	nil	—	—	7	3	2.3
8.	19	3	6.3	16	—	—	6	—	—	11	2	5.5	21	2	10.5	13	3	4.3
Sub-total	451	41	—	599	31	—	315	27	—	448	35	—	276	31	—	589	43	—
All hhs	1020	67	—	763	51	—	646	57	—	722	59	—	698	58	—	924	62	—

of the total number of households listed in our census survey. In our tables and discussions, we shall be referring only to population estimates. No sample values have been presented separately.

A comprehensive investigation into all socio-economic conditions would have been too tall an order to match with the available resources. That would also have been unwieldy for a single project. We had, therefore, to limit our enthusiasm to what was feasible. Our resources did not also permit us to adopt the cost accounting method, used in farm management studies, requiring either a continuous presence of investigators in the concerned villages throughout the year or atleast fortnightly visits and interviews. Though such a method is ideal for recording information free from recall lapses, sample size would have to be far too restricted here. Even then, a comprehensive investigation requiring a large questionnaire would not be feasible. We sought a middle path between an all comprehensive survey and a limited survey of the farm management type, and also between a once-for-all visit and frequent visits/continuous presence.

We first made a preliminary visit to all the selected villages and gathered rich field impressions based on informal discussions with a cross-section of the rural society and officials. The author also personally visited all the villages for the purpose and held detailed discussions. This was followed by a census survey lasting about two months. Four investigators were sent to each district, and all the three districts were covered simultaneously, with a total of 12 investigators in the field. Villages within a given district, however, were surveyed one after the other. The investigators were closely supervised by the author and two Research Analysts. The latter were also continuously in the field with the investigators. A similar procedure was followed during the sample survey also, but it took much longer lasting about 6 months. The longer stay in the village enabled us to scrutinise schedules in the villages ourselves and cross-check with interviewed households again where doubts arose.

Though we had a fairly dependable information for estimating the income of households, it was deficient and not so dependable for estimating consumption levels of households and employment measured in terms of mandays of work. Though information on hired mandays was available, it was not so in the case of self-employed family labour. Even if it was possible to record all the mandays of self-employment, it would have been of doubtful use as an indicator of productive employment. A member of a poor farm family may be busy throughout the day collecting twigs and sticks or cowdung for fuel, but it can hardly constitute remunerative employment. Income earned by households is a better indicator of family's socio-economic condition in general.

Though we tried to probe into incidence of illness, data gathered were rudimentary and recall lapses were high. Only serious illnesses requiring professional medical attention were recalled, but such cases were not significant enough in number.

We have, however, recorded broad field impressions in such cases, so that even if hard data are not available, these impressions are not lost. In sum, our analysis and presentation had to be less ambitious than the questionnaire itself. The data used in our presentation, however are dependable and adequate enough to derive conclusions that are drawn. We have desisted from analysis of data which we felt to be deficient. We have, therefore, depended more on the estimation of income, than of consumption levels and employment in terms of mandays.

We have also desisted from analysis of aspects where we were not qualified or competent enough. We could not, therefore, assess the availability of water and ground water potential in each of the districts and in this light examine the need for transfer of water from outside. We felt that it was a technical aspect, which is better handled by engineers. We have, however, used secondary information available to us for the districts selected for survey. We also could not make an estimate of actual consumption of drinking water in villages and compare it with their needs. We have only recorded broadly our field impressions of the situation in the district and village profiles presented in a subsequent chapter.

Though obviously we could not probe into socio-economic conditions with the same depth and comprehensiveness that is possible for an investigator staying in a single village throughout the year, this was compensated by the fact that our method has enabled us to obtain wide contrasts in the levels of rural development both across regions and strata. This much of a variation could not have been obtained by confining to only one or two villages. And it is the analysis of this variation which is the basic thrust of our study. Even in assessing the impact of variation, such a method of comparing a cross-section of villages would give a more realistic picture, than one which is content with comparing irrigated holdings with unirrigated ones within a village. After all, the impact of irrigation or other strategies of development should be felt on the villages as a whole including the poor and assetless households, and not direct beneficiaries alone. Our method of studying inter-village contrasts on a fairly wide scale also would be more dependable than the one relying on a comparison of only two neighbouring villages, one wet and the other dry. There could be differences even among wet (or dry) villages, depending on the impact of the region concerned, its industries, agrarian structure and so on.

References

1. Montek Ahluwalia—'Rural Poverty in India', in Ahluwalia *et al.*, *India: Occasional Papers*, World Bank Staff Paper No. 279, 1978.
2. See Boudhayan Chattopadhyay and Moonis Raza, 'Regional Development: Analytical Framework and Indicators', *Indian Journal of Regional Science*, 7, 1979.
3. See Michael Lipton, '*Why Poor Stay Poor—A Study of Urban Bias in World Development*', *London*, 1977; V.M. Dandekar, 'Nature of Class Conflict in the Indian Society in the Marxian Framework', *Artha Vijnana*, 20 (2), June 1978; S. Chakraborty, 'Urban Economic Base: A Contemporary Indian Experience', paper at the Indo-French Seminar on Problems of Urban Growth, New Delhi, 1978.
4. Krishna Bharadwaj, 'Regional Differentiation in India—A Note', *Economic and Political Weekly*, **17** (Nos. 14-16), Annual Number, April 1982, pp. 605-616.
5. See Pradhan H. Prasad, 'Limits to Investment Planning', in Ashok Mitra (ed.) *Economic Theory and Planning*: *Essays in Honour of A.K. Dasgupta*, Calcutta, Oxford University Press, 1974, esp. pp. 264-5.
6. Hans P. Binswanger, 'Risk Attitudes of Rural Households in Semi-Arid Tropical India', *Economic and Political Weekly*, Review of Agri., 24 June 1978.
7. See N.S. Jodha, 'Effectiveness of Farmers' Adjustment to Risk,'

Economic and Political Weekly, Review of Agri., 24 June 1978; also V.V. Borkar and M.V. Nadkarni, *Impact of Drought on Rural Life*, Bombay, Popular, 1975.

8. Net irrigated area as per cent of net sown area. The reference to Bijapur and Coimbatore also is in terms of a similar proportion.
9. Selection of districts was done on the basis of statistics for the latest years available before conducting the survey. Our analysis of secondary data has, however, been updated later.
10. Officially, 553 mm is reported as normal for the district which comes close to Anantapur average. This normal is reportedly the average for 1901-50.

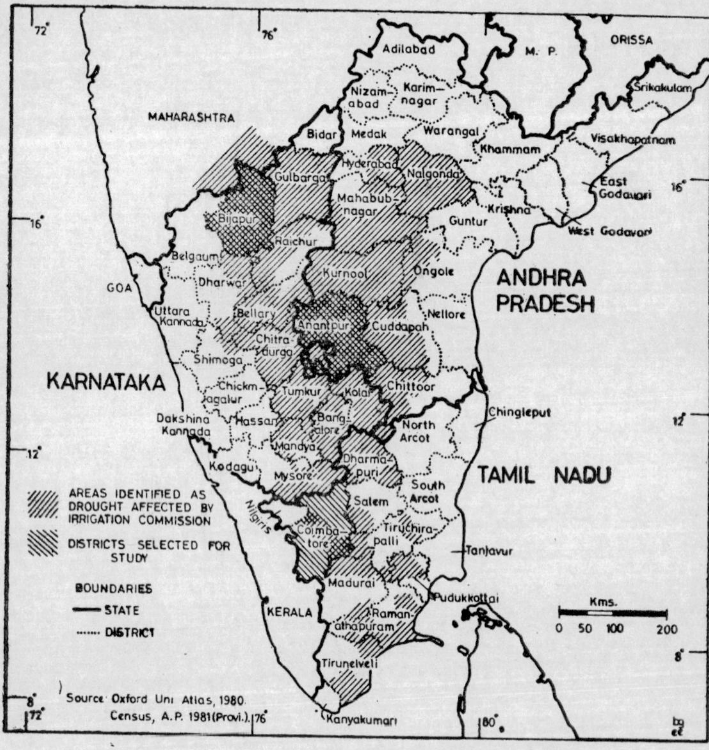

MAP 1 : *Drought-prone areas in Karnataka, Andhra Pradesh and Tamil Nadu*

2

DIMENSIONS OF DROUGHT-PRONE ENVIRONMENT

CONTRASTING THE AREAS

THIS chapter is devoted to an analysis of how and to what extent drought-prone regions are different from non-drought-prone regions. In a country where agriculture continues to be the most dominant sector both in terms of income generated and people dependent on it, droughts and drought-proneness of regions emerge as one of the important problems affecting the lives of millions of people. We have to see in what ways drought-proneness affects the demographic and socio-economic features of the region, as well as its agrarian structure and development. We have also to see if in spite of adverse climatic factors, drought-prone regions have achieved some agricultural growth comparable to state average and the performance of other districts. We have also to see whether the differences between drought-prone and other regions have been reduced in the course of economic development in general. In other words, we can see whether and how far drought-proneness as a growth or development inhibiting factor has been overcome. In overcoming drought-proneness and initiating development in such regions, how far the strategies of irrigation, animal husbandry and rural industry have succeeded would be the thrust of subsequent chapters, based on a study of contrasts within drought-prone regions themselves.

The drought-prone areas have been identified by the

Irrigation Commission (1972) up to the taluka level for the country as a whole. Areas where the frequency or probability of failure of annual rainfall by more than 25 per cent from the normal was found to be 20 per cent or more for the observed years, were considered as drought-prone. Areas where the frequency exceeded 40 per cent were considered as chronically drought-prone. The state governments had given lists of talukas to the Commission for considering them as drought-prone out of which the following were excluded: (a) talukas having more than 30 per cent of cropped area under irrigation, (b) those which received an annual rainfall of over 1000 mm and were considered outside the broad drought-zone, and (c) taluks which comprised a small portion of a district having adequate rainfall and irrigation. The areas thus identified broadly covered those with adverse water balance, as calculated on the basis of potential evapotranspiration. The state governments had apparently taken into account the frequency of droughts in each area from the point of view of remissions of land revenue and annavari estimates, but this does not necessarily tally with the more objective criteria based on rainfall and irrigation. The drought-prone taluks within each district have been listed by the Irrigation Commission,[1] which broadly form the basis of our analysis here. It may be noted that drought-prone areas in our study region comprising the three states are semi-arid, and not arid. They are not chronically drought-prone as in arid tracts, though some of them have more frequent failures in rainfall than others among the semi-arid areas.

This list of course, is not necessarily identical with the list adopted by the state government for implementing drought-prone area programmes. They have included more taluks, giving the benefit of development programmes to more areas. Our assessment is that such inclusion has often been due to local pressures, and also to accommodate small drought-prone portions within an otherwise nondrought-prone zone. In the light of state governments' lists and also their own information, the Central Water Commission has also a list of drought-prone districts, which covers more areas than listed by the Irrigation Commission. When funds for programmes for vulnerable areas and weaker sections are limited, one could question the necessity for liberal extension of target areas even before the core areas have benefited from the programmes. However, since we could not probe deep enough into the identification problem, we do not intend to question the new list of drought-prone areas. For the purpose of our analysis, however, we felt that the list provided by the Irrigation Commission was more suitable as it provided greater contrasts between drought-prone and nondrought-prone areas.

Since the identification of drought-prone areas was basically at the taluk level, it would have been proper to make an analysis at the taluk level rather than at the district level. However, most of the data are available on a dependable basis only at the district level. Let alone data on agricultural output available only at the district level, even data on rainfall are not available on a continuous basis at taluk levels. Some of the census data like death rate, are also not available at taluk level. We have, therefore, taken districts as units of observation in our analysis.

Since quite a few districts were of a mixed character having both drought-prone and other taluks, and since wholly drought-prone districts were extremely limited in number, we have treated those districts as drought-prone where over 55 per cent of their taluks were identified as drought-prone.* On the other hand, those districts were treated as nondrought-prone where none of the taluks therein were drought-prone. These two groups of districts have been contrasted with each other in respect of different characteristics studied, by taking average values and testing the difference for its statistical significance. Other districts were isolated as those of mixed character whose inclusion would have distorted the results. We have modified this rule only in two cases—Belgaum and Mandya both in Karnataka. The Irrigation Commission had identified all taluks as nondrought-prone in the former and 57 per cent as drought-prone in the latter. We have, however, treated both as of mixed nature. Belgaum has quite

*There were only 6 totally drought-prone districts, 3 in Andhra Pradesh (Kurnool, Anantapur and Nalgonda) and 3 in Karnataka (Bellary, Bijapur and Gulbarga). Some of them (like Bellary and Gulbarga) later received significant irrigation in some of its taluks, and could not be considered wholly drought-prone.

a few taluks with low and uncertain rainfall, and has therefore been identified as drought-prone subsequently. On the other hand, Mandya had over 30 per cent irrigation (40% in 1981-82), which has transformed the economy of the district. Even the districts considered as drought-prone had some nondrought-prone taluks (though less than 45 per cent of total number of taluks). The latter were considered as nondrought-prone mainly because of irrigation, but were otherwise a part of the broader drought-prone region sharing many of its macro characteristics. In our judgement, therefore the inclusion of a minor nondrought-prone portion among otherwise drought-prone districts for the purpose of contrasting them with totally nondrought-prone districts, would not lead to distorted results. Table 2.1 below (under notes) indicates which districts have been treated as drought-prone (DP) and non-drought-prone (NDP).

TABLE 2.1 : **Demographic and socio-economic features of drought-prone (DP) and nondrought-prone (NDP) districts**

(Average value of Indicators)

Indicators and year		Average value for DP@	NDP @@	Ratio (3)÷(2)	t Statistic for difference of means
(1)		(2)	(3)	(4)	(5)
1. Density of population (No. per sq. km)					
All :	1971	153	223	1.46	1.75*
	1981	196	271	1.38	1.66^{ns}
AP :	,,	145	237	1.63	2.25**
Ka :	,,	218	161	0.74	0.80^{ns}
2. Growth of population (in per cent)					
All :	1961-71	23.1	22.2	0.96	0.62^{ns}
	1971-81	24.9	22.0	0.88	1.60^{ns}
AP :	,,	22.3	22.6	1.01	0.10^{ns}
Ka :	,,	27.4	23.8	0.87	0.96^{ns}
3. Net in-migration as per cent to total population					
All :	1961-71	4.75	4.23	0.89	0.31^{ns}
AP :	,,	7.90	6.40	0.81	0.65^{ns}
Ka :	,,	3.80	17.83	4.72	1.90*
4. Literacy rate in per cent to total population					
All :	1971	24.9	31.6	1.27	2.14**
	1981	30.9	36.6	1.18	1.65^{ns}
AP :	,,	27.1	28.2	1.04	0.30^{ns}
Ka :	,,	33.7	44.4	1.32	2.17**

5. Rural population as per cent to total					
All :	1971	78.6	80.8	1.03	0.58^{ns}
	1981	77.7	77.8	1.00	0.06^{ns}
AP :	”	82.7	79.5	0.96	0.98^{ns}
Ka :	”	72.1	78.9	1.09	1.02^{ns}
6. Proportion per cent of total workforce in agriculture					
All :	1971	71.2	64.8	0.91	1.52^{ns}
	1981	72.7	64.1	0.88	2.00^{**}
AP :	”	74.9	70.3	0.94	2.16^{**}
Ka :	”	69.2	57.1	0.83	1.50^{ns}
7. Number of agricultural workers (cultivators and labour) per 100 ha of cultivated area (net sown area and current fallows)					
All :	1971	78.3	125.7	1.61	3.19^{***}
	1981	95.6	139.4	1.46	2.94^{***}
AP :	”	99.0	149.3	1.51	2.46^{**}
Ka :	”	101·4	125.9	1.24	0.85^{ns}
8. Birth rate					
All :	1971	24.4	23.1	0.95	1.26^{ns}
	1979	22.2	20.7	0.93	0.75^{ns}
AP :	”	20.9	20.7	0.99	0.12^{ns}
Ka :	”	24.5	18.7	0.76	1.05^{ns}
9. Death rate					
All :	1971	9.2	8.3	0.90	1.87^{*}
	1979	8.3	7.1	0.86	1.65^{ns}
AP :	”	6.8	7.4	1.09	0.67^{ns}
Ka :	”	9.9	6.0	1.65	2.71^{**}
10. Infant mortality rate					
All :	1971	40.3	43.1	1.07	0.97^{ns}
	1979	35.1	32.9	0.94	0.60^{ns}
AP :	”	24.8	32.8	1.32	1.60^{ns}
Ka :	”	43.6	25.7	0.59	3.09^{***}

Source : Derived from the Census of Population and Vital Statistics of India

All—Districts in all the three states together
AP—Separately for Andhra Pradesh districts
Ka—Separately for Karnataka districts

*, ** and *** indicate significance at 10, 5 and 1 per cent levels respectively.

@ In AP —Anantapur, Chittoor, Cuddapah, Kurnool, Mahboobnagar and Nalgonda.

In Ka —Bangalore, Bellary, Bijapur, Chitradurga, Gulbarga, Kolar, Mysore, Raichur and Tumkur.

In TN —Dharmapuri

@@In AP —Adilabad, East Godavari, Guntur, Karimnagar, Khammam, Krishna, Medak, Nellore Nizamabad, Srikakulam, Vishakapatnam, Warangal, and West Godavari.

In Ka —Bidar, Chikmagalur, Dakshina Kannada, Kodagu, Shimoga and Uttara Kannada.

In TN—Chinglepet, Kanyakumari, Nilgiris, North Arcot, South Arcot and Tanjavur.

In any case, our analysis of interregional differences does not stop here. The analysis of household data in the chapters that follow, based on village types at different levels of development is at a much more disaggregated level and would complement the analysis at the district level.

The contrasts have been provided at two points of time, 1971 and 1981. Some districts were reorganised between the two years, but the contrasts are between districts as prevailing during the concerned years. Sometimes problems arose in comparing growth rates, where we had no comparable data for the reorganised districts over the time periods concerned. We had to leave out such problem cases in studying growth rates. Growth rates are not averaged for the purpose of contrasts, but the distribution of DP and NDP districts according to various levels of growth rates (intervals) has been presented.

DEMOGRAPHIC AND SOCIO-ECONOMIC FEATURES

Demographic features as revealed from the Census of Population and Vital Statistics of India have a great socio-economic significance and indicate different dimensions of the level of development reached by the concerned areas. Table 2.1 here presents the average values of these indicators for DP districts as against NDP districts and also the statistical significance of the difference between the two. This is done pooling together the districts from all the three states together, as well as separately within Andhra Pradesh and Karnataka. No such separate figures within Tamil Nadu could be given as there was only one drought-prone district there (Dharmapuri). The districts of Tamil Nadu also have been included, however, in the pooled calculations.

Density of population is often a proxy indicator of level of development in making cross-section comparisons, if not as between two years for the same region. The semi-arid character of DP districts can be expected to a result in a lower density in such areas. It is interesting that though the difference between DP and NDP districts in this respect was significant in 1971, it was no longer so in 1981, suggesting that disparity in overall levels of development between the two could have come down. The difference however was significant in the case of Andhra Pradesh in 1981. Interestingly, the density of population was actually higher on an average in DP districts in Karnataka, though the difference was not statistically significant. The two types of districts showed no significant difference in respect of growth rates in population, both in the sixties and seventies.

It is generally expected that out-migration takes place from DP areas into NDP areas on a net basis. As we shall see in our village profiles below (in Chapter 4), we had also some evidence that the 1972-73 drought pushed out quite a few households from several villages who did not come back even after normal years set in. However, during the sixties at least, at the aggregative level of districts in the three states together, both DP and NDP districts showed some marginal in-migration on a net basis* on an average, and there was no statistically significant difference between the two groups. While in Karnataka, DP districts showed only a marginal net in-migration, the NDP districts had a much higher level of the same, and the difference in the averages was statistically significant. We could not calculate these rates for 1981, and do not like to hazard a prediction of migration behaviour during the seventies. The two droughts in 1972-73 and later could have unsettled quite a few families, but it is difficult to say whether it resulted in net in-migration because such droughts had occurred during mid-sixties too. Economic development and attraction of employment opportunities have not been entirely determined by climate or ecology, and they do not seem to be universally less in the case of DP districts. A few districts did show net out-migration but more from NDP districts (7 out of 26) than from DP districts (3 out of 18).*

---

*The net in-migration rates were calculated for each district on the basis of the difference between actual increase in population and the natural increase in population derived from the birth rate and death rate in 1971. The difference was expressed as per cent of total population. This was not calculated for the seventies, since at the time of writing we did not have figures on birth and death rates for 1981.

**They were Srikakulam, Dakshina Kannada, Uttara Kannada, Belgaum, Nilgiris, Kanyakumari and North Arcot among NDP, and Anantapur, Kolar and Bijapur among DP districts.

Literacy rate is an important indicator of development and quality of life. It is interesting to note that though DP districts had significantly lower literacy rate in 1971, by 1981 the difference became non-significant. However, literacy levels in both DP and NDP are still quite low, and it is a poor consolation that the disparity has been reduced. In Karnataka, the disparity was still significant in 1981.

There was no significant difference between the two types of areas in respect of urbanisation. The proportion of rural population were close to each other between the two types, not only when pooled, but also within Andhra Pradesh and Karnataka. The number of towns and cities relative to area and population also did not throw up significant differences.

Though the extent of urbanisation was almost the same, the extent of diversification of the economy was different. Dependence on agriculture seems to be more in DP districts, as indicated by the proportion of workforce engaged in agriculture. Actually, the difference was not significant in 1971, but became so in 1981. The difference was also significant within Andhra Pradesh, but not in Karnataka since there were considerable variations within DP and NDP districts in the latter. On an average, however, DP districts had a higher proportion of workforce in agriculture even in Karnataka.

Though the proportion of workforce in allied agricultural activities like dairy was a little higher in NDP districts, the difference was not statistically different in 1971. The change in 1981 could not be noted as these data were not available at the time of writing. However, animal husbandry as indicated by the number of cows and she buffaloes per 1000 population also was not significantly different between the two types, both in 1971 and 1977. We have not, therefore, presented these figures in the tables here. It was only in Karnataka that DP districts had on an average 108 cows per 1000 people in 1977, while the NDP had 151 cows, and the difference was statistically different at 10 per cent level. The small ruminants like sheep and goats, however, dominated only in DPs. But this hardly made an impact, at least as indicated by the proportion of workforce engaged in animal husbandry. We thus see that even animal husbandry has not helped so far in diversifying the economy of DP districts. This could suggest that even for a proper diversification of the rural economy, agriculture needs to be at a more developed stage and more dependable, and capable enough to provide fodder on the one hand and demand for the output from animal husbandry. This is in spite of the fact that urbanisation in DP districts does not seem to be very much constrained by the level of agricultural development on the whole. The metropolitan cities particularly have gained a momentum of their own, which may have to some extent stimulated animal husbandry only in areas surrounding them. But elsewhere, animal husbandry in DP districts is in a depressed state.

The drought-prone areas have generally less agricultural workers per unit of cultivated area than nondrought-prone areas. This is partly a reflection of lower density of population there and lower productivity of land. We should remember, however, that pressure of population of land was no less in DP areas since other opportunities of employment there were less.

The statistics of birth rate, death rate and infant mortality rates are also an indicator of development and quality of life. Birth rates can be generally expected to be lower in more developed areas. However, there was no statistically significant difference between DP and NDP districts in this respect, not only when all the states were pooled but also within AP and Karnataka. However, death rate was significantly higher in the case of DP districts in 1971 but not in 1979 for the three states together. The disparity has come down, owing perhaps to improvement in medical infrastructure in DP districts. The problem, however, remains in Karnataka where death rates in DP districts were significantly higher. Infant mortality rates were also significantly higher in DP districts in the state. In Andhra Pradesh, infant mortality rates were actually lower in DP districts but the difference was not statistically significant. The disparity in the state of health as between the two types of districts was mainly a problem in Karnataka at least in 1979, but not in the three states taken together. Higher mortality rates in the DP areas of Karnataka may not necessarily be due to adverse climate; they appear more due to lower level of development of medical infrastructure and such other facilities in DP districts.

AGRARIAN STRUCTURE AND DEVELOPMENT

It is clear that the NDP districts are on the whole better endowed in terms of resources, which has also influenced their agrarian structure (see Table 2.2). They have not only higher

TABLE 2.2 : **Indicators of agrarian structure and development of DP vis-a-vis NDP districts**

(*Average values*)

Indicators and year		Average value for DP	Average value for NDP	Ratio (3)÷(2)	t Statistic for difference of means
(1)		(2)	(3)	(4)	(5)
1. Proportion of agricultural labourers among agricultural workers					
All	1971	43.5	51.3	1.18	2.14^{**}
	1981	43.3	51.5	1.19	2.09^{**}
AP	,,	50.2	53.7	1.07	0.64^{ns}
Ka	,,	41.7	41.5	1.00	0.04^{ns}
2. Average size of holding (operational) in hectares					
All	1970-71	3.4	2.2	0.65	3.02^{***}
	1976-77	3.1	2.0	0.65	3.04^{***}
AP	,,	3.2	2.0	0.63	3.17^{***}
Ka	,,	3.3	2.6	0.79	0.88^{ns}
3. Proportion (%) of operated area under holdings of					
(i) below 2 hectares					
All	1970-71	19.1	30.2	1.58	2.48^{**}
	1976-77	21.9	32.1	1.47	2.23^{**}
AP	,,	17.4	28.5	1.64	2.37^{**}
Ka	,,	20.6	25.9	1.26	0.67^{ns}
(ii) above 10 hectares					
All	1970-71	29.2	21.3	0.73	1.88^{*}
	1976-77	25.3	18.6	0.74	1.62^{ns}
AP	,,	30.6	18.5	0.60	2.82^{**}
Ka	,,	26.1	22.0	0.84	0.54^{ns}
4. Gini concentration ratio for operational holdings (excluding landless labour) :					
All	1970-71	0.52	0.57	1.10	3.72^{***}
	1976-77	0.52	0.56	1.08	2.43^{**}
AP	,,	0.56	0.58	1.04	1.05^{ns}
Ka	,,	0.50	0.54	1.08	1.57^{ns}

5. Proportion of leased in area (%)					
All	1970-71	5.45	11.16	2.05	2.03**
AP	,,	5.10	6.50	1.27	0.51^{ns}
Ka	,,	4.13	3.06	0.74	0.33^{ns}
6. Net irrigated area as per cent of net sown area					
All	1970-71	15.7	37.6	2.39	3.64***
	1980-81	18.1	39.4	2.18	3.36***
AP	,,	20.6	45.0	2.18	2.54**
Ka	,,	13.7	20.4	1.49	0.63^{ns}
7. Double cropped area as per cent of net sown area					
All	1970-71	8.1	20.1	2.48	3.43***
	1980-81	8.4	20.4	2.43	3.02***
AP	,,	6.4	21.4	3.34	2.47**
Ka	,,	6.7	13.8	2.06	1.39^{ns}
8. Draught livestock (over 3 years) per 100 ha of net sown area					
(i) Bullocks					
All	1972	43.7	66.1	1.51	2.82***
	1977	47.2	67.4	1.43	2.14**
AP	,,	49.8	57.3	1.15	0.05*
Ka	,,	48.7	81.3	1.67	1.85*
(ii) He buffaloes					
All	1972	3.2	16.4	5.13	3.62**
	1977	2.9	16.0	5.52	3.31***
AP	,,	5.9	16.4	2.78	1.88*
Ka	,,	1.2	20.5	17.08	2.00*
9. Number of tractors per lakh hectares of net sown area					
All	1972	52.1	106.9	2.05	2.41**
	1977	81.7	144.7	1.77	1.92*
AP	,,	86.0	155.2	1.80	1.03^{ns}
Ka	,,	85.6	77.5	0.91	0.26^{ns}
10. Fertiliser consumption in kgs per hectare of net sown area					
All	1970-71	16.4	39.8	2.43	2.85***
	1980-81	39.2	71.6	1.83	2.40**
AP	,,	35.0	73.6	2.10	1.50^{ns}
Ka	,,	36.5	53.6	1.47	1.08^{ns}
11. Average yields per hectare in kgs					
All	1956-57 to 1970-71	585	1021	1.75	4.00***
	1971-72 to 1980-81	864	1339	1.55	3.43***
AP	1956-57 to 1970-71	629	869	1.38	1.32^{ns}
	1971-82 to 1980-81	863	1143	1.32	1.15^{ns}
Ka	1956-57 to 1970-71	560	1088	1.94	3.22***
	1971-72 to 1980-81	864	1383	1.60	2.77**

Note : All, AP and Ka as in Table 2.1.

normal rainfall but also higher level of irrigation (item 6 in the table). The disparity in the proportion of irrigation was not significant, however, in Karnataka. There is some indication that the irrigated areas particularly through major irrigation projects have been expanding faster in the DP areas since the sixties. Even in Karnataka, the disparity was significant earlier, but was reduced on account of the thrust of irrigation in DP areas. The disparity still remains to be reduced in Andhra Pradesh, though the level of irrigation there is higher than in Karnataka.

The higher level of development in NDP districts has been reflected in their agrarian structure in several ways. First of all, it has produced a higher level of proletarianisation there as compared to DP areas. This is seen, however, more in the pooled data particularly because of the inclusion of Tamil Nadu districts. Within Karnataka and AP, however, the difference in the proportion of agricultural labourers among agricultural workers was not statistically significant in 1981. This is not surprising because the contrasts in the level of development became sharp only with the inclusion of Tamil Nadu districts in the pooled data. This is reflected in the primary data as well, analysed in the subsequent chapters. The higher level of proletarianisation at higher levels of development results both from higher demand for labour and higher wage rates, and from inducements offered by richer farmers to tiny holdings to sell off or lease out their land. Tiny holders may find it more remunerative to be full-time labourers, rather than cultivate their nonviable holdings.

But this has not led to the average size of holdings being higher in NDP districts, at least in nonstandardised form. The average size of holding was actually higher in DP districts both in pooled data and in Andhra Pradesh. The difference, however, was not significant within Karnataka because of variation within the two types of districts. The proportion of area under small holdings was also considerably higher in NDP districts particularly in Andhra Pradesh, though not in Karnataka. Correspondingly the proportion of area under large holdings above 10 hectares was higher in DP areas particularly in Andhra Pradesh. This dominance of large holdings and higher size of holdings in DP districts is not necessarily indicative of higher concentration in the control on land. Actually, the Gini ratios indicating concentration in operational holdings were higher in NDPs. This was at least in the pooled data, though not in AP and Karnataka. Gini ratios have been calculated excluding landless labour, and suggest concentration within holdings only. On the whole, in spite of lower average size of holdings in NDP districts, they had a more inegalitarian agrarian structure indicated both by the proportion of agricultural labourers and concentration within operational holdings. The contrast comes out clearly only when Tamil Nadu districts are pooled together with others.

Though the proportion of leased in land is on the whole marginal it was significantly higher, being 11.2 per cent in NDPs compared to only the 5.5 per cent in DP areas. The difference however was not significant within Andhra Pradesh and Karnataka taken separately. Generally lease market for land develops only in areas where productivity of land is high and is indicative of higher demand for land. However, even in DP areas this can exist, particularly since enlarging the size of holding through leasing can improve the capacity for survival in droughts. Small holders are particularly vulnerable to droughts. But there were variations regarding who leased in more. As we shall see later, whereas large holders leased in more in Bijapur, it was the small holders who leased in more in Anantapur. Leasing in of land need not necessarily be a non-capitalist or pre-capitalist feature. However, the extent of leasing has drastically declined in the last three or four decades, and proletarianisation is taking the place of tenancy. We shall probe further into this while analysing primary data.

The higher level of rainfall and higher proportion of irrigation has made possible a higher cropping intensity in NDP districts. The difference in the same was statistically significant both in 1976-77 and 1980-81 on the whole, but it was not significant in the case of Karnataka. This was not because the DP districts had a higher cropping intensity in Karnataka, but unfortunately even the NDP districts had a low cropping intensity. Even on the whole, taking all the states together, the level of cropping intensity in NDP districts—though higher than in DP districts—was hardly impressive.

Another distressing feature common to both DPs and NDPs was a fairly high proportion of idle land, comprising current fallows, cultural waste and other fallows. In 1981 DP districts had 18 per cent of their culturable land under current fallows, 11.2 per cent under culturable waste and other fallows, together making 29.2 per cent of land held idle. The NDP district had 13.4 per cent as current fallows and 12.5 per cent culturable waste and other fallows during the same year, together forming 25.9 per cent as idle land. This is a fairly high level of underutilisation of land, considering the general scarcity of land and demand for it. It was not necessarily due to climatic factors. The difference in idle land was not statistically significant between the two types of districts both in the pooled data and separately in Andhra Pradesh and Karnataka. A study of fluctuations even over time did not suggest that climate played a very important role in under-utilisation of land. The study suggested that institutional factors like dominance of large holders may be more relevant here.[2] We shall probe more into these aspects in the light of findings from primary data later, particularly in the context of introduction of irrigation.

Even in cultivated areas, the crop pattern in DP districts is generally dominated by low value and low yield crops like millets and pulses. If they also happen to have dominantly black cotton soils, even the introduction of irrigation would not enable them to raise high value and high yield crops like paddy and sugarcane. However, DP areas do raise commercial crops like oilseeds and cotton. Unfortunately, they are subject to high instability both in respect of yields and prices. Though irrigation tends to make their yields a little more stable if supply of irrigation itself is stable, it does not solve the problem of instability in prices. The markets for food-grains are generally better organised and less monopolistic than the markets for commercial crops like groundnut and cotton. Though sugarcane is also a commercial crop grown mostly in NDP areas, its growers are better organised to fight exploitation by mills.

Though crop pattern in DP areas has thus some disadvantage, it has been evolved to reduce risks as much as possible. Crop combinations and rotations are thus more prominent in

DP areas, and hence their crop patterns are more complex.[8] Cotton, for example, is combined with either pulses or oilseeds. Similarly, jowar is combined with cotton, oilseeds or pulses. There are tremendous variations over the regions in such crop combinations. One of the effects of introduction of irrigation and HYVs has been that it has to some extent upset traditional cropping patterns, though overall growth in production has indeed resulted. The leguminous crops which used to naturally enrich soils through nitrogen implantation and also provided protein rich pulses even to the poor, are slowly being replaced by high yielding crops which generally are sown as pure crops. There is some opportunity cost, therefore, of introduction of HYVs in DP areas. We may note, however, that these changes are often not observable through secondary data on changes in areas under different crops over time, particularly because of tremendous fluctuations obliterating trends.

The NDPs on the whole have more resources even in terms of draught power, which is not surprising because of a higher level of development there. They had significantly more bullocks and he-buffaloes per 100 hectares of net sown area (see item 8 in Table 2.2), and also significantly more tractors per unit of net sown area (item 9) as compared to DPs both in 1972 and 1977. The difference in respect of tractors, however, was not statistically significant within AP and Karnataka, but the inclusion of Tamil Nadu with higher level of tractorisation would have contributed to a greater contrast in the pooled data. Though the more developed character of agriculture in NDP districts may need more tractors, it may very well be due to higher prosperity resulting in more demand for a prestige asset like tractors, and not because DP districts *need* less tractors. We may recall that DP districts have a lower proportion of agricultural labour, and also less agricultural workers and less draught animal power per unit land. These factors and also the more arduous nature of cultivation in DP areas, greater need for soil conservation and bunding can step up the demand for tractors in DP areas. These tractors may have to be under government owned service units charging fees for their use, if not necessarily under private ownership. A study by Jodha has indicated that tractors can play an important role in the agriculture of DP areas also.[4] Possibly this is borne out by the lack of statistically significant difference in the tractors per unit of land between the two types of districts within Andhra Pradesh and Karnataka if not in the pooled picture.

Fertiliser consumption was also higher in NDP areas though the disparity has somewhat declined during the seventies. On the whole, even in 1980-81 the DP districts consumed only 39 kgs of fertilisers per hectare of net sown area compared to 72 kgs by the NDP districts. The averages were similarly higher in the latter both in Andhra Pradesh and Karnataka but the difference was not statistically significant because of the variation within types. Moreover, the inclusion of Tamil Nadu with its higher level of consumption would have influenced the pooled results.

Though on the whole the DP districts have a lower level of agricultural development, this has not prevented them from achieving higher rates of growth. Table 2.3 here presents the distribution of both DP and NDP districts separately according to growth rates per annum in production and yield of foodgrains during a quarter century of 1956-57 to 1980-81. The table shows that on the whole 79 per cent of DP districts showed growth rates of above 1.5 per cent in production per annum, as compared to 70 per cent of NDP districts achieving such growth rates. In respect of growth in yield per hectare also, all of the DP districts had achieved growth rates of higher than 1.5 per cent per annum, whereas only 75 per cent of the NDP districts were in this category. (See also Appendix II to this chapter). The better performance of DP districts comes out, even if we consider the proportion of districts achieving more than 3 per cent growth in production and yield. This experience was shared both by Andhra Pradesh and Karnataka considered separately. This would suggest that in spite of adverse environmental factors and lower endowment of resources, the DP districts had succeeded in achieving fairly high rates of growth, and that higher yield uncertainty in these districts has not acted as a growth inhibiting factor. If risk aversion is more a trait of small farmers than of the large, the dominance of large holdings in the DP districts may have helped in this matter.

TABLE 2.3 : **Distribution of districts (number) according to growth rates per annum in production and yield of foodgrains during 1956-57 to 1980-81**

Type of district and state	Intervals of Rates of Growth* in								Total number of districts studied
	Production				Yield per hectare				
	Non significant	Up to 1.5 per cent	1.6 to 3.0 per cent	Above 3.0 per cent	Non significant	Upto 1.5 per cent	1.6 to 3.0 per cent	Above 3 per cent	
Drought-prone									
AP	2 (40)	1 (20)	1 (20)	1 (20)	nil	nil	4 (80)	1 (20)	5 (100)
Ka	nil	nil	5 (56)	4 (44)	nil	nil	5 (56)	4 (44)	9 (100)
Total DP	2 (14)	1 (7)	6 (43)	5 (36)	nil	nil	9 (64)	5 (36)	14 (100)
Nondrought-prone									
AP	nil	1 (11)	4 (44)	4 (44)	1 (11)	1 (11)	5 (56)	2 (22)	9 (100)
Ka	nil	3 (50)	nil	3 (50)	nil	1 (17)	2 (33)	3 (50)	6 (100)
TN	2 (40)	nil	3 (60)	nil	nil	2 (40)	3 (60)	nil	5 (100)
Total NDP	2 (10)	4 (20)	7 (35)	7 (35)	1 (5)	4 (20)	10 (50)	5 (25)	20 (100)

* There were no districts with negative and statistically significant growth either in production or yield of foodgrains. Districts considered here are the same as listed under the Notes to Table 2.1, except that the following are excluded (since comparable time series were not available owing to reorganisation of districts): Kurnool, Dharmapuri, Guntur, Nellore, Srikakulam, Visakhapatnam and Tanjavur.

Note : Figures in brackets are percentages.

This growth has not, however, eliminated the disparity in the yields per hectare of foodgrains (see item 11 in Table 2.2). The disparity remained significant both during the earlier period of 1956-57 to 1970-71 and during the seventies, though the ratios of yield in NDP over DP districts declined somewhat not only in the case of all districts together, but also within Andhra Pradesh and Karnataka separately. Andhra Pradesh alone had no significant disparity in this respect as between the two types of districts, due to wide variation within the types. On an average, however, the yields were higher in NDP districts even here, but the disparity was lower. This was because whenever irrigation was introduced in DP areas in Andhra Pradesh, a good portion of it was used for paddy.

This growth performance of DP areas has been achieved in the context of higher instability in agriculture. We find from Table 2.4 that the 64 per cent of DP districts were in the highest range of instability indicated by the co-efficient of variation in production adjusted for trend being above 20 per cent. In contrast, only 35 per cent of NDP districts were in this range. Similarly a higher proportion of DP districts (viz., 29 per cent) were in the range of highest instability in yield compared to only 4 per cent of NDP districts in this range. A study of growth and instability in agriculture in Karnataka showed, however, that growth did not have to be necessarily associated with instability though on the whole there was a positive association between the two. A DP district like Bijapur combined growth with stability, though its yield levels were still low in spite of their growth.[5] A judicious combination of traditional practices like soil and water conservation with modern practices like the use of fertiliser and HYVs, could lead to a happy state of combining growth with stability.

Unfortunately, even before the problem of instability was solved, growth received a setback during 1970s, though there was positive growth at least up to 1978-79. The setback was mostly due to stagnation at the end of the seventies. Both types of districts seem to have shared this unfortunate outcome, though possibly there was a reversal to growth recently —particularly in 1983-84. Even in the more developed Tamil Nadu, *every* district suffered stagnation in foodgrains

TABLE 2.4 : **Distribution of districts (number) according to instability in production and yield of foodgrains during 1956-57 to 1980-81**

Type of district and state	Intervals of CVT in							
	Production				Yield			
	Below 10 per cent	10.1 to 15 per cent	15.1 to 20 per cent	Above 20 per cent	Below 10 per cent	10.1 to 15 per cent	15.1 to 20 per cent	Above 20 per cent
Drought-prone								
AP	nil	1 (20)	nil	4 (80)	nil	2 (40)	3 (60)	nil
Ka	nil	nil	4 (44)	5 (56)	nil	nil	5 (56)	4 (44)
Total DP	nil	1 (7)	4 (29)	9 (64)	nil	2 (14)	8 (57)	4 (29)
Nondrought-prone								
AP	nil	3 (33)	4 (44)	2 (22)	1 (11)	5 (56)	2 (22)	1 (11)
Ka	1 (17)	1 (17)	2 (33)	2 (33)	1 (17)	1 (17)	3 (33)	1 (17)
TN	nil	nil	2 (40)	3 (60)	nil	3 (60)	2 (40)	nil
Total NDP	1 (5)	4 (20)	8 (40)	7 (35)	2 (10)	9 (45)	7 (35)	2 (10)

CVT—Co-efficient of variation adjusted for trend.
Note : Figures in brackets are percentages.

production during the period 1971-72 to 1980-81, and only one district—Coimbatore—recorded a positive and statistically significant growth (viz., 3 per cent p. a.) in yields. The record of Karnataka was a little better. Only 4 districts out of 19 recorded positive and significant growth rates in production, two of them being DP and two of mixed nature; but seven districts recorded positive and significant rates of growth in yield of which four were drought-prone. Even in Karnataka growth rate suffered a setback after 1978-79. In Andhra Pradesh, 10 out of 15 districts studied recorded significant and positive growth in production, and 11 districts in yields. They were from both DP and NDP categories.

It may be noted that most of the growth in agriculture of drought-prone districts came about as a result of irrigation, increased consumption of fertilisers and adoption of high yielding varieties both in irrigated and rainfed conditions. In fact, the drought-prone districts which recorded conspicuous rates of growth over 3 per cent per annum in production and yields were also the districts which recorded conspicuous growth in irrigated area. This was true of both the seventies and the earlier period. However it should also be noted that most of the districts which faced a severe setback in growth as in Tamil Nadu, were also the districts which had significant irrigation and also recorded increase in irrigated area. This would suggest that even from the narrow point of view of growth, irrigation need not produce an automatic positive impact, let alone the impact on socio-economic conditions in general. The impact of irrigation needs therefore, a close scrutiny, so that factors that hinder positive impact are identified and overcome. This justifies a critical look at irrigation in the chapters that follow. The intention is not to deny the importance of irrigation in drought-prone areas. There is no such prejudice against irrigation in the present study.

A few points coming out of this chapter need to be noted before we conclude, even at the risk of repetition. Even drought-prone areas have shown a dynamism for growth in spite of lower endowment of resource, both natural and man-made. They have indeed a lower level of development and lower of quality of life in general, but the disparity between drought-prone and other areas is getting narrowed. This is not necessarily due to irrigation alone, which is still at a very low level in the former. The process of economic development in general, and the thrust on improvement of infrastructure and services in particular would have produced this impact. However, there is still a long way to go both in drought-prone and other areas, particularly in the former, in improving general levels of living and reducing poverty.

References

1. Government of India, Irrigation Commission Report, 1972, pp. 420, 422-4.
2. See M.V. Nadkarni and R.S. Deshpande 'Underutilisation of land—Climatic or Institutional Factors?', *Indian Journal of Agricultural Economics*, April-June 1979.
3. Barbara Harriss, *et al.* also have referred to greater complexity of crop pattern in dry land areas. See their '*Exchange Relations and Poverty in Dry Land Agriculture*, New Delhi, Concept Publishing Company, 1984, Chapter 5.
4. N.S. Jodha, 'A Case of the Process of Tractorisation', *Economic and Political Weekly*, Review of Agriculture, 28 December, 1974.
5. M.V. Nadkarni and R.S. Deshpande, 'Agricultural Growth, Instability in Productivity and Rainfall—Case of Karnataka', *Economic and Political Weekly*, Review of Agriculture, December 1982.

APPENDIX-1

SOCIO-ECONOMIC AND OTHER INDICATORS—FOR THE SELECTED DISTRICTS AND STATE AVERAGES

Sl. No. of indicator	Year	Anantapur	Andhra Pradesh	Bijapur	Karnataka	Coimbatore	Periyar	Tamil Nadu
Demographic and Socio-Economic Indicators (Serial numbers in the same order as in Table 2.1)								
1	1981	133	195	141	194	410	252	372
2	1971-81	20.3	22.8	22.0	27.7	18.8	15.1	17.5
3*	1961-71	—1.6	5.6	—9.4	2.7	3.3@	—	1.4
4	1981	29.0	29.9	31.9	38.5	53.1	39.8	46.8
5	1981	79.2	76.7	75.9	71.1	49.5	78.0	67.0
6	,,	76.0	69.5	72.8	65.0	47.4	66.0	60.9
7	,,	99	147	55	90	181	228	216
8	1979	19.7	21.9	25.1	25.0	19.6@	—	21.9
9	,,	6.0	7.1	10.3	9.0	6.2@	—	7.1
10	,,	32	32	41	39	36@	—	39

Indicators of Agrarian Structure and Development (Serial numbers in the same order as in Table 2.2)

1		1981	47.0	52.9	52.2	41.2	66.8	57.3	52.1
2		1976-77	4.08	2.34	5.27	2.98	2.22@	—	1.25
3	(i)	,,	11.5	22.1	6.1	40.4	25.5@	—	41.9
	(ii)	,,	39.5	24.8	17.2	31.7	17.4@	—	10.4
4		,,	0.58	0.60	0.46	0.56	0.54@	—	0.57
5		1970-71	7.4	7.0	8.2	7.4	5.4@	—	8.7
6		1980-81	13.6	32.2	8.6	13.7	45.9	57.8	48.0
7		,,	3.8	14.4	2.1	7.7	11.6	22.3	20.7
8	(i)	1977	43.3	50.9	18.1	33.6	51.7@	—	77.3
	(ii)	,,	2.9	12.0	0.3	3.2	2.6@	—	6.4
9		,,	32	119	58	85	147@	—	142
10		1980-81	15	54	10	35	176	94	92
11		See under the last two columns in Appendix 2.							

* Negative sign indicates net out-migration. State averages here are averages of district level net in-migration and not as in the state as a whole from outside the state. Calculated for the state as a whole, net in-migration rates were —1.8 in Andhra Pradesh, 1.3 in Karnataka and 1.9 in Tamil Nadu.

@ Including the newly formed Periyar district.

APPENDIX-II

GROWTH IN FOODGRAINS PRODUCTION AND YIELDS—DISTRICT-WISE

A : In Andhra Pradesh

District	Annual Growth Rates (per cent) in Foodgrains				Average Yields in kgs per hect.	
	Production		Yield per hect.			
	1956-57 to 1980-81	1971-72 to 1980-81	1956-57 to 1980-81	1971-72 to 1980-81	1956-57 to 1970-71	1971-72 to 1980-81
(1)	(2)	(3)	(4)	(5)	(6)	(7)
Drought-prone districts						
Anantapur	0.21^{ns}	—2.30^{ns}	1.58***	0.81^{ns}	479	638
Chittoor	0.91^{ns}	—0.17^{ns}	1.82***	—0.45^{ns}	1018	1385
Cuddapah	1.19***	1.68^{ns}	2.11***	2.37*	699	934
Mahboobnagar	2.11***	7.66**	1.92***	7.64***	450	541
Nalgonda	3.26***	3.99**	3.51***	5.88***	501	818
Nondrought-prone districts						
Adilabad	0.98***	1.89^{ns}	0.16^{ns}	2.33*	563	578
E. Godavari	1.97***	4.78**	1.58***	3.84***	1255	1603
Karimnagar	4.88***	5.97**	4.11***	5.31***	629	1058
Khammam	2.68***	2.40^{ns}	1.74***	2.19^{ns}	585	748
Krishna	1.66***	3.21*	1.05***	—1.39^{ns}	1339	1555
Medak	1.87***	6.84**	1.76***	6.66**	636	752
Nizamabad	3.54***	9.13***	3.02***	8.50***	968	1264
Warrangal	3.35***	4.02*	2.81***	3.87***	602	860
W. Godavari	3.01***	4.37**	2.78***	2.85**	1382	1980
State	1.90***	3.57**	2.11***	—0.39^{ns}	729	1030

Note : Linear growth rates presented as per cent at mean.

B : In Karnataka

(1)	(2)	(3)	(4)	(5)	(6)	(7)
Drought-prone districts						
Bangalore	2.47***	3.31ns	2.48***	2.87ns	739	1043
Bellary	4.31***	2.96ns	4.33***	2.10***	531	900
Bijapur	2.14***	0.47ns	2.75***	1.93ns	322	452
Chitradurga	5.42***	3.12ns	5.38***	3.29***	558	1185
Gulbarga	2.45***	5.53**	3.15***	4.28*	362	499
Kolar	1.69*	—3.76ns	1.55*	—3.74ns	732	1037
Mysore	3.39***	1.71ns	2.63***	1.85ns	743	1093
Raichur	4·32***	3.44**	3.76***	2.99**	425	687
Tumkur	1.58**	—1.63ns	1.80***	—0.90ns	624	882
Nondrought-prone districts						
Bidar	3.29***	4.34ns	2.08**	3.95ns	423	640
Chikmagalur	3.22***	3.08ns	1.93***	2.79ns	902	1229
Dakshina Kannada	1.00***	—0.54ns	2.28***	1.95**	1101	1506
Kodagu	1.15**	1.25ns	0.15ns	2.55ns	1647	1769
Shimoga	4.25***	1.74ns	3.25***	1.26ns	1126	1701
Uttara Kannada	1.21***	1.14ns	0.84***	1.11ns	1328	1454
Others (Mixed)						
Belgaum	1.35***	0.79ns	1.74***	1.40ns	551	698
Dharwad	1.14**	3.22ns	1.46***	3.26ns	578	690
Mandya	4.19***	4.46ns	3.20***	4.17**	845	1337
Hassan	3.94***	5.68*	2.42***	4.89*	812	1154
State	2.68***	2.10ns	2.55***	2.24*	577	868

Appendix-II (Contd.)

C : In Tamil Nadu

(1)	(2)	(3)	(4)	(5)	(6)	(7)
Nondrought-prone districts						
Chinglepet	2.91***	0.49^{ns}	2.86***	0.34^{ns}	1185	1780
Kanyakumari	0.27^{ns}	-3.96^{ns}	1.30***	0.54^{ns}	1663	1994
Nilgiris	0.96^{ns}	-2.00^{ns}	1.21**	1.00^{ns}	909	1145
North-Arcot	1.79***	-0.56^{ns}	2.18***	0.84^{ns}	1191	1652
South-Arcot	2.62***	-0.84^{ns}	2.52***	-0.61^{ns}	1277	1825
Others (Mixed)						
Coimbatore@	1.02**	2.31^{ns}	1.48***	3.07***	866	1028
Madurai	1.54***	2.14^{ns}	1.65***	5.59^{ns}	1102	1385
Ramanathapuram	0.81***	-1.70^{ns}	0.52^{ns}	-1.06^{ns}	834	911
Tirunelveli	1.77***	0.51^{ns}	2.15***	1.60^{ns}	1111	1516
State	1.64**	0.17^{ns}	1.65***	0.82	1084	1365

Note : Reorganised districts for which comparable time-series were not available, have been excluded here.

*, ** and *** indicate significance levels at 10, 5 and 1 per cent respectively.

ns—not significant.

@ including the newly formed Periyar district.

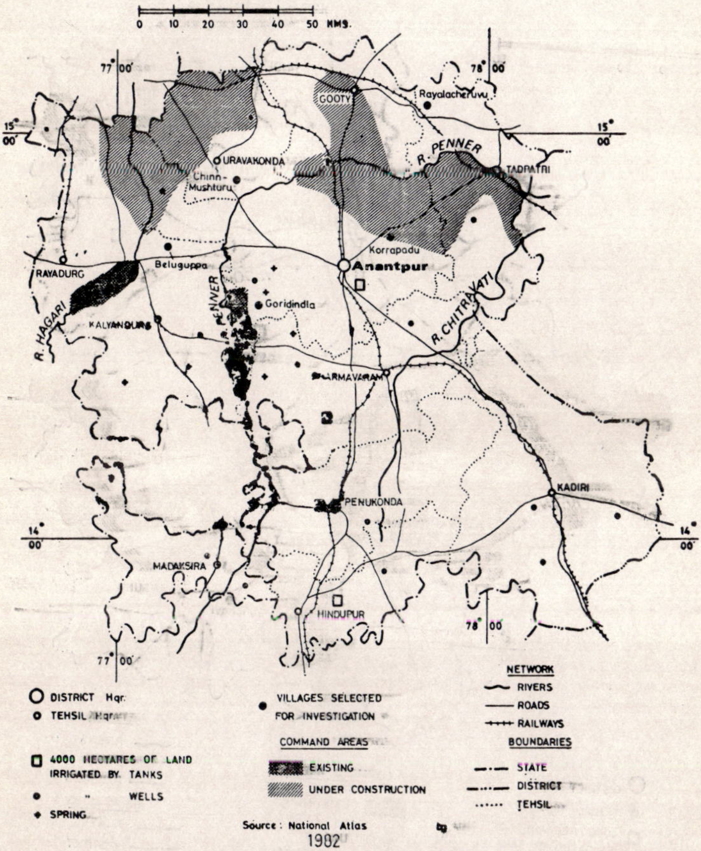

MAP 2 : *Anantapur district*

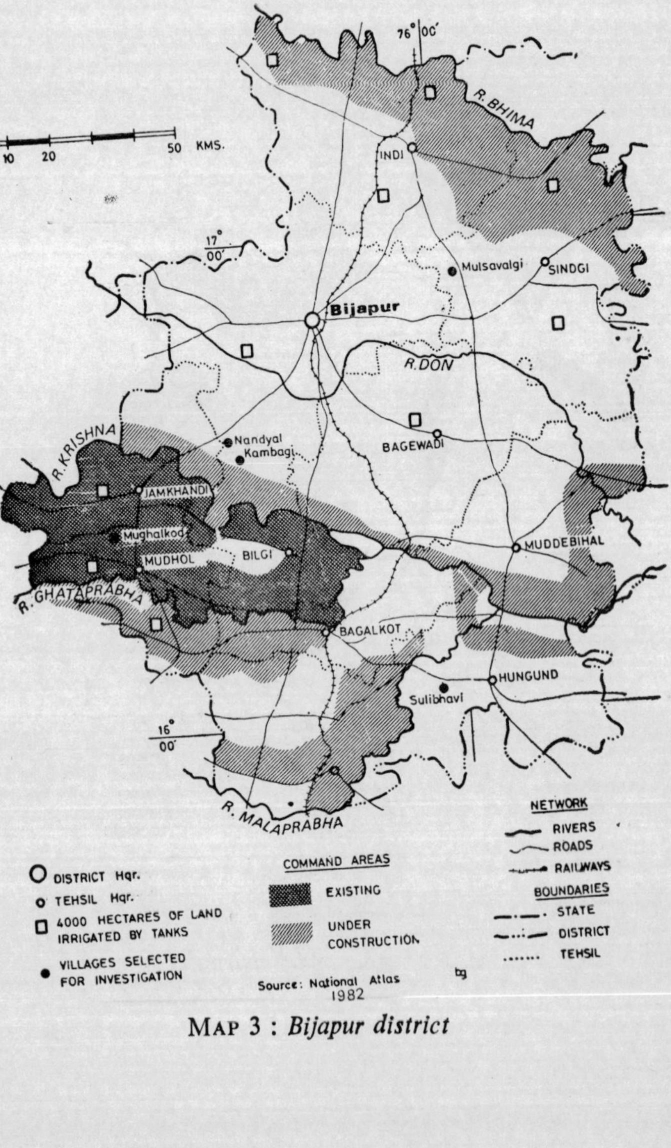

MAP 3 : *Bijapur district*

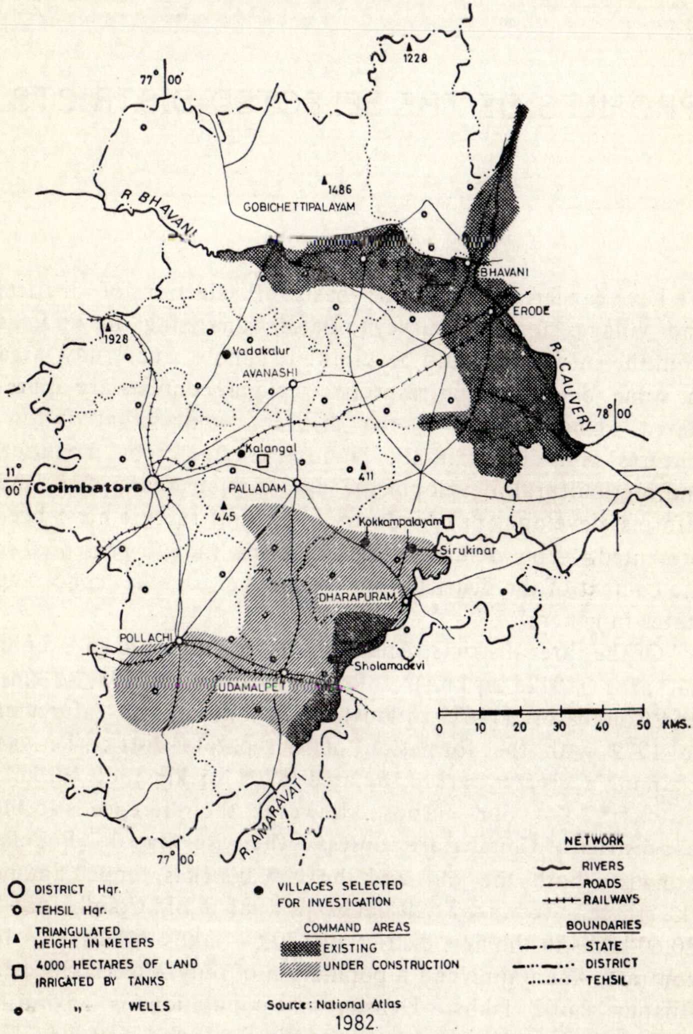

MAP 4 : *Coimbatore district*

3

PROFILES OF THE SELECTED DISTRICTS

We have earlier explained the basis of selection of districts and villages for our survey. Before analysing the findings from the survey, it would be useful to know our study area in some detail so that respective regional contexts are appreciated. Under each of the district profiles that follow, features regarding rainfall, landuse, leading crops, irrigation and agricultural development, agrarian structure and land reforms, development of industry and infrastructure have been presented. The details of land reforms, though presented in the context of the district, have relevance for the concerned states in general.

Of the three districts, Anantapur is the largest in geographical area (19125 sq kms), followed by Bijapur (17056 sq kms) and Coimbatore (15673 sq kms). Coimbatore was bifurcated in 1979 with the formation of a separate district, Periyar, claiming a greater part of the area (8208 sq kms) of the old district.* For our purpose, however, the reference is to the old district of Coimbatore, unless otherwise stated. Populationwise, both the old and the new districts, topped among the three. It was 51.29 lakhs in 1981 in old Coimbatore—30.60 lakhs in the new district and 20.68 lakhs in Periyar. In contrast, Anantapur had a population of only 25.48 lakhs, and Bijapur 24.02 lakhs. Density of population is obviously highest in Coimbatore among the three selected districts—321

*Periyar consists of 6 taluks—Satyamangalam, Gobichettipalayam, Bhavani, Erode, Peruntherai and Dharapuram. Out of the 5 villages selected for survey two come under Periyar.

per sq km for the old district including Periyar, 410 in new Coimbatore and 252 in Periyar as in 1981. It was only 141 in Bijapur and 133 in Anantapur during the same year. Density is a broad or proxy indicator of the level of development as noted earlier. It was lower in Anantapur and Bijapur, not only than in Coimbatore, but also compared to their respective state averages. Some of the statistical details about the three districts can be seen from Appendex I in the preceding chapter.

ANANTAPUR

The district was under direct British rule before Independence and formed a part of the Madras province before States' Reorganisation. It is known for its hot and dry climate and is a part of the semi-arid interior Deccan. It gets its rains mostly from May to November from the South-West Monsoon. The variation in normal rainfall across talukas is not very wide, ranging from 499 mm in Kalyandurg to 617 mm in Kadiri. All talukas in the district are recognised as drought-prone, the frequency of droughts varying from 6 to 12 times in 20 years.

An interesting feature of its agriculture is that net sown area in the district has been conspicuously low, and had hardly increased over the years. It was 47 per cent in 1902-3, and 48 per cent in 1977-78 as a proportion of total geographical area. Area under forests also has been practically stationary at about 10 per cent. Arable but uncultivated land has shown no trend, but fluctuated widely in response to weather. Generally, fallows increase during droughts. But even in 1977-78, which was a relatively good year for the district, such lands—current and other fallows—amounted to 21 per cent, indicating a high proportion of idle land. It is surprising that they are not even brought under tree crops or afforestation, even if they may not be suitable for normal cultivation. Even areas officially under forests did not have noticeable vegetation. Pastures and grazing lands accounted for a mere 1.4 per cent in 1977-78, hardly enough to support a thriving animal husbandry.

Dominant crops of the district are groundnut, korra (an

inferior millet) and jowar, which accounted for 31, 13 and 12 per cent of gross sown area respectively in 1977-78. Area under groundnut has been increasing over the years, as it fetches good price. Jowar and cotton have been losing in area. These are all dry crops. Paddy is the most important crop in irrigated area, accounting for over 60 per cent of it. Red soils dominate in the district and can bear relatively heavy irrigation, unlike Bijapur. The use of irrigation for paddy has pushed up the average productivity of the district in terms of total foodgrains. Ragi is the next major irrigated crop, accounting for about 16 per cent of irrigated area. Wheat and maize are also grown mostly under irrigation.

HYV technology has affected this district too. There is a Dry Farming Agriculture Research Station here which has been trying to improve the adoption of high yielding technology suitable to the region. Groundnut, jowar and bajra—though mostly rainfed—have come under this technology. HYV areas under paddy, ragi and wheat, however, were wholly irrigated. (There can be no rainfed paddy in any case in such a district.) By mid-seventies, about 40 per cent of the cropped area was reported to be under the new varieties; the proportion was expected to have increased to over 50 per cent by early eighties.

Growth in the production of foodgrains has occurred wholly due to increase in productivity. Area under foodgrains actually declined by 30 per cent between 1955-56 and 1978-79, whereas production increased by 18 per cent during the period. In spite of the drought-prone status of the district, principal crops including groundnut and cotton registered a fairly significant increase in yields from mid-sixties to mid-seventies, notable among them being jowar and cotton. Yields of only pulses and chillies, however, declined. In spite of a higher growth in the district than in the state as a whole, particularly in the case of cereals, their average yields are still lower here. But this was more because of the dominance of low yield crops in the crop pattern than because of lower yields in individual crops. Some individual crops like bajra and wheat also had lower yields here. This is not surprising because of lower rainfall, lower irrigation and relatively poor soils. Fertiliser consumption has also been low because of these factors; it was only 15 kgs per hectare of net sown area here, as compared to 54 kgs in the state as a whole in 1980-81. In 1973-74 it was only 5 kgs per hectare here, as against 22 kgs in the state. Though fertiliser consumption has increased in the district, yields have increased mainly due to better seed selection and soil conservation practices and of course increase in irrigation.

The proportion of net sown area irrigated nearly doubled during the decade preceding 1977-78 though even in this year it was only at 14.2 per cent. Wells accounted for 49 per cent of irrigated area, canals coming next with 23 per cent, and tanks with 19 per cent. The role of tank irrigation has declined both relatively and absolutely. Even by 1980-81, the proportion of irrigation had not crossed beyond the 1977-78 level. Though the district has North Pennar and Chitravati rivers, major parts of their beds are dry. Channels to these rivers in some regions have, however, provided irrigation and helped raising even fruit gardens. There are a few other streams too, which have helped tank irrigation. However, it is the Tungabhadra high level canal which is the major project benefiting the district.

The known water potential of the district from its own sources has been less than its utilisation, according to data made available by the Central Water Commission.* The total potential (both surface and ground water) was estimated as 1526.82 M Cum, while utilisation was 2035.60 M Cum. This would suggest that the only hope of expanding irrigation here is through transfer of water from river basins elsewhere. According to another report, however, as much as 31 per cent of ground water resources were underutilised.[1]

In any case, the district has a grave water shortage. It has considerable difficulty in summer in obtaining drinking water particularly in black soil areas of north and north-west taluks—Gooty, Uravakonda, Rayadurg and Kalyandurg. People have to utilise water from small shallow pits on stream-beds in summer, and when they dry up, water has to be obtained by lorries from distances as far as 7 to 10 kms.

*As per information received in March 1980 from the Hyderabad Office of CWC (DAS-1).

Ground water is being exploited in many areas by borewells now for drinking purposes.

Encouraging animal husbandry—both dairy and sheep development—has been an important part of DPAP here. Between 1972 and 1977, however, total livestock population declined from 22 to 17 lakhs, which was most conspicuous in sheep. In certain taluks like Kadiri, which is less drought-prone and has relatively more pasture land, animal husbandry is better developed. A great constraint on development of animal husbandry has been lack of fodder and water and uncertainty in their availability.

Being a drought-prone district, the average size of holding here has been large, viz., 4.41 hectares in 1970-71 and 4.08 hectares in 1976-77, compared to 2.51 and 2.34 hectares in the state as a whole during the same years respectively. The largest size class of 10 hectares and above claimed nearly 47 per cent of the total area, as against only 31 per cent in the state in 1970-71, though these shares declined to 39.5 and 24.8 per cent respectively during 1976-77. The role of small holdings both in number and area is much less in the district than in the state, just as the role of large holdings is much more here. This is typical of drought-prone areas.

However, the small holdings appear to try to be viable by leasing in more land. As per the 1970-71 census of holdings, holdings below 1 hectare had nearly 18 per cent of leased in area here, as against only 8 per cent in the state. This proportion declined here steeply with an increase in the size of holdings, but only gradually declined in the state. The average proportion of leased in area, taking all holdings together, has been marginal at a little over 7 per cent in 1970-71, both in the district and the state as a whole.

The dominant tenure pattern in the district was based on ryotwari principles, but there was a significant proportion of *inam* villages too. Under the Inams (Abolition and Conversion into Ryotwari) Act of 1956, the tenure of *inam* lands was converted into Ryotwari. The Andhra Tenancy Act of 1956 sought separately to protect tenants from unjust eviction, and provided for up to six-year agricultural lease, payment and fixation of fair rents and their remission. It should be noted that the Act gave the landlord the rights to resume land from the tenant after the lease period, and 'personal cultivation' included cultivation with the help of wage labour and cultivation through relatives. The Act gave no pre-emptive right to the cultivating tenant, and there was no attempt to help tenants to become owners.[2]

The Amendment in 1970 allowed resumption subject to the ceiling provided in 1961 Act, viz., three family holdings which meant a range of 18 to 216 acres. This gave a good scope for resumption, apart from the fact that ceiling itself could be circumvented. The 1970 Amendment also sought to restrict the growth of big tenants by prohibiting lease where the tenant already owned more than two family holdings. The Amendment provided pre-emptive right to the cultivating tenant, subject to the above clause. The 1974 Amendment raised the level of rates of rent (30 per cent of gross produce in irrigated land except where irrigation is by baling of water, and 25 per cent in other cases); fixed 6 years as the minimum period for lease and, provided for automatic renewability of lease. Rights of tenant were declared heritable. Tenant has also the right of first purchase in case landlord desires to sell land and the right of mortgaging land for raising loan. The right of landlord for resumption under personal cultivation without insisting on a residency clause, however, went against the interest of tenants.[3] The ceilings fixed in 1973 ranged from 4.05 hectares (10 acres) for double cropped wet land to 54 acres of dry land for a family unit of five members. Implementation, however, is another matter.

The district is dominantly rural, and the proportion of rural population has hardly declined over the last two decades being 82.6 per cent in 1961, 82.2 per cent 1971 and 79.2 per cent in 1981. It is higher than the state level proportion of 76.7 per cent in 1981. Similarly, the proportion of workforce in agriculture has been higher here at 76.9 per cent in 1981, than the state level proportion of 69.5 per cent during the same year. This indicates a low level of diversification and development of the economy as a whole. In such an economy, the proportion of agricultural labourers among total agricultural workers is also low. It was 47 per cent in this district, as against 53 per cent in the state as a whole in 1981.

On the whole, the district is such that when the drought

strikes, there is little to depend upon. Agriculture itself is uncertain and is dominated by large holdings. Nevertheless, the district has recorded significant growth rate in production and yields, though the yield levels are still low by the state and national standards.

BIJAPUR

Bijapur district was a part of the erstwhile Bombay Province before the States' Reorganisation. It receives most of its rain during June to October. Taking the average of 25 years during this century, annual rainfall has increased in the district from 558 mm during 1901-25 to 564 mm during 1926-50, and then rather noticeably to 622 mm during 1951-75. Equally interestingly, the co-efficient of variation in annual rainfall declined conspicuously from 34.2 per cent to 20.0 per cent between the first two periods, and remained almost at the same level at 20.9 per cent during the last. Admittedly, even the increased level at present is quite low and uncertain and the district is still very much a part of the semi-arid Deccan Plateau, and noted for frequent droughts. During every year between 1950-51 and 1972-73, some villages or the other—varying from 22 to 742 out of a total 1247—were declared as scarcity affected in the district.[4] Scarcity relief works have been almost continuously undertaken every year here. As in Anantapur, all talukas are drought-prone. Though average rainfall is slightly higher in Bijapur than in Anantapur, the co-efficient of variation also is higher, indicating that it is more uncertain in Bijapur.

It is interesting that Bijapur has reacted differently to frequent droughts. Whereas the proportion of net sown area in Anantapur was low (48 per cent in 1977-78), it was as high as 80 per cent in 1978-79 in Bijapur. Actually net sown area has shown a slight declining trend over the years, but it still remains high. Perhaps this is one of the reasons for yield levels being higher in Anantapur than in Bijapur. The former's sown area is in selective regions—the less fertile tracts not being cultivated at all.

The district thus has only a little area which is arable but not cultivated. Current fallows have increased corresponding to decline in net sown area, but accounting for only 6.5 per cent in 1978-79. 'Forest land' is marginal, being only 4.9 per cent during this year. Of the 75,000 hectares under the Forest Department, only 7400 are reported to be under forests.[5] Rural people face severe shortage of fuel wood, who have to be content with jowar stalks and cowdung cakes for the purpose. Since black cotton soils here are rated as deficient in organic matter, farm trees at least can play an important role in providing green manure and enabling more cowdung to be used for manure. Soil conservation was undertaken here almost on a war-footing in the form of contour bunding. Farmers have started planting 'bhutale' or sisal fibre plant on bunds to prevent soil erosion. They are being encouraged to grow 'subabul' also both to meet fuel and fodder needs.

Dominant crops of the district are jowar, bajra and cotton accounting respectively for 33, 18 and 14 per cent of cropped area as in 1978-79. The district is also dominant in rabi crops, with 53 per cent of foodgrains area under the rabi season. Area under rabi foodgrains first increased from 6.0 to 7.0 lakh hectares between 1955-56 and 1962-63 and then declined to 5.2 lakh hectares in 1977-78. This is rather contrary to the general trend of increase in rabi area in the country as also in Karnataka in the wake of introduction of HYVs. In Bijapur, however, HYVs recorded greater success in bajra and maize, both kharif crops, both of which gained in area, particularly the latter.

HYVs have not been restricted to irrigated crops here. In all about 1.6 lakh hectares or 11.3 per cent of cropped area was under HYVs here in 1978-79, which is more than the proportion of cropped area irrigated (viz., 9.4 per cent). This was particularly so in the case of bajra, wheat and maize. The bulk of area under HYVs of these crops was rainfed. This can be seen from the following table for 1978-79:

	HYV area as per cent of total area under the crops	Irrigated area as per cent of total area under the crop
Bajra	27.2	5.8
Wheat	42.9	27.4
Maize	86.0	49.6

Source: Calculated from the data from the Directorate of Agriculture, Karnataka.

As in Anantapur, growth in the production of foodgrains has been only due to increase in productivity in Bijapur also. Between 1955-56 and 1978-79 area under foodgrains actually declined from 10.4 lakh to 9.9 lakh hectares (i.e. by 4.7 per cent), but production increased from 2.8 lakh to 5.2 lakh tonnes (i.e. by 83.6 per cent). Productivity per hectare increased in the period from 271 kgs to 549 kgs (i.e. by 102.6 per cent), which is a larger increase than in Anantapur. But even this impressive increase has not improved the yields above average, since Karnataka too recorded impressive gains in yields during the period. This is not just because high productivity crops like paddy are relatively absent here. Even in the case of jowar, the dominant crop of the district, yield per hectare here was only 537 kgs, compared to 852 kgs in the state as a whole in 1978-79. The district, however, has higher yields in the case of wheat, minor millets and pulses.

Fertiliser consumption in the district is extremely low, being a mere 9.8 kgs per hectare in 1980-81 as compared to the state average of 34.7 kgs. In 1973-74, it was only 1.8 kgs in the district, which improved to 8.2 kgs in 1978-79. This is understandable in a district with only 8.6 per cent of net sown area irrigated as late as 1980-81, which is much lower than even in Anantapur. It was a mere 2.1 per cent in 1960-61 and 8.5 per cent in 1978-79. Whatever irrigation is available is mostly used for lightly irrigated crops, since most of the district cannot stand heavy irrigation and is unsuitable for crops like paddy and sugarcane. This has meant low value and low yield crops.

Wells provide dominant portion of irrigation, viz., 56.3 per cent of net irrigated area in 1978-79. Their relative role however has declined through the years, their contribution being as high as 83 per cent in 1960-61. Canals have been playing an increasing role, their share being 28 per cent in 1978-79. Tanks provided 7.4 per cent and other sources 8.3 per cent during the same year. The paradox of Bijapur is that it has no dearth of even perennial rivers, and yet has very little irrigation. In a way, this district too is a land of five rivers*—each with several tributaries, but a distant and poor cousin of the prosperous Punjab.

*Krishna, Ghataprabha, Malaprabha, Dhone and Bhima, the last being on the northern border only.

The district has been covered by a programme to provide drinking water to all villages through borewells. As per official statistics, only 91 out of 1239 inhabited villages had no adequate supply of water as in March 1979. By now, almost all villages were reported to be having drinking water facility. In summer, however, clean drinking water seemed to be continuing as an important problem in many villages.

Concerted efforts are being made in the district, particularly as part of DPAP, to develop animal husbandry. The district, however, has less animal wealth than Anantapur, except in respect of female buffaloes, where Bijapur has a slight edge. The district has a mere one per cent of its area under pastures and grazing land, which is hardly adequate to support a thriving animal husbandry. These lands are also hardly productive of fodder. Jowar stalks, however, serve as a good feed for bovines, in which the district has an advantage. The number of working and breedable bovine population per agricultural family (including labourers) was only 0.96 in the district in 1972, which improved to 1.02 in 1977. This was accompanied by a little qualitative improvement, in so far there was an improvement in the proportion of milch cattle from 54 to 58 per cent during the period.

As in most other drought-prone regions, average size of holdings in Bijapur also is higher, viz., 5.9 hectares in 1970-71 and 5.3 in 1976-77, compared to the state level average of 3.2 and 3.0 hectares respectively in the same years. The role of large holdings both in area and number is also much larger here than even in Anantapur. The size-class of 10 hectares and above in the district claimed 47.2 per cent of operated area in 1970 71 and 40.4 per cent in 1976-77, compared to 31.7 and 28.8 per cent in the state as a whole in the same years respectively. The share of this size-class in number was 16.6 and 13.5 per cent during the same years, compared to 6.2 and 5.2 per cent in the state as a whole. Correspondingly, the role of small holdings was smaller.

Incidence of tenancy is only marginal in Bijapur. Taking all the holdings together, 8.2 per cent of area was rented in 1970-71 in the district, compared to 7.4 per cent in Karnataka. Generally smaller holdings lease in more land; it was particularly so in Anantapur. What is peculiar in Bijapur is that it is the larger holdings which lease in land a little more than even the smaller holdings. The share of rented land was 8.6 per cent in the largest size-group, which declined to 7.6 per cent in the smallest holdings (below 1 hectare) in 1970-71. We have no data on leased in land from the census of holdings in 1976-77. In any case, it appears to be a case of dominant farmers trying to further increase their area by leasing in. Under such circumstances, 'tenant' need not necessarily belong to weaker sections, nor need a 'landlord' to the dominant class.[6]

An interesting dimension of the agrarian structure of the district is the higher proportion of agricultural labour among cultivators, which is unlike drought-prone areas. It was 52.2 per cent in 1981 in the district, as compared to 42.2 per cent in the state as a whole. Cultivation through labourers is apparently more important in the district than through tenancy, irrespective of a little higher share of rented area than in the state as a whole. Though commercialisation of agriculture also tends to increase the proportion of agricultural labour, in this district frequent droughts were the main factor to drive small farmers to sell or lease out their lands, reverting to the status of labourers in the process. While in Anantapur small holdings leased in more, in Bijapur it was the big who did so. It is interesting that even within drought-prone areas, there are almost opposite types of tendencies. Landlord capitalism was more evident in Bijapur.

The district was mainly under ryotwari tenure. The District Gazetteer has noted that only 14 per cent was under *inam* tenure, the rest being under *ryotwari* tenure. The *inams* were subsequently abolished and by the mid-sixties they disappeared. But even the *ryotwari* tenure had problems as elsewhere. Unrestricted rights of transfer and sub-letting of lands prevailed, intermediaries enjoyed absolute rights and peasants were reduced to status of tenants-at-will. The erstwhile Bombay Province took the lead in the matter as early as 1939, by trying to provide fixity of tenure, protection from eviction and rights to house sites. No lease could be made for less than 10 years according to the 1939 Act. A tenant who held land continuously for not less than 6 years before 1.1.1938 became a protected tenant. Tenancy was made heritable. The landlord, however, was given the right to resume land for personal cultivation even from a protected tenant. This right was subjected to a ceiling by a more comprehensive legislation enacted after Independence, through the Bombay Tenancy and Agricultural Land Act, 1948. Also, the landlord could not claim resumption, if the protected tenant became a member of a co-operative farming society. If the landlord failed to cultivate within a year, the land would be restored to the tenant according to this Act. The 1952 Amendment reduced maximum rent to 1/6th of the crop, irrespective of whether the land was irrigated or not. It also made a provision for purchase of land by the tenant on payment through instalments. The right of the landlord to evict the protected tenant was restricted to cases where the income from land was the main source of income for the maintenance of the landlord.[7]

The 1955 Amendment defined an economic holding as 16 acres of Jirayat land, or 8 acres of seasonally irrigated land, or 4 acres of perennially irrigated land. The ceiling on holdings was placed at three times the size of an economic holding. On a day known as Tiller's Day (1.4.1957), every tenant—whether permanent, protected or otherwise—was deemed to have purchased from the landlord land held by him as tenant free from encumbrances, subject to the condition that he cultivated the land personally. This was not applied to the lands leased by a person who did not hold more than an economic holding and where annual income from all sources including the rent of the land did not exceed Rs. 1500.[8] The 1957 Amendment, enacted after States' Reorganisation, suspended the operation of the Act relating to resumption by landlords and purchase by tenants, and required that all surrenders should be registered at the Tehsildar's office. A Committee headed by Shri B.D. Jatti was simultaneously appointed to take a comprehensive view of land tenure and legislation throughout the new state, which inherited different systems. The Committee's recommendations helped in enacting a new legislation for the state—the Mysore Law Reforms Act, 1961, as amended again in 1965.

The 1961 Act for the first time banned leases, except under cases like widows, minors, the disabled, defence personnel and small holders for whom the ban did not apply. The Act permitted resumption 'if the landowner *bonafide* intended to take up personal cultivation or if the tenant had committed defaults like nonpayment of rent or causing damage to land or unauthorised sub-letting or noncultivation for over 2 years.[9] Resumption was permitted also if the land was needed for nonagricultural purposes. There were constraints on resumption regarding extent of area. Also, resumption was not allowed if tenant were rendered landless. The Act placed a ceiling on holdings at 27 standard acres for each family—one standard acre being equal to one acre of first class irrigated land or 8 acres of dry land under regions where rainfall was less than 25" (i.e. 635 mm) per year. Though the Act came into force in 1965, even by 1972 its implementation was lagging and suffered from several drawbacks which contributed to in built delay.[10] In practice, few tenants were actually able to secure ownership rights and landlords enjoyed substantial facilities for displacing tenants. The ceiling too was substantially high; it could go up to 432 acres of dry land per family.

The 1974 Act followed the all-India pattern and directive.[11] It also went beyond central guidelines, as far as tenancy was concerned. Under this Act, none except a soldier or a seaman can lease out land. Concessions to other parties provided under the earlier Act were abolished. The law, however, permits 'personal cultivation' through wage labour. For this purpose, wage could be in kind or cash but not in crop share; and, there has to be supervision of labour by the owner or members of his family. If land is leased in contravention of the law, it would be forfeited to the government without compensation. The Act also abolished resumption by landlords. Tribunals were appointed under the Act to ascertain facts and settle issues. Compensation payable to landlords is based on annual rent or estimated annual net income from land and not on market value of land—20 times the annual net income for dry land and 15 times for irrigated land. Tenants cannot sell or alienate land in any way for 15 years, except by way of mortgage with credit institutions. If a tenant has to, he can surrender it to government in return for premium paid earlier by him for acquiring ownership rights (plus depreciated value of improvements effected by him).

The Act also provided for ceilings, but adopted the concept of a unit (equal to one acre of the land of the highest value or 5.4 acres of D class i.e. dry land), replacing the earlier concept of a standard acre. The ceiling applicable to a family of man, his wife, his minor sons and unmarried daughters, is 10 such units. If the size of family exceeds 5, two extra units are allowed for every additional person, subject to a maximum of 20 units for any single family. Lands under plantation crops like coffee are exempted from the provisions of this Act. Persons with an annual income of more than Rs. 12,000 from sources other than agriculture are debarred from acquiring agricultural land. But this provision is not applicable to cases where by inheritance or personal law, a person acquired agricultural land though having substantial income from non-agricultural sources.

According to official sources, in all only 10,874 hectares of surplus land were distributed as in March 1979, in the district. By the same date, 28,678 applications were decided in favour of landlords, as against 6752 tenants on whom the ownership rights were conferred in the district. The extent of land involved which went in favour of landlords was 23.97 lakh hectares, as against only 41 thousand hectares assigned to tenants.[12] Though this would apparently suggest that land reforms benefited the dominant class of the rural society more than the weaker sections, we may recall the peculiarity of Bijapur, viz., that large farmers held even more rented land than small farmers.

As can be expected, this district too is dominantly agricultural, and the economy is not much diversified. As much as 72.8 per cent of workforce was agricultural in 1981 here, as against 65.0 per cent in the state as a whole. However, this proportion is a little less than in Anantapur (when it was 76 per cent). Household industry is more dominant here than in Anantapur, thanks mainly to handlooms. Bijapur has a great tradition in weaving and several villages and towns have grown because of this activity. This is particularly prominent in Hungund, Jamakhandi and Badami taluks. Ilkal sarees of the district are very popular in the countryside in North Karnataka, Maharashtra and even Andhra Pradesh. The district, however, had only six per cent of its workforce in household industries, though higher than four per cent in the state in 1981.

The factory sector has yet to develop in the district. In 1977-78, it had 403 factories and 7550 factory workers.[18] Anantapur, on the contrary, had 346 factories and 6229 factory workers in 1976. Cotton growing and pressing is the most prominent industry of the district. Vegetable oil industry comes next. Since limestone is available in the district, cement industry has also been started. Slate industry is another based on raw material available in the district. A District Industries Centre has been started in Bijapur in 1978 to encourage industries and meet the needs of entrepreneurs. To further improve and encourage the working of small and cottage industries, training programmes for artisans have been started. Two industrial estates—one in Bijapur and one in Jamkhandi—have been established.

In respect of infrastructure, the district is much less developed than the state, though not so in the proportion of villages electrified. The district had 99 primary schools per lakh of population, as compared to 112 in the state. But this is much higher than in Anantapur. It had only 6 medical institutions per lakh of people in 1971, as compared to 13 in the state. It had only 35 per cent villages electrified in 1971, as compared to 48 per cent in the state. But by 1978-79, the proportion improved to 71 per cent both in the district and the state as a whole.

Literacy rate in this district was only marginally higher than in Anantapur, being 31.8 per cent in the former as against 29.0 per cent in the latter 1981. However, this was lower than the literacy rate of 47.7 per cent in Karnataka.

On the whole, in spite of its handloom units and a few factories, the district has an underdeveloped character. Its agriculture is still one of the most backward, with one of the lowest yield levels in the whole of south India in spite of a significant growth recorded till the end of seventies at least. Its low rainfall, should have been more than compensated by its river resources and also mineral and material wealth. Its industrialisation has been marginal at the most.

COIMBATORE

This district was also under direct British rule at the time of

Independence, and was in the Madras state before the States' Reorganisation. It is undulating, sloping down from hill ranges in the north and west to the Kaveri river in the east. The district gets its rainfall both from the south-west monsoon upto September, breaking through the Palghat gap, and also from the north-east monsoon from October to December. The rainfall here has thus a better spread over the year than in the other two districts selected. Though its annual average is higher, it is more uncertain in any given period. The south-west monsoon here is even more uncertain. Even in terms of annual rainfall, its co-efficient of variation is higher here than in the other two districts. But almost all of its taluks—except Avanashi—have more than 30 per cent irrigation, and even Avanashi has an annual rainfall of over 700 mm. The district as a whole cannot therefore be considered as drought-prone, but its unirrigated parts—forming 57.5 per cent of the net sown area in 1978-79—are subject to greatly uncertain and scanty rainfall. The district provides an example of a drought-prone district, having transformed itself through irrigation. However, it is among the most successful examples. Even when rainfall failed here by more than 25 per cent from the normal level—as it happened in 1958-59, 1967-68 and 1968-69, the district did not witness a marked decline in either production or yield of foodgrains. The need for scarcity relief works does not arise here, certainly not on the scale or dimension as in Anantapur or Bijapur.

Thanks to its irrigation, agriculture is much more prosperous here than in the other two districts, and has a more diversified crop pattern. Jowar, paddy and groundnut were the principal crops, accounting respectively to 24.5, 13.1 and 8.7 per cents of cropped area in 1978-79. Three crops of paddy are raised here, as in several other parts of Tamil Nadu. While cropping intensity was nominal in Anantapur and Bijapur (around 103 per cent), it was 119 per cent in Coimbatore. For an irrigated district, however, this is not impressive. Even irrigation intensity was only 132 per cent, which was not conspicuously higher than the Anantapur level of 123 per cent.

Net sown area here was 46.1 per cent of geographical area in 1978-79 which is lower than in even Anantapur. Though cultivable wastes and other fallows accounted for a small proportion (viz., 1.9 per cent) current fallows were high, viz. 16.1 per cent in the same year. The latter have significantly increased over the years, being only 6.6 per cent in 1955-56, a trend which has occurred with increasing irrigation. On the other hand, pastures and grazing have been nominal, being 1.1 per cent in 1955-56, and only 0.6 per cent in 1978-79. Forests have, however, occupied 25 per cent of land as in the same year, particularly in hilly regions. This proportion was even higher at 32 per cent in 1955-56.

The district appears to be more heterogeneous in soil types than the other two. Soils here are chiefly red sand and gravel, with a moderate area of red and black loam, or sometimes black clay according to the District Gazetteer. Red sandy soils occur in 68 per cent of area. Soils are generally poor, but portions of Udumalpet, Palladam, Avanashi and Coimbatore taluks have black cotton soils.

Production and yields per hectare, however, have recorded significant gains in the district. Production of foodgrains increased in spite of a decline in area under them from 6.1 to 5.3 lakh hectares between 1955-56 and 1978-79. But production increased from 3.95 to 5.69 lakh tonnes, and yield per hectare from 695 to 1081 kgs during the same period. This rate of growth, viz., 55.5 per cent in 23 years, was however, lower than in the drought-prone Anantapur, and Bijapur. Incidentally, Bijapur's average yield of foodgrains even in 1978-79 (viz., 549 kgs per hectare) was lower than in Coimbatore of even 1955-56 (viz., 695 kgs). Even Anantapur's average yield in 1978-79 was only marginally higher (at 734 kgs), than Coimbatore's level in 1955-56. However, the yields of Coimbatore itself were lower than the average in Tamil Nadu, except in paddy, bajra, ragi and cotton.

Irrigation has no doubt played an important part in keeping the yields higher in Coimbatore in comparison with other drought-prone districts, if not with other districts in Tamil Nadu itself. It has enabled the district to raise high value and high yield crops like paddy, cotton and sugarcane. Even as early as 1955-56, a quarter of net sown area was already irrigated, and by 1980-81, over half of the area was irrigated. The completion of Lower Bhavani Project in 1955 was a landmark, which particularly increased the role of canal irrigation. The district is blessed with Kaveri, Bhavani, Nayyal, Amaravathi and Aliyar rivers, which are principal sources of its irrigation, Bhavani being particularly so. Water potential has been tapped mostly through private irrigation in the form of wells. They have been traditionally the most important source of irrigation, providing 56.1 per cent even in 1978-79 followed by canals (42.1 per cent).

One of the interesting features of canal irrigation in some parts of the district is the supply of water on rotational basis in alternative years. At the time of our field work, this was in operation only in the ayacut area of the Parambikulam-Aliyar project, which benefits the southern taluks of Pollachi, Udumalpet, Palladam and Dharapuram. The affected farmers have resented this practice and have even formed an association to press for a regular supply every year. Their contention is that there is considerable under-utilisation of irrigation potential due to slow development of land in ayacut areas; and that if land development is expedited, all ayacut areas can be given water regularly every year. The official contention is that even in the years when irrigation is not given, wells in ayacut areas can make up for the loss to some extent, since the ground water levels have increased due to the project. Rotational supply has also made water available to a large number of farmers, and—theoretically—could help in preventing water logging—a phenomenon which has already affected many irrigated parts of the district. In practice, however, even areas covered by rotational supply had the problem of water logging, mainly due to inefficient management of water supply, inadequate land development and drainage. While ayacutdars were organised to press their claims, they did not show the same enthusiasm for organisation to have a systematic drainage net work and equitable distribution.

In the wake of irrigation development, Coimbatore agriculture has been considerably modernised. This is reflected both in fertiliser consumption and tractor use. The former was in high as 176 kgs per hectare in 1980-81, compared to 92 kgs in Tamil Nadu as a whole. The district had 1.47 tractors per thousand hectares of net sown area in 1977, which however was close to the state average figure of 1.42. But this was much less than a mere 0.32 and 0.58 tractors per thousand hectares in Anantapur and Bijapur respectively in the same year. Tractors are concentrated in Bhavani, Erode, Pollachi and Coimbatore taluks. Tractors are not strongly associated with irrigation; multiple cropping and above all the size of holding also have influenced their use. One could easily notice tractors used for dry farming too.

Bullocks are also in greater use here. Male cattle (over 3 years old) per hectare of cultivated area (net sown area and current fallows) amounted to 0.4 in Coimbatore district in 1977, compared to 0.3 in Anantapur and 0. 2 in Bijapur. Total livestock here was over 24 lakhs, as against only 17 and 16 lakhs respectively in Anantapur and Bijapur. Relatively to human population, however, Coimbatore had actually less female bovines. The milk economy is more cattle-based here (accounting for 63 per cent female bovines over 3 years old, as against 61 per cent in Anantapur and 53 per cent in Bijapur). In terms of sheep and poultry also, Coimbatore is more developed, suggesting that animal husbandry economy also is more diversified here. It had 5.8 lakh sheep in 1977, compared to 4.9 lakhs in Anantapur and 3.1 lakhs in Bijapur. Similarly, it had 8.8 lakhs poultry, compared to 6.8 lakhs in Anantapur and 5.1 lakhs in Bijapur.

The average size of holding in this district was only 2.8 hectares in 1970-71 and 2.2 hectares in 1976-77 as against the state average of 1.5 and 1.25 during the same years respectively. Though this is smaller in Coimbatore than in Anantapur and Bijapur, it has to be seen in the context of higher irrigation. Though compared to Anantapur and Bijapur the dominance of large holdings also appears to be less here, it is more than in Tamil Nadu as a whole. The largest size-class of 10 hectares and more claimed 23.5 per cent of area and 3.8 per cent of holdings in this district in 1970-71, compared with 12.9 per cent of area and 1.2 per cent of holdings in the state as a whole, though it is close to the state average in irrigation. The proportion of area under these holdings declined in 1976-77 to 17.4 per cent in the district and 10.4 per cent in the state.

Tenancy as such is much less in the district than in Anantapur and Bijapur, and also as compared to Tamil Nadu. On the whole, rented land accounted for only 5.4 per cent here, compared to 8.7 per cent in the state. But the rented portion tended to increase somewhat with the size of holding here as in Bijapur, but unlike in the state as a whole. The rented portion ranged from 3.9 per cent in the smallest size-group to 5.8 per cent in the largest size-group and in the size-group of 4 to 10 hectares. In Tamil Nadu, there was no pattern of increase and decrease in rented area as the size of holding increased and fluctuated in a narrow range of 7.5 to 9.7 per cent.

The proportion of agricultural labourers among total agricultural workers is an interesting dimension of agrarian structure. It was as high as 66.8 per cent in Coimbatore (reorganised) as compared with 52.1 per cent in Tamil Nadu in 1981. This was higher than in Anantapur and Bijapur too. While tenancy was marginal, cultivation was mainly through labourers. Being much more irrigated, labour requirement of even small farmers is higher here. Through manpower requirement in Coimbatore agriculture is obviously greater, the dominant form it has taken is not necessarily of small farms operated mainly or entirely through family labour, but of farms operated mainly through hired labour. The household level data would give more insights into this situation.

The dominant tenure system in the district had been *ryotwari* even during the British days, though this did not obviously exclude sub-letting or hired labour. A significant part of the area was also under inam and zamindari or palayam systems, which were treated as estates. The Madras (Estates Abolition and Conversion into Ryotwari) Act of 1948 transferred estate lands, commercial lands, forests, and streams etc. within estates to the government, after which the estates were surveyed and resettled on ryotwari basis. Landholders including *zamindars* were entitled to *ryotwari pattas* in respect of private lands held by them.

Though the extent of tenancy as per the 1970-71 Census of Agricultural Holdings appears marginal, it must have been much more extensive in the past. It prevailed under different forms. The District Gazetteer for Coimbatore has given a brief account of the same (p. 566). Apart from the usual fixed rent and crop sharing (*varam*) systems, there was a system known as *kootu*, under which the landholder also worked with tenant and took an additional one-fourth of crop share apart from the usual half *varam.* Two alternative systems prevailed when land was mortgaged to a creditor. Under one system, creditor himself cultivated land, paid taxes and enjoyed the harvested crop till the loan was repaid with interest. Under the alternative system, mortgager was allowed to cultivate the land on the execution of a lease bond for rental equivalent to the interest on the loan.

Rents were quite high, ranging from one-third to three-fourths, and covered not only the main crop but also straw and subsequent crops. Rents were reported to be higher in irrigation projects areas than in other areas. Suits for ejecting tenants were significantly high. The proportion of absentee landlords was said to be about 10 per cent as per official reports around 1949 (See District Gazatteer, p. 567).[14] But absentee landlords were not necessarily urban residents. They often resorted to 'self cultivation' in the villages where they lived, and leased out their land in other villages. 'Self cultivation through labour was also common, irrespective of whether the land was located in villages of residence or elsewhere.

An Act was passed in 1955, aimed at protecting tenants from eviction. Sonachalam has indicated that few tenants benefited from this Act at least through court settlement, as very few complaints were made. A further Act in 1956 fixed fair rents, and the 1969 Act provided for maintaining records of rights. Mencher has remarked that neither of these were quite effective in practice, since there was no awareness of legal provisions; even if it was there, the weaker tenants could not decide the terms. (Mencher, pp. 112-113).

If this was the fate of tenancy reform, the impact of ceilings legislation was no brighter. The first land ceilings legislation in Tamil Nadu was passed in 1961, which set a ceiling of 30 standard acres for a family of 5 members and exempted plantations, orchards, garden land under sugarcane etc. from the scope of the ceilings. Very little land reportedly was available as surplus. For Coimbatore district, the estimated surplus amounted to a mere 14,975 acres, most of which (viz., 14,429 acres) was dry land. For the state as a whole, the surplus estimated was 2,40,068 acres, of which 88,964 acres were dry land. (Sonachalam, p. 70). Actually, however, only 2648 acres were declared as surplus in the district by 31.3.1967, and only 25,153 acres in the state as a whole. (Sonachalam, p. 82).

In 1972, the ceiling was reduced to 15 standard acres for a family of five members. The ceiling could be higher for larger families, but not beyond 30 standard acres. One standard acre was equal to 0.8 acre of best class of wet land and 4 acres of the most inferior dry land. Several exemptions were withdrawn, but those relating to plantations, religious trusts and orchards continued, subject to some conditions. Mencher has presented interesting details of how in practice the ceiling was circumvented and has indicated requirements for a change in the system of maintenance of records of land owenership (pp. 117-125).

According to a recent report, about 1,20,000 acres were expected to be available as surplus under the new ceilings legislation. Unlike as in Karnataka, tenancy has legally continued in Tamil Nadu. Under the 1969 Act, 4,09,645 tenants were registered so far in the state as a whole, involving 6,16,504 acres.[15]

Leaving aside Madras, Coimbatore (new district) had the lowest production of rural population at 49.5 per cent in the entire state in 1981, Periyar, the new district, is more rural—the proportion being 78 per cent, and in the two districts together it was 61.0 per cent, compared with the state level proportion of 67 per cent. Even in 1971, the old district had 64.4 per cent of its population in rural areas, as against 69.7 per cent in the state. Coimbatore is urbanised in a more fundamental sense than is indicated by the proportion of urban population. Even its villages are more urbanised, more developed, and have more amenities and infrastructure than taluk headquarters in Bijapur. Coimbatore villages are better connected by roads and buses, and more developed in terms of non-agricultural activities. Its villages are also much bigger than those in the other two districts. The average size of population per village in Coimbatore even in 1971 was 3022, compared to 1870 and 1262 in Anantapur and Bijapur respectively. This could have given a viable base for rural infrastrcuture in Coimbatore.[16] Every taluka, moreover, has one town or city (except Udumalpet which has only one). In all, the district had 58 towns or cities even in 1971, compared with only 11 in

Anantapur and 17 in Bijapur. The district represents a case of of rural and urban development—or agricultral and industrial development—having proceeded hand in hand, each reinforcing the other, and providing development stimuli spatially on a wider scale than in Anantapur and Bijapur. We find evidence of this in terms of dispersal of factories, schools, medical institutions and workforce engaged in non-agricultural activities. An interesting feature of industrial development of the district is that while the expansion of the large sector slowed down here, the small-scale sector rapidly increased between 1960 and 1970, which was contrary to trends in the states as a whole. While employment in the small-scale sector increased only by 31.5 per cent in the state, it increased in the district by 100.4 per cent during the period.[17] This is consistent with a wider spatial spread of industries, development of small towns, and involvement of even villages in industries.

The higher level of development is reflected in terms of literacy rates too. Compared to Anantapur and Bijapur, both the new district of Coimbatore and Periyar have higher levels of literacy—the former with 53.1 and the latter with 39.8 per cent as in 1981. The state average was 46.8 per cent. Interestingly, the number of primary schools per lakh of population has been no higher in Coimbatore. It was only 24.2 in 1971, compared with 57.1 in Anantapur and 99 in Bijapur. Of course, we do not suggest a negative association between this and literacy!

On the whole, Coimbatore is more developed in agriculture, industry and infrastructure, than either Anantapur or Bijapur. Both agriculture and industry again are highly diversified here. Perhaps the thrust of the large scale sector and also towards diversification weakened by 1970, but inspite of this the district retains its eminent position. It cannot be attributed to irrigation alone, since there are other districts in the state which have the same or even higher level of irrigation since long, and yet not as developed. Entrepreneurial qualities of the trading community and certain other elite communities like Naidus, greater importance of cash crops like cotton and, other factors too would have contributed to the development of the district. It remains to be seen in our subsequent chapters how the benefits of this are shared by different sections of its people, and by unirrigated areas within the district.

References

1. *Commerce*, Annual Number, 1975.
2. G. Damodar Reddy, 'Tenancy Reform in Telangana and Andhra Regions, in B. A. V. Sharma (ed.) *Political Economy of India: A Study of Land Reforms Policy in Andhra Pradesh*, New Delhi, Light and Life, 1980, pp. 356-357.
3. For details, Ibid, pp. 345-362.
4. Govt. of Karnataka, 'Economic Development of Bijapur district—Under 'Drought-prone Areas Programme with World Bank Assistance', Bangalore 1973, Table 3, p. 310.
5. Ibid., p. 121.
6. This was found to be so by the author also in drought-prone areas of Marathwada, Maharashtra. See M. V. Nadkarni 'Tenants from the Dominant Class—An Emerging Contradiction in Land Reforms,' *Economic and Political Weekly*, Review of Agri., December 1976.
7. For details see Chapter XI, 'Revenue Administration', in the District Gazetteer, Bijapur op.cit.
8. Ibid., p. 334.
9. See M.A.S. Rajan, *The Land Reforms Law in Karnataka: A Descriptive Account*, Govt. of Karnataka, Bangalore, 1974, p. 4.
10. Ibid., p. 9.
11. The account of the Act here is based on Rajan, Ibid.
12. 'Talukawise Plan Statistics—Bijapur District', Planning Department, Govt. of Karnataka, Bangalore, 1979 pp. 12 & 13.
13. In 1978-79, there were 429 factories and 10,088 factory workers. Cf. 'Bijapur District 1978-79—An Economic Review', issued by the District Statistical Officer in 1980.
14. Apart from the Coimbatore District Gazetteer (1966), for an account of the agrarian and tenurial conditions in Tamil Nadu, see also Joan P. Mencher, *Agriculture and Social Structure in Tamil Nadu*, Allied, New Delhi, 1978, pp. 74-125, and K. S. Sonachalam, *Land Reforms in Tamil Nadu*, Oxford & IBH, New Delhi, 1970. Mencher has discussed different forms of tenure in detail which prevailed in Tamil Nadu, particularly in Chingleput district.
15. See 'Implementation of Land Reforms', special issue on Rural Development in Tamil Nadu, *Kurukshetra*, vol. 27, No. 11, March 1,1979 pp. 4 & 5.
16. V.K.R.V.Rao has since long emphasised the importance of the size of the village as an important factor in rural development, as it provides a viable base for infrastructure & industries. See his, *Neglected Factors in Integrated Rural Development*, Convocation Address, IARI, New Delhi, 1977.
17. See C.T. Kurien and Josef James, *Economic Change in Tamil Nadu*, Allied, New Delhi, 1979, esp. pp. 110 & 124.

4

PROFILES OF THE SELECTED VILLAGES

WE present here brief profiles of selected villages, drawn both from village level data and field impressions obtained by us during the survey. The profiles include location, infrastructure, conspicuous features of social and economic structure, and activities, and situation regarding drinking water and sanitation. Table 4.1 presents the number of households and population in the villages, taken from the Censuses of 1961 and 1971, and the growth rate between the two years. It shows which of them have been fast growing. The table also presents literacy levels. (See the district maps for their locations.) Most of these villages have hamlets. Our survey covered them too, in addition to the main villages.

Rayalacheruvu

Rayalacheruvu is a large village which had 644 households and 3323 people in 1971. As per our census survey, it had 697 households and 3746 people in 1978-79. According to local history, the village was built by Krishnadevaraya of Vijayanagara. It is on the rail-line connecting Guntakal and Renigunta (Madras-Bombay broad gauge) and, also on the state highway connecting Guntakal and Jammalmadugu. It is a Panchayat Headquarter, and located at a distance of 32 kms from Tadapatri, its taluka headquarter. The main village has also two hamlets (Ramarajupalli and Kurmajipet) connected by a kutcha road.

It is a significantly irrigated village, with well over half of the cultivated area under irrigation by tanks, wells and other minor sources. It had no canal irrigation. It has a large tank irrigating over 500 acres, mostly under small holdings. There were complaints that the tank was not looked after well due to the pressure from large holders, since in the absence of dependable irrigation the small holders would be forced to provide labour as a source of living and the large holders would get cheap labour. The large holders got their irrigation mostly from wells. Since several large holders had no irrigation, an element of jealousy also had allegedly led to the neglect of tank maintenance.

No household in the village owned tractors, but 67 electric pumsets were in operation in 1977-78 according to village records. There were 77 iron ploughs out of 188 owned.

The village has a diversified economy, mining and quarrying being the main activity other than irrigation. Some minerals used in chemical industry, limestone and mosaic chips are mined from the surrounding area and exported from the village railway station. About 200 wagon loads were said to be departing every month with minerals. Mining, loading and transport absorb a significant amount of manpower.

The village had no significant programmes apart from normal agricultural schemes for credit, seed and fertiliser distribution. The village has a post office, two private dispensaries and only primary schools. There was a multipurpose co-operative society, having 336 members, only Rs. 10,000 as deposits and Rs. 74,100 as advances during 1977-78. A commercial bank was expected to open a branch during our field work. The village had 7 groceries, 15 tea/coffee stalls, 3 cloth shops, 9 tailoring shops, 5 artisan shops and 7 hair cutting saloons. For a village, this looked impressive, and has been the result of mining and transport activities.

The village had no protected water. Wells provided the main source of drinking water. There were about 12 public and 10 private wells used for the purpose. A tank too was used for drinking water. The sheduled castes had separate settlements and also separate facilities for drinking water, with one ordinary well and one borewell. There were no complaints of any severe scarcity of drinking water. Even during droughts, they have not faced serious difficulties. In view of the increasing population in the village, schemes for stepping up drinking water supply have been reportedly drawn up. The village has electricity, used both for lighting and irrigation. Only a few houses had electric connections.

Our field investigators, who had to stay in the village for quite a few days for investigation, noticed fairly widespread *matka* gambling. It seems to have affected large sections of population irrespective of age and sex. Even children who earned only Re. 1 or Rs. 1.50 per day through limestone picking used to bet at least ten paise a day. Average amount spent on betting per day amounted to Rs. 200 to 250 totalled for all people. An interesting aspect of the phenomenon was that even the poorest sections were involved in betting, with fond hopes of making at least small fortunes.

Korrapadu

This is comparatively a medium size village. It had 280 households and 1668 people in 1971. As per our field survey, it had 366 households and 2031 people in 1978-79. It is only 14 kms from Anantapur, but about a kilometre from bus stop on the main road connecting Anantapur with Tadapatri. It is accessible by a kutcha road, greeting the visitors with fine greenery and orchards. A hamlet—Neelareddipalli—about one and a half km away is a part of this village.

The village has come under irrigation mainly during the seventies through canal water. As per the Districts Census Handbook 1971, the village had only 6 per cent irrigation; when we visited, it had nearly half of the net sown area under irrigation. Canals provided 69 per cent of irrigation, wells providing the rest. Canal irrigation had only 43 beneficiaries according to village records, whereas there were 95 beneficiaries from well irrigation, of whom 20 benefited from community wells. No tractors were reportedly owned by any in the village, but there were 75 pumpsets of which 40 were oil engines in 1977-78, according to village records. Only one iron plough was reported out of 151 during the same year. Cultivation was dominated mostly by the Kapu caste—a prosperous peasant community. In fact, two Kapu families seemed to control major portions of fertile and irrigated land in the village, though they did not live under single roofs. They held an important position in the village, and lived in a style totally different from the others. Some of the houses were quite large and luxurious and stood apart from others in every respect. A few other castes, Kamma, Kuruba, Brahmins, Vysyas and Devangas also seemed to have moderately good living styles and houses, and shared a certain amount of cultivated area. The scheduled castes came at the bottom having very poorly built small 'houses'.

The economy of the village was not very diversified in the sense of having rural or other industries. However, quite a few households had dairy, based on cattle. Sheep husbandry has not been popular, but encouragement to it has been given recently particularly through provision of credit by a commercial bank. DPAP schemes are in operation here, covering dairy, sheep, pasture development and soil conservation. Among these, only dairy development seems to be conspicuous. A co-operative milk society has been formed in 1976, which is active in the Neelareddipalli hamlet. Milk is sent mostly to Anantapur.

The village was electrified in 1976 and 80 households had domestic connection by 1978. Both oil and electric pumpsets were used for irrigation. The village had a primary school with about 86 students and two teachers, teaching up to the Vth standard. There were 26 students from scheduled castes and tribes. For further secondary education, they had to travel eight kms by bus. The village has a post office, but no credit society or dispensary, which are available only 8 to 10 kms away. The village does not have satisfactory drainage and sanitary facilities. Drinking water is a problem in summer, from April to July. No plans for alleviating this scarcity were reported to be in existence.

Trading facilities even for purchasing petty goods were far too limited within the village. It had only 5 petty shops selling beedies, lottery tickets, *paan* and so on operating both on barter and cash basis.

Goridindla

Goridindla is a cluster of 7 settlements at a distance of 1.5 to 9 kms three of which are *thandas* of scheduled tribes. Together, it is a fairly large village. It had 669 households and 3676 people in 1971. As per our survey, it had 707 households and 3789 people. The village is quite in the interior, accessible by a kutcha deviation road at a distance of 10 kms from the main road junction at Atmakur. Atmakur is on the state highway connecting Anantapur with Kalyandurg, about 26 kms from the former. A few of the hamlets of Goridindla are even more in the interior. The main village has the benefit of a bus service daily, with only one trip to and from Anantapur. People prefer bullock carts to go to Atmakur, where they have more frequent services.

No hamlet has significant irrigation. There were, however, 52 irrigation pumpsets in the village in 1977-78 of which 22 were run on electricity, irrigating in all about 160 hectares, which was less than 10 per cent of cultivated area. No tractors were reported. Only 4 iron ploughs were recorded out of 824 during 1977-78. The village has been covered by soil conservation schemes.

The economy of the village, however, is moderately diversified, thanks mainly to DPAP schemes for promoting sheep husbandry, involving both breeding and rearing. A co-operative society has been formed for the purpose and, veterinary services have been provided, apart from sheep, sheds and credit. Dairy, however, has not developed mainly due to scarcity of fodder. Even sheep husbandry has been mainly adopted by cultivating households, in the sense that the sheep are owned by them; the task of tending them is done by labourers.

Sheep husbandry, has not spread to the thandas of scheduled tribes. They have depended so far mainly on agricultural labour and limestone burning and selling. In the three scheduled tribe hamlets particularly, limestone burning and selling has been a main source of income. But this is a seasonal and not a year-round, activity. Under DPAP schemes, some cattle have been distributed to the thandas, but this has not made an impact.

Infrastructure conditions differed widely as between hamlets of this village, but quite underdeveloped on the whole. Sanitation and drainage were almost nonexistent and housing was in a poor shape except a few belonging to the rich. However, government schemes for housing the weaker sections have made some impact on one of the scheduled tribe hamlets, where they had moderately pucca houses. Drinking water was a problem particularly in summer, but the condition was not quite bad in at least 3 hamlets where they had good wells. Goridindla-main was worse off in this respect, along with two out of three scheduled tribe hamlets.

The village had nominal electricity, mainly confined to Goridindla-main and Muttala—the latter being the largest of the hamlets. It had two post offices, and also a co-operative credit society. It had no bank and medical facilities within the village, for which it depended on Atmakur and Anantapur. The village was served by primary schools, one in each hamlet; one of them was being conducted in a temple, not having its own building. In one of the scheduled tribe hamlets, though there was a provision of a school and a teacher, it did not seem to be functioning.

It was difficult to say that the scheduled tribe hamlets alone had inferior infrastructure, compared to others. In fact, only 2 out of 7 hamlets had somewhat better infrastructure, neither of them being a ST hamlet. Among the remaining there were both ST and non-ST hamlets.

Chinnamushturu

This is rather a small village. It had only 204 households and 1124 people in 1971, but only 190 households and 1057 people as per our field survey. This is a singular village and not a cluster of hamlets, unlike other villages surveyed by us in the district. It is only 6 kms from the taluk headquarters, Uravakonda. It is also on the state highway between Anantapur and Uravakonda and can be said to be well located. But it appeared also to be relatively backward having dry agriculture, which was not even covered by soil conservation. Though a few rich farmers tried to dig wells, water level was not adequate and only seasonally available. As such, it could not lead to a shift to high yielding for high value irrigated crops significantly. There was evidence of several families having migrated, some of them permanently, and some seasonally. No tractors were reported from the village. There were, however, 26 electric pumpsets during 1977-78. Only 86 ploughs were reported, none of which was made of iron. A few Kamma households seemed to be dominating most of the land.

On the whole the economy of this village could not be considered as quite diversified. Though it had some non-agricultural activities, they have either been only supplementary sources of income or not remunerative enough to attract workforce. 'Thread-reeling' has been an important industry here mainly confined to women. The concerned families buy cotton thread, process, dye and reel it, and then supply it to merchants of Uravakonda for saree weaving units there. However, it is not the main source of income for these families any longer. Two communities—Vaddars and to some extent Boyas have taken to quarrying from small hillocks nearby, which has emerged as a noticeable activity of the village in the last decade. Recently, a quarry workers' co-operative society has been formed. Dairy activity was being encouraged, but the village has fodder scarcity impeding its progress.

The village has electricity, a primary school, a post office, and a milk co-operative society. Being close to Uravakonda and having bus facilities, the village has access to higher education, medical facilities and so on.

The village has acute scarcity of drinking water during summer. It has two public wells, and two more borewells in the scheduled caste and Vaddar settlements respectively have been commissioned recently. But water level declined significantly in summer.

Beluguppa

This is the largest of the villages surveyed in Anantapur district, which had 751 households and 4314 people in 1971, and 846 households and 4961 people as per our survey for 1978-79. It is a slow growing village, its population having increased by only 9 per cent between 1961 and 1971. It is located on the Anantapur-Rayadurg road, and is at distance of 28 kms from Kalyandurg (taluka headquarters) and 54 kms from Anantapur. It is well connected by bus, both to Anantapur and Kalyandurg. It is a *firka* or *hobli* headquarter and also a Panchayat headquarter. It is almost a singular village, but for a hamlet (a scheduled tribe thanda) attached to it.

It is a very dry village with practically no irrigation. But its main activity is *kambli* (coarse rug) weaving, for which it is a famous centre. Beluguppa *kamblis* have a good market in rural areas even outside the district and the state. As such, the village has impressive amenities and infrastructure. It had 3 primary schools, one secondary school, a post office with telegraph and telephone facilities, a primary health centre, veterinary dispensary, a commercial bank, co-operative credit society, and even a police station. A kambli weavers' co-operative society had been formed, but was as good as defunct during our visit. The scheduled tribes, consisting mainly of Banjaras were somewhat organised. There was a Banjara Welfare Association, and also a Banjara Women's and Children's Welfare Association.

Apart from kambli weaving, sheep rearing—a related activity is also significant here. Being a large village with a rural industry, quite a few artisans also thrived here, including carpenters, blacksmiths, potters and tailors. But agriculture too was not negligible, and was still the main occupation in the village. Groundnut and cotton were conspicuous crops, apart from jowar, korra etc. Land appeared to be concentrated mainly in the hands of a dominant peasant caste—Kapus. Apart from these activities, there was also lime-stone burning, involving mainly the scheduled tribe families. Dairy was only a marginal activity.

Two private tractors and 104 pumpsets were reported to be in existence during 1977-78 according to village records; of the latter 64 were run on electricity. During the same year, there were 987 ploughs, 65 of which were made of iron. Considering the marginal character of irrigation, the higher number of pumpsets reported could look surprising. Only about 84 hectares were reported under irrigation in 1977-78.

The main activity of the village—kambli weaving and sheep-rearing—was dominated by Kuruba (shepherd) community, with a marginal involvement of Banjaras as well. But the former community was also said to be diversifying, quite a few families engaged in cultivation too. The weavers were hard pressed both for raw material and finance to purchase it. A co-operative society, which was fomred to help the weavers in this respect and also in selling their product, did not succeed in this task. Its place was reportedly taken over by a private individual belonging to the same Kuruba community, who advanced loans and supplied raw material; in return, the weavers had to sell their produce to him at prices fixed by him, the proceeds being adjusted against loans taken. A local commercial bank has hardly been able to take his place as creditor.

Sheep rearing in the village is hardly adequate to meet the raw material needs of the weaving industry. A few enterprising weavers go out in search of raw material themselves. Most of the weavers are poor and are not able to rear sheep themselves except on a marginal basis. It is the cultivators who mostly own the sheep, though tending sheep may be done through Kuruba labour. Weaving does not provide year-round employment, and many weavers have to seasonally migrate in search of raw material or work.

In terms of drinking water, the village is better off than Chinnamushturu or Gorindindla. Apart from a few ordinary wells, there were four tubewells and four borewells. The village, however, faced some scarcity during three months from March to May. Though it is a large village with even Panchayat headquarters located here, sanitary conditions were not satisfactory. There were only six public and seven private toilets in the whole village, and they did not have water connections. No proper drainage system existed.

In terms of other infrastructure, however, the village was better off. It had 16 groceries, four fair price shops, 11 tea/coffee shops, 12 cloth shops, 25 tailor shops, two chemist shops, a mutton stall, a cycle shop. two toddy/arrack shops, 15 pan-beedi stalls, and seven vegetable shops. It had also two playgrounds and a tent cinema, which are not a normal feature of villages. These details are mentioned, because it would show that even when a large village attracts all these amenities, it may still be deficient in proper drainage and sanitation facilities and a clean environment. Probably, that is because it needs community interest and help. Even the richer sections in villages have no particularly keen interest in community sanitation.

Mughalkhod

This is a medium size village which had 324 households and 2253 population in 1971, and 368 households and 2117 population in 1978-79 as per survey. It is about $1\frac{1}{2}$ kms off the main road connecting Mudhol (taluka headquarter) with

Mahalingapur in Bijapur district. It is midway between these two towns, at a distance of eight kms from each. It is served by bus both way on the main road. It is a singular village, with no hamlets attached.

The village is highly irrigated, benefiting from Ghataprabha left bank canal. Most of the increase in irrigated area took place during the seventies only. Earlier, at the end of the sixties, about 17 per cent of area was irrigated, half of which was by private wells. When we visited, about 61 per cent of the area was irrigated mostly by canals. Irrigation was available mostly in the kharif season. Maize was the most important irrigated crop, followed by sugarcane.

The village had 3 private tractors during 1977, 180 pumpsets (electric), 13 sugarcane crushers, and 110 ploughs (50 iron).

The village economy was hardly diversified, agriculture being the single most dominant occupation. Dairy has developed a little recently, based mostly on buffaloes. A few families maintained sheep, goats and poultry too. But these were subsidiary activities, and have not been significant enough to absorb manpower from cultivation as such.

For most of its needs, the village has to depend on Mudhol or Mahalingapur, 10 kms away. There were, however, two primary schools, a post office, a consumer co-operative serving as a fair price shop, and also 5 private groceries.

The village has electricity, and about 150 houses had domestic connections. The village had no problem of drinking water even in summer. Normal wells and borewells were the source for the same. Though water was not a great problem, the general sanitary conditions were poor. There was no drainage system, nor any public or private toilets.

Nandyal

This is the smallest village in our entire sample, having had only 97 households and 702 people in 1971 and, only 111 households and 731 people in 1978-79 as per our field survey. Though located in Bijapur taluka itself, it is rather in the interior not being near any main road. Nearest busstop was 2 km away at Chikkalki in Jamakhandi taluka. It is a singular village, without any hamlets attached.

The village had about 32 per cent of area under irrigation

through wells in 1978-79. There were 104 irrigation wells in the village irrigating 108 hectares in 1977-78. There were 30 pumpsets, 16 of which were run by electricity. No tractors were reported, and out of 70 ploughs, 21 were made of iron. Though soil conservation programme is being extensively implemented in the district, this village had not come under the same atleast till 1978-79. There were no large land-holders here with 20 hectares or more, unlike other villages in Bijapur and Anantapur. Holdings were mostly small or medium below 10 hectares.

The village economy was hardly diversified, cultivation being the mainstay. Dairy, based both on cows and buffaloes, and goat rearing have made some progress. In 1977, the village was reported as having only 21 cows, 45 female buffaloes, 60 goats and 332 poultry.

There were no amenities to speak of within the village. However, there is a primary health centre in Gunadal, a village which is 2 kms by walk and also dispensaries in Chikkalki also 2 kms away by walk. Gunadal also has a veterinary centre. There was a one-teacher primary school in Nandyal, and for higher schooling the children had to go to Chikkalki. There was not even a post office in the village. No acute scarcity of drinking water was reported in the village. No sanitary or drainage facilities were found. However, the village appeared fairly clean and well maintained. Muslims formed the largest part of the population here.

Mulsavalgi

This is a medium size village which had 488 households and 2751 population in 1971, and 523 households and 3067 population in 1978-79 as per our survey. Dairy is its prominent economic activity, supplying milk to Bijapur, Though it is in Sindgi taluk, the village borders on Bijapur taluka. The village is rather in the interior, the nearest road—where buses run—being 5 kms away approached through a mud track. Even the nearest road is a diversion route connected to Bijapur-Indi road. A bus came to the village once daily in good weather conditions; when it rained, the village was cut off. A milk van came, however, every day to collect milk. Very few owned bullock carts and as such transport problems of the majority were not solved by these carts. A hamlet—a Lambani thanda—consisting of about 35 families is also attached to this village. But it is about 5 kms away from the village, and not quite well integrated with the main village.

The village had some irrigation through a PWD tank and private wells. During 1978-79, nearly 18 per cent was reported to be under irrigation, most of which was developed during the seventies. The village is electrified, but power was used only for irrigation and no domestic connections were reported during our visit. There were 50 oil engines, 25 irrigation pumpsets and 29 persian wheels. Though as a proportion, irrigated area looked rather small, in absolute terms it amounted to 360 hectares in 1978-79.

The dairy economy was based both on buffaloes and cows. In 1977, 235 cows and 164 she-buffaloes (over 3 years old) were reported. There were also 549 goats, 354 sheep and 369 poultry. A dairy co-operative was formed some time back, but it was defunct during our visit. The daily collection of milk for sale outside was not impressive, amounting to only about 50 litres a day at that time. The major complaint was scarcity of fodder, and it was felt that the co-operative should have solved this difficulty. A commercial bank, 10 kms away at Hippargi, had been giving loans for livestock purchase to some of the persons here.

The village has a primary and middle level school, and also a post office. But for this, the village infrastructure is poor. Medical and veterinary facilities were available only 10 kms away at Hippargi. There were only about 6 shops in the village, including groceries, tea stalls and a cloth shop.

Drinking water posed some difficulties in summer, but the problem did not appear to be quite severe. There were 4 borewells. No plans of improving drinking water supply were reported. As usual, no drainage or sanitary facilities existed.

Kambagi

Kambagi is a medium size village. It had 472 households and 1877 people in 1971, but only 378 households and 2234 people in 1978-79 as per our field survey. This is inclusive of a hamlet Hanumanthasagar attached to it, located about 3 kms away. It is an interior village, served by a kutcha road linking Chikgalgali with Bijapur, the latter being its taluka headquarter 45 kms away.

Most of the cultivated land here is rugged and rocky, and was converted at some stage from pastures. Kambagi had only a marginal level of irrigation of only 7 per cent during 1978-79 as per our survey. Wells were the exclusive source of irrigation as in Nandyal.

The village is quite drought-prone. During the 1972-73 droughts, many families were forced to migrate. Productivity being one of the lowest and also subject to great instability, a few families have migrated even thereafter—particularly the landless labour. Some of these migrants are seasonal and were not available during our survey. The hamlet, Hanumanthasagar, appeared to be a little more developed, which had the lion's share of irrigation wells.

The economy of the village was hardly diversified. Only 44 cows and 24 female buffaloes were reported in 1977; there were also 57 goats, 49 sheep and 207 poultry during the same year. There were hardly any artisans in the village. There were in all 8 shops, including grocery, *paan-beedi*, saloon, tea-shop, and a cycle shop. There was no fair price shop. For banking, credit, medical and market facilities, they had to go to other villages beyond 6 kms. There was a school, however, teaching from Ist to VIIth standards, manned by 3 teachers.

The village faced serious scarcity of drinking water in summer. There were 2 borewells, and one more was planned for construction during our survey. The scheduled caste settlement had a separate borewell and one protected well. Sanitary conditions were not good, and epidemics were reported to be common. *Kajji* (Itch) and to some extent even leprosy were also said to be prevalent. In sum, the village gave a very dismal picture, and the people lacked enthusiasm and looked gloomy.

Sulibhavi

Sulibhavi offered a tremendous contrast to Kambagi. It was vibrant and more lively. It was actually treated as an urban area in 1961, as part of a bigger complex including Amingad 2 kms away on the main road connecting Hungund (taluka headquarter) with Bagalkot. Sulibhavi is connected to Amingad by an asphalted road towards Gajendragad. The village has a regular bus stand and has the benefit of fairly frequent buses.

This is the largest of the villages selected here which had 969 households and 5881 people in 1971, and 1020 households and 6431 people in 1978-79 as per our survey data. It is a singular village without any hamlet attached to it.

For several decades, the village has been known as a handloom centre. Its sarees have a good rural market in north Karnataka and Maharashtra. Devangas and Kurubas were the dominant castes here, the former being mostly weavers and the latter being mostly cultivators and labourers. There were Muslim weavers too. Devangas seemed to be the more prosperous of the lot.

The village has a very successful weavers' co-operative society. Though there were attempts to involve weavers in a co-operative organisation earlier, a major thrust was given by a weavers' conference in 1957 at Guledgudda which was presided over by Dr V.K.R.V. Rao. The event was recalled by the office-bearers of the society when we visited. The society purchases raw material from outside and distributes among members. A member got Rs. 26 for weaving a saree as a return for his labour. The society had 447 members—both Devangas and Muslims—during 1978-79, and a share capital of Rs. 2.61 lakhs. They had 650 looms with a turnover worth Rs. 22.3 lakhs and a profit of nearly 74 thousand rupees. This success enabled the society to undertake a number of welfare measures including distribution of house sites and Provident Fund schemes. The society even advanced consumption credit of up to Rs. 100 per member, though this was regarded as rather measly. There were also a few weavers who were not members of this co-operative and served under master weavers or merchants of Ilkal to whom they have been traditionally indebted. Weavers themselves were not a homogeneous class; some of them worked on looms owned by others. There was a noticeable variation in their levels of living and annual earnings; several weavers were cultivators too simultaneously, who naturally enjoyed a higher social status.

Though weaving and dyeing were the main activities of the village, cultivation too was an important profession, dominantly under rainfed conditions. Only 2.5 per cent of area was under irrigation, which was through wells. Only 22 pumpsets were reported in 1977-78 as per village records, of which 20 were run on electricity. They irrigated about 48 hectares.

The village has good amenities. It had two government higher primary schools (up to VIIth std.) for boys and girls, from a few lower primary and nursery schools. The schools had a good strength both in terms of teachers and students. A local Mahila Mandal was running a nursery and a tailoring school. For higher schooling, students went to Amingad (2 kms), and for college to Hungund (14 kms). There was a primary health centre, apart from four private medical practitioners. The retail market structure is also fairly well developed. There were 35 to 40 shops, including two fair price shops. The handloom industry has also stimulated the settlement of a few other artisans, 25 tailors, 3 blacksmiths, 4 carpenters and 2 goldsmiths. There were also quite a few mat makers and basket weavers. Due to raw material shortage, basket weaving seems to be on the decline. The Khadi Board has set up a yarn making unit in the village, employing over 50 persons. There was also a ginning mill employing about 12 persons. Apart from a co-operative credit society, there was also a commercial bank within the village.

Wells provided drinking water to the village. There was no general scarcity of drinking water in any season, but some difficulties are experienced in June and July in a few areas. The village panchayat has a plan of initiating tap water system, mobilising water from wells.

The village had some animal husbandry, but not significant enough compared to the size of the village. A dairy co-operative and also a sheep rearing and wool weaving co-operative were functioning in the village, which had been started recently. Only a little over 100 litres of milk were reportedly being collected daily by the dairy co-operative and sent outside during our survey. The DPAP scheme here had been encouraging farmers to rear goats and sheep also.

In spite of the fairly developed character of the village, sanitary conditions were bad. Toilet facilities were extremely limited. Except in the premises of the weavers' co-operative society and commercial bank, there were no private toilets, an there was only one public toilet.

Sholamadevi

This village, which belongs to Udumalpet taluk of Coimbatore district, is fairly large, with 840 households and 4027 people in 1971. However, a smaller number of a households, viz., 763, and 3893 people were recorded in 1978-79 as per our survey, though every effort was made to cover all the households in the village. Our enquiries revealed that quite a few muslim farmers had left the village and set up business in Udumalpet. The village is well located, only 2 furlongs from the main road running between Dharapuram and Palani. The Coimbatore-Madurai highway is only one and a half km away. The river Amaravati is nearby, which is the main source of irrigation. The village derives its name from the Mahadevi temple constructed by the Cholas, which is live even today and maintained fairly well. It has no hamlets as such attached to it. The local panchayat is located in the village itself.

The village is highly irrigated—the highest in our sample. It was reported as 100 per cent irrigated as per 1971 District Census Handbook. During 1978-79, it was 88 per cent irrigated as per our data gathered from households. This has been mainly due to inclusion of new land brought under cultivation at a little higher elevation, which was not yet irrigated. Apart from crops like paddy, sugarcane, cotton, jowar (*cholam*) and groundnut which are grown under irrigation, betel vines and coconut gardens are also a conspicuous feature of the village. Betel leaves are exported to Coimbatore. Farmers complained that the river Amaravati was polluted due to industrial effluents, which has adversely affected the quality of betel leaves. They said that even the yield had declined of late.

This is also a dairy village, based mainly on buffaloes. According to village records, there were 75 cows and 780 she-buffaloes, over 3 years old. There were also 120 sheep, and 135 goats. No poultry was reported.

This is a village of small and semi-medium land holders. There was no holding with more than 6 hectares. Cultivators usually tried to supplement their income through other activities like dairy, trade, basket weaving etc. Muslims dominated the social structure, but there were also other castes including Harijans and Brahmins. The diversification of household economy was more in evidence among Muslims, some of whom had good trade connections with Udumalpet and Coimbatore. Unlike the migration from drought-prone areas, migration from here was on the part of relatively more well-to-do-cultivators also who accumulated some capital through cultivation and trade, and invested it in towns and cities and ultimately migrated thereafter leasing out or selling their land mostly to relatives. But for this migration, the average size of holding would probably have been smaller still.

Amenity-wise, the village is well off and has good access to market centres and higher education. The village has a panchayat dispensary, primary and middle schools and a post office. It had a co-operative credit society too, but it was under liquidation when we visited due to allegedly bad loans. The village was not merely electrified, but there were also as many as 225 domestic connections. The village panchayat maintained a drinking water scheme too, by pumping well water into a tank and distributing through pipes. Some farm houses located within fields, preferred to have their own source of drinking water. Unlike the village in Anantapur and Bijapur, the village even had a drainage scheme. Several houses had private toilets, again unlike the villages in the other two districts. In spite of this, the village is not well laid-out, the roads being narrow and not maintained clean. Cholera was reported to be recurrent here in epidemic form.

Kokkampalayam

This is a village with as many as 9 dispersed hamlets, all significantly irrigated. A stream and also an irrigation canal of the Parambikulam Aliyar Project run through the village. This has made the access of one hamlet to another a little difficult, particularly in the rainy season. The stream had no bridge, and one had to wade through it. The village is near Kundadam town (5 kms.) in Dharapuram taluk. The Coimbatore-Dharapuram highway passes through one of the hamlets—Mettukadai. The highway to Tirupur runs through another hamlet—Edaiyapatti. Kokkampalayam-main is connected to Mettukadai through a kutcha road. The main village is in the interior and inter-hamlet transport is mainly by walk, cycle or cart. The village as a whole had 611 households and 2789 people in 1971, and 646 households and 2920 people in 1978-79 as per our census survey data.

The village was highly irrigated both through canals and wells, the former accounting for about 65 per cent of irrigated area. Canal irrigation came under rotational system discussed earlier in the profile on the district. Canal irrigation was available in the kharif season only, but well irrigation was used in more than one season. There were 302 wells, 226 electric pumpsets and 73 oil engines. During the reference year 1978-79, canal irrigation was available and about 68 per cent of area was irrigated; but during 1979-80, there was much less irrigation, our crude estimate being 30 per cent. The soils are dominantly red loam, but in some parts of the village black soils occur. The lime content of the soil and availability of irrigation, made tobacco cultivation a conspicuous feature of the village. Cotton, onion, chillies, gingelly, groundnut, castor seeds and turmeric were also raised. It is the nonfood crops which dominated the crop pattern. Among the food-crops, paddy, ragi, bajra, jowar and red gram were notable. The well irrigation got a fillip through the supply of canal water. Since canal water is available in alternate years, there is variation in the level of well water too. Crop pattern consequently changed from year to year, depending on the magnitude of irrigation.

In spite of rotational irrigation, there was water logging in areas around branch canals. No accurate estimate of water logged area could be made; there were no records about it, though farmers complained of the same. There did not seem to be proper drainage.

There was also the problem of equitable and rational distribution of water. Quite a few complained of inadequate water, and others of unnecessary water through seepage which even led to crop losses where dry or lightly irrigated crops alone were to be cultivated. The general impression was that there was no proper water management and the farmers complained that they received no proper guidance and help in this respect.

The large farmers had their own pucca storage facilities, which others lacked. In the case of commercial crops, particularly tobacco, traders themselves visited the village and purchased the farm produce, through almost regular contracts. In spite of the village access to market facilities at Kundadam and through it to Dharapuram and Tirupur, quite a few transactions took place in the village itself. There was a mini *sandy* (weekly market), where the poorer sections purchased their requirements and also to some extent sold their produce. But for this, the market infrastructure is hardly developed. There was hardly any shop in Kokkampalayam-main, and even in other hamlets there were hardly any except for a small cloth shop, paan-beedi stalls and a tea stall. There were no groceries or fair price shops. It had of course a post office and a co-operative credit society. The latter was under severe strain due to a bad recovery position.

Apart from cultivation, dairy was one of the main activities here, but did not seem to be significantly commercialised and not much milk was exported outside the village. During 1977-78, 345 cows and 167 she-buffaloes (over 3 years old) were reported. Sheep, goats and poultry too were reported to be significant. Though the village as a whole did not have a significant rural industry, one of the hamlets (Valayampudur) had an artisan community engaged in saree weaving through handloom. They were mostly landless, and worked under merchants of Tirupur who supplied yarn to weavers and got the sarees woven, by paying Rs. 20 to 24 per sari. There was an association of weavers, but not a co-operative society as such. The association was meant to demand year-round employment, fixed wages rates and loans for weavers to purchase looms. There were also toddy tappers-cum-agricultural labourers in the village. A significant area in the village was under palmyra groves which were tapped for both jaggery and liquor.

The farmers were organised here and had formed Kokkampalayam Village Farmers' Association about a year prior to our visit, affiliated to a similar district level association under Narayanaswamy Naidu. The main objectives of the association were to lobby for higher farm prices and reduction in taxes to obtain more facilities, and to resist pressure from agricultural labour for a wage rise. The association was rather distrustful of government officials and had exhibited notices in several places outside the village, which read, "Government officials should obtain permission of the

President of Association to enter this village". It was reported that one of the immediate impacts of the association was almost a stoppage of recoveries of loans given by the co-operative credit society.

There was also an Agricultural Labourers' Association, the majority of its members belonging to the scheduled caste. This was owing to the efforts of the CPI(M) and the taluk level Harijan Association, who lent support to the local labour class. This was also formed recently, mainly to demand a minimum wage of at least Rs. 6 per day for male labour and Rs. 4 for female labour. The demand for even this low level of wage had been resisted, and there was evidence of a bitter struggle between landless labour and farmers. This was particularly so in one of the hamlets where the scheduled castes mostly resided. The farmers have resisted this association in various ways—particularly by boycotting the members of this association, using outside agricultural labour, and by physical violence even against women. Quite a few scheduled caste labour households were reported to have migrated. Since most of the rich farmers belonged to a particular caste (Vellala Gounders), what was basically a class struggle appeared in the form of a caste struggle too. These scheduled castes reported that before their Association was formed, they had to work not only at low wages in fields but also without remuneration on domestic and other non-agricultural tasks for the farmers' families. With the formation of the labourers' association, such exploitation has stopped, though they had to live under constant tension. Farmers also made systematic attempts to see that scheduled caste labour was isolated from government officials intending to give them loans, livestock etc. When one of our investigators, Mr K. Muthayan, asked an activist of the farmers' association about this his justification was as follows:

> If the SC people get monetary or material benefits or loans from the government, they cannot repay the loans but spend the money on liquors,...or *they would concentrate on their own activities* (like livestock rearing) *and would not come for agricultural coolie work.* Agriculture would then suffer without coolies. (Emphasis added).

The village people used irrigation wells for drinking purposes too. Two hamlets in the village had constructed water tanks for supply of piped water. Though drinking water for men and cattle was no problem on the whole, the village experienced scarcity in April and May. Village sanitation was not quite satisfactory on the whole. A few rich farmers had private lavatories, but not others. There were no public lavatories, nor any civic drainage system.

Kalangal

This is a fairly large village. It had 688 households and 3265 people in 1971, and 722 households and 3379 people in 1978-79 as per our census survey. It is only 4 kms from Sulur town, and 25 kms from Coimbatore. Its taluk headquarter, Tirupur, is about 35 kms far. The Coimbatore-Sultanpet highway passes through this village. A private transport company and also Cheran operate buses daily, serving the village. The technological celebrity and industrialist, Mr G.D. Naidu, hailed from this village.

The village had about 45 per cent of area irrigated during 1978-79, through wells. The village had 134 electric pumpsets during previous years as per village records. More than cultivation, the village derives its prosperity through its other activities including animal husbandry and industries. As per village records, however, there were only 121 cows and 119 buffaloes (over 3 years old) in 1977; there were also 126 sheep, 268 goats and 111 poultry. Milk was sent daily to Coimbatore. Kambli weaving was an important activity here in which several households were engaged seasonally. There were also two mills for carding wool, where wool was processed not only from this village but also from surrounding areas. Weaving, however, was done by hand. A 'sheep-rearing and kambli weaving society' had been formed in 1971, but it was not reported to be functioning properly, though the industry as such was not on the decline. In fact, it was reported that the community which had been traditionally engaged in sheep-rearing and weaving, the Kurubas (shepherds), of late had become more prosperous and had been dominating the village economy and agriculture, replacing in the process, the erstwhile dominance of the Naidus. The village is also known for pottery.

Because of the developed transport network and easy access to Sulur and Coimbatore, the village has more than made up for any deficiency in local infrastructure. The village, however, has a primary and middle school, post office and telephone facilities. Medical facilities are available at Sulur.

The village has the facility of piped supply of drinking water, fed by a tank, apart from several wells. Yet, there were difficulties in April and May. Sanitary and drainage facilities, however, did not exist. The village, however, presented, a relatively clean environment, and broader approach roads than in other villages. The houses of larger farmers were quite spacious and well built, who were also more urbanised and involved in non-agricultural activities. Even the housing conditions of the poorer sections looked somewhat better here than in Sholamadevi or Kokkamapalayam.

Sirukinar

Sirukinar is located on the main road connecting Dharapuram with Erode, at a distance of 15 kms from the former—its taluka headquarter. It had 671 households and 2679 people in 1971 and, 698 households and 2760 people in 1978-79 as per our census survey. The village is a cluster of as many as 10 dispersed hamlets. Buses pass through the hamlet Nochipalayam, 2 kms from Sirukinar main, on the highway.

The village was practically dry up to 1970, but by 1978-79, 28 per cent of its area was under irrigation through wells. All the hamlets together had 314 private wells irrigating about 255 hectares involving 265 farmers. As per village records, it had 148 pumpsets in 1977-78, of which 142 were run on electricity. No tractors and iron ploughs were reported. Tobacco, groundnut, cotton paddy, gingelly were grown under irrigation, whereas, bajra, jowar and pulses were grown under rainfed condition. The major part of the area was rainfed. The village was reported to be quite drought-prone, and even area under irrigation was not stable. One result of this is that only one-third of the land was under cultivation in the village.

Livestock economy was hardly developed. The village was reported as having only 26 cows and 18 she-buffaloes (over 3 years old), 109 sheep, 58 goats and 90 poultry in 1977-78. Except for Sirukinar-main having some weavers, rural industry has also not developed. Bed sheets are woven through handlooms under labour contract with merchants from outside. Recently, Khadi Sarvodaya Sangha has taken initiative in setting up 45 spinners in a hamlet on the highway, intended to provide jobs to women. The same hamlet also has some carpentry and blacksmith units for producing and repairing agricultural implements. Though the economy of the village is at present not diversified much, it has the potential for it and the trend towards diversification has already set in.

The village itself does not have much infrastructure but it has a fairly good access to other places through buses. The dispersed location of hamlets (in a range of 2 to 6 kms) and lack of proper roads between hamlets has put some hamlets at a disadvantage. It has a post office in the hamlet on the highway, and also a co-operative credit society. Except for 2 or 3 petty shops near the highway, there were no shops in the village. Though a primary health centre was available at a village 9 kms away, villagers preferred to go to the more distant Dharapuram which have better facilities and to which buses were also available. There was a small maternity centre within the village. There were schooling facilities within the village up to Vth standard.

The village got its drinking water through wells but faced difficulties in summer. There were no drainage or sanitary facilities. Though the village had electricity, only 6 houses had domestic connection in 1978. There were only 39 street lights, and the villagers complained that they were hardly adequate and that the panchayat has been rather indifferent to the problem of providing light in all areas.

The farmers of the village were organised to press their demands, but agricultural labourers were not.

Vadakalur

Vadakalur is a large village, which had 1034 households, and 4730 people in 1971, and 924 households and 4207 people in 1978-79. The decline was due to a significant migration of scheduled caste labour from one of the hamlets (Punjamadai), and also of a few weaver households to Coimbatore during the decade due to shortage of looms and employment. The village is a cluster of 6 hamlets including Vadakalur main.

It is located only 7 kms from Annur town in Avanashi taluka and is well connected by buses from Avanashi, Satyamangalam, Mettupalayam and Coimbatore. The Panchayat headquarter is located in Kariyagoundanur, one of the hamlets attached to Vadakalur.

This is the least irrigated of the villages selected by us in Coimbatore district, with only 14 per cent of area irrigated in 1978-79. Wells are the dominant source of irrigation, though there was also a tank irrigating about 16 hectares. There were 237 wells irrigating 190 hectares in 1977-78. As per village records, 134 electric pumpsets but no tractors were reported. There has been practically no increase in irrigated area here. Though cultivation is an important occupation of the village, the village is known for handloom weaving and oil extraction industry.

Devanga weavers are concentrated in Mookanaur hamlet. They were migrants from Karnataka once upon a time, and have been organised in a co-operative. There is also a bank here which finances this industry, apart from other economic activities in the village. Another hamlet—Kariyagoundanur, had nine oil extraction units and 2 rice mills. Two oil mills were not in working condition when we visited. They got groundnut for oil extraction both from the village itself and outside.

The livestock economy, both bovine and others, was being promoted, though its impact on the village as a whole was yet to be felt. The village has grazing lands around, and is also well connected to Coimbatore. Its potential for dairy development can be rated as high. A veterinary centre has been set up in the village.

The village is fairly well developed in terms of infrastructure, having post office, schools credit society, bank, and quite a number of shops. There were no proper medical facilities within the village. In terms of drinking water, the village faced difficulties in summer, though Bhavani river is only 14 kms away. There is piped water supply in some areas, and wells were the main source for this purpose. Sanitary facilities were also developed in some areas, about one-third of houses having their own lavatories. There was no civic drainage system as such.

Scheduled castes formed an important part of the

population here. Though they were dispersed in different hamlets, most of them were in Vadakalur main. As usual, they provide casual agricultural labour. The migration of agricultural labour households to towns and the presence of small industries here has created seasonal shortages of labour. During busy seasons, outside labour came here daily by bus. There seemed to be a lot of daily commuting to and from the village.

TABLE 4.1: **Village particulars from population census**

Villages	Total households			Total population			Literacy %	
	1961	1971	Increase %	1961	1971	Increase %	1961	1971
1. R'vu	517	644	24.6	2321	3323	43.2	27.9	29.0
2. K'du	219	280	27.8	1272	1668	31.1	16.0	14.4
3. G'la	591	669	13.2	3083	3676	19.2	11.7	11.1
4. C'ru	184	204	10.9	966	1124	16.4	7.6	16.0
5. B'pa	728	751	3.2	3951	4314	9.2	29.2	30.4
6. M'hod	263	324	23.2	1586	2253	42.1	8.5	11.5
7. N'yal	73	97	32.9	415	702	69.2	14.7	8.4
8. M'lgi	430	488	13.5	2428	2751	13.3	20.0	21.7
9. K'gi	305	472	54.7	1605	1877	16.9	14.6	14.2
10. Su'vi	NA	969	NA	NA	5881	NA	NA	30.6
11. Sh'vi	643	840	30.6	3021	4027	33.3	31.9	34.2
12. K'yam	464	611	31.7	1964	2789	42.0	20.0	26.4
13. K'gal	609	688	13.0	2696	3265	21.1	15.4	26.5
14. S'nar	660	671	1.7	2548	2679	5.1	21.3	29.7
15. V'lur	838	1034	23.4	4230	4730	11.8	25.4	38.5

Note : Sulibhavi village was treated as part of a bigger complex and as a town in 1961. Separate figures for 1961 for the present village *not available (NA)*.

5

STRUCTURE OF RURAL ECONOMY AND HOUSEHOLDS

INTRODUCTION TO SURVEY FINDINGS

WE shall analyse, from this chapter onwards, the findings from our survey of households in the selected villages. While both the present chapter and the next would be based on our Census Survey, the subsequent chapters would be based on the sample survey of households. While presenting the findings, we shall follow the village typology discussed in the first chapter above.

A comparative analysis of different village types in terms of indicators of structure of rural economy, or level of living, can be done in two ways. One is to take a simple average of the villages in the given type in respect of the concerned indicators and then compare the averages across village types. Such a procedure has the merit of being simple, but when the number of observations are very limited within a given type—e.g., only two in the case of D (a)—we have no means of assessing the statistical dependability of the averages. Also, we cannot derive parameters in the sense of being able to predict (subject to usual limitations) what happens when a determinant variable—such as irrigation, animal husbandry and industry—is introduced into a village, given other variables. We have, therefore, generally followed Regression analysis, except where it gave statistically not significant results or was considered unnecessary. For this, dummy variables are used to indicate the relative presence (=1) or absence (=0) of irrigation, animal husbandry and rural industry (See Table 1.1). Even when variables overlap, the analysis enables isolation of the impact of particular variables provided that inter-correlation among determinant (i.e. independent variables) is not very high. Fortunately in our case, the inter-correlations among dummy variables are not at all statistically significant. The equations used in each chapter are presented in the Appendices of respective chapter. Incidentally, for economising on space, we have not presented all village-wise tables,[1] though some important ones have been presented. The equations, actually, amount to summarising them in an analytical form.

We have to interpret the results of regression analysis with caution. For example, if (hypothetically speaking) the impact of irrigation on levels of living is not found to be significant, it cannot be interpreted to mean that irrigation has no such potential. Absence of the impact may very well be due to the way irrigation is managed.

Ultimately, apart from the analysis of village as a whole, impact of development differentials on households would be of vital importance. In particular, it is necessary to see how far a higher level of development of a village as a whole also had a positive impact on its weaker sections. We have to understand the structure of rural economy in this case and identify different types of households, particularly the weaker sections among them. In this chapter, we shall focus on the *occupational, social* and *agrarian structure* of the households in different types of villages, the last being viewed mainly from the angle of land distribution. We shall see how rural structures differ in these dimensions between these village types and what class structure ultimately emerges.

The structure of the rural economy can be said to be much more complex than that of the urban or industrial economy. This is not merely due to the subsistence motive being combined with the profit motive in family enterprises but also due to the fact that rural households cannot afford an exclusive specialisation in one economic activity. They derive income from several sources, and it is again not quite necessary that income derived from and time spent on different economic activities are strongly and positively correlated, so that identification of a household in terms of its main economic activity becomes complex.

For presenting the structure of the rural society in what follows, we have followed mainly economic criteria, though a little later we shall also juxtapose economic classification of households against social classification based on caste. We have two main groups of households—cultivating and non-cultivating. The former include all those who cultivate some land, owned or leased in irrespective of whether cultivation is the main economic activity or not. Grouping them together helps us to analyse the activities and economic status of different categories of cultivators. This is particularly helpful in analysing their agricultural production and income. Dependence on cultivation as a source of income—major or minor—distinguishes them from the other groups from the point of problems faced. The cultivators were classified in terms of seven size-classes of operated land, as shown in Table 1.2 above.

The non-cultivators were classified according to their main economic activity as reported by the households, as shown in Table 1.2. In doing this, we followed the criterion of the largest source of income of the household, according to the respondent. No particulars of income were asked from them during the census survey. But the respondents were themselves asked to identify main and secondary sources of income for the household as a whole, and they were classified according to their major source. To be qualified as a main source, it is not necessary that the source should provide more than half of the total income. It is simply the largest of all the sources of income. We found this criterion more convenient for classification than time spent, since different members of the household would have different time pattern of their activities and this was not amenable to an easy summation for the household as a whole. Income presented no such problems.

OCCUPATIONAL STRUCTURE

It would be interesting to see here how occupational structure responds to introduction of irrigation, animal husbandry and industry. The questions that arise here are : Do higher levels of development through these strategies bring about a sharper division of labour among households ? Does this division of labour take the form of only proletarianisation—the role of small cultivators or cultivating labourers being reduced and that of non-cultivating labour being increased ? Or, does it involve specialisation even among the self-employed households—cultivators, artisans, traders, animal husbandry keepers etc ? Diversification of rural economy may be achieved either through a greater division of labour among households, or through a diversification of the household economies themselves where households derive income from more than one source of income.

A diversification of the household economy as between agriculture and non-agricultural sources of income can spread the risk of drought to some extent, provided that different sources of income are not derived ultimately from the same agricutural activity. Diversification is itself of two types (i) diversification of the weak or the poor, or forced diversification; and (ii) diversification of the strong. An agricultural labour household, unable to secure a decent living from agricultural employment, may be forced to collect firewood or cow dung and sell them as fuel to others (when they are themselves short of fuel). Or, a marginal farmer, unable to make both ends meet from his meagre holding, is forced to hire out labour. These are instances of diversification of the weak.[2] A large farmer, who also collect agricultural produce from others and sells, or maintains dairy cattle as a source of income, or is able to find salaried jobs for his son or brother, provides instances of diversification of the strong. We had instances of both among one surveyed households.

A few sailent features of the impact of introduction of irrigation, animal husbandry and rural industry on rural occupational structure can be seen from Table 5.1 below, derived from Equations 1 to 9. Irrigation by itself also tended to decrease the proportion of cultivating households and increase the proportion of non-cultivating households. While the decrease in the former was not statistically significant, increase in the latter was significant. (See Equations 1 and 4 under Wet). There was no significant difference between wet and dry villages in the *total* proportion of agricultural labour households (both cultivating and non-cultivating together), but the difference was significant in the case of *non-cultivating*

TABLE 5.1 : **Occupational structure: Village type-wise**

Village types	Proportion (per cent) of households in each category* to village total								
	Cultivating		Agri. Labour		Artisans		Traders		White collar and salaried
	All	Mainly	Cultivating	Non-Cultivating	Cultivating	Non-Cultivating	Cultivating	Non-Cultivating	
Village type-wise	(values derived from regression equations)**								
Dry - a	75.7	57.8	12.3	13.5	3.2	6.1	1.0	2.3	Nil
- b	68.0	47.6	14.1	18.5	2.8	2.7	1.1	3.1	2.0
- c	48.9	35.9	3.7	22.0	4.4	15.4	1.8	4.3	3.9
- d	41.2	25.7	5.5	27.0	3.9	12.0	1.8	5.2	5.9
Wet - a	69.6	55.5	10.9	23.2	1.1	0.9	0.6	2.1	1.0
- b	61.9	45.3	12.7	28.2	0.7	Nil	0.7	2.9	3.0
- c	42.8	33.6	2.3	31.7	2.3	10.2	1.4	4.1	4.9
- d	35.1	23.4	4.1	36.7	1.8	6.8	1.4	5.0	6.9
Location-wise	(average of respective villages)								
Anantapur	53.6	38.5	9.0	25.2	2.5	4.8	1.4	5.0	5.1
Bijapur	68.4	52.9	11.5	16.6	3.4	6.1	1.1	1.6	1.5
Coimbatore	41.5	31.5	2.9	31.9	2.2	11.0	1.3	4.1	4.1
All villages	55.5	41.0	7.9	24.6	2.7	7.3	1.3	3.6	3.6

* Except for all cultivating households, the categories are according to the main source of income. Where they are classified as cultivating and non-cultivating, cultivation is a secondary source to the former.

** Equations 1 to 9 respectively; See the appendix to this chapter.

agricultural labour. There was a strong tendency on the part of wet villages to attract non-cultivating labour, which could be both through immigration from dry villages and conversion of cultivating labour into non-cultivating labour. Between the two, immigration seemed to be the stronger tendency.

Introduction of rural industry showed a sizeable effect on occupational structure. It lowered the proportion of cultivating households—total as well as mainly cultivating, and also of cultivating agricultural labour households (see Equations 1 to 3 under 'Rural Industry'). It may be noted here that rural industry reduces the proportion of cultivating households with labour as a source of income, both where labour income is a major and minor source (see Equations 4 and 10 respectively). But it increased the proportion of non-cultivating agricultural labour households and also of non-cultivating artisans. The impact on cultivating artisans—atleast proportionwise—was not significant (see Equations 4 to 6). Rural Industry introduced a sharper diversification and division of labour in the rural economy than irrigation and animal husbandry. A village with rural industry also had a significantly higher proportion of white collar and salaried class, but not necessarily of trading class (See Equations 7 to 9). Interestingly, none of the three variables had a statistically significant impact on the proportion of trading class—cultivating and non-cultivating, though rural industry tended to increase their proportion somewhat. The *local* trading class was also marginal in every village, and that was so even in the more developed Coimbatore. This would suggest that outside traders play an important role in the sale of village produce—agricultural and non-agricultural, and the role of traders within the village is generally restricted to retail sales and purchases. However, there were exceptions, and though traders were numerically marginal in proportion, some of them were powerful, and had a hold in their villages.

Animal husbandry did not appear to be a major factor in sharpening occupational distribution. It was more a source of secondary income than main income. Equations 11 and 12 below show that it made no impact on the proportion of households following it as a major source of income. In the least developed village type Dry-a, it could be considered as zero, both for cultivating and non-cultivating households. (Intercepts were negative but not statistically significant). Even with the introduction of animal husbandry, this proportion—together for cultivating and non-cultivating households—could be said to be only 4.2 per cent of all households. But it was not statistically dependable.

It is only when households with animal husbandry as a minor source of income were considered, that some impact coefficients emerged with statistical significance. (See Equations 13 and 14). In the Dry-a (least developed) village type, only the non-cultivating households had interest in animal husbandry (see under Intercepts)—mainly in tending sheep, goats etc. But when animal husbandry programmes were introduced significantly, particularly involving dairying, it is the cultivating households which emerged to the fore. As a proportion of all households, cultivating householdings with animal husbandry as a minor source of income increas ed by 6.9 percentage points, whereas a similar proportion of non-cultivating households increased only by 1.1 percentage points, both co-efficients being significant. Rural industry, however, tended to reduce this proportion by 0.9 percentage points, but it had no such statistically significant impact on cultivating households. Non-cultivating households appeared to prefer rural industry where such opportunity arose, to animal husbandry. Though in quite a few villages like Sulibhavi and Beluguppa, both rural industry and animal husbandry co-existed, the latter was more in evidence among cultivating households. This is understandable because, animal husbandry needs a minimum land base, and cultivating households find a complementarity between cultivation and animal husbandry. In the case of non-cultivating households, no such advantage is available. Community assets like grazing land either do not exist; or even if they are nominally there, they have practically lost their productivity long ago. Programmes, trying to involve landless households in link production, appear, therefore, to have only hopes as their main base. This is not to say that they go entirely untouched by animal husbandry programmes.

The opposite effects of animal husbandry and rural industry

on the diversification of household economies come out clearly from Equation 15. While 54.1 per cent of households have only one source of income in the least developed (D-a) village, it *decreases* further in a dry village with animal husbandry by 11.2 per cent points, while it *increases* with the introduction of industry by 9.5 per cent points. The introduction of irrigation, however, had no significant impact.

The differences in the impact on the diversification of the households economy as between cultivating households as a whole, marginal cultivators (with one hectare and below), and agricultural labour households can be seen from Equations 16 to 18. Neither irrigation nor rural industry affects the proportion of households having only one source of income among the respective categories. However, the introduction of animal husbandry reduces this proportion significantly only among cultivators as a whole, but such a reduction is not significant statistically among marginal cultivators and also among agricultural labour. This shows that only the cultivators other than the marginal are in a position to benefit more and diversify their household economies with the introduction of animal husbandry.

The bulk of artisans have a single source of income in every village. Even where artisans had more than one source, it was the main source in the bulk of cases. In Dry-a type of village, 84.2 per cent of artisans had artisanship as the main source of income, which did not significantly increase even in Dry-c villages (with rural industry), but decreased by 13.5 per cent points in Dry-b villages. The diversifying impact of animal husbandry was seen even among artisans. Or one could say, that cultivators with animal husbandry tended to go in for artisanship too—either as main or secondary source of income. Among artisans with more than one source, it was only the cultivators who dominated. But this does not mean that bulk of farmers benefited from rural industry spreading the risk of drought. Though in general rural industry seemed to absorb only a marginal proportion of rural work force—particularly of cultivators, Sholamadevi in Coimbatore district was an exception. Almost 22 per cent of cultivators—all in the smallest two size-classes—depended on some rural industry or the other as a secondary source of income.

On the whole, the impact of both animal husbandry and rural industry on diversifying household economy was only marginal—the latter in fact being actually negative on the whole. Even the marginal and positive impact of animal husbandry may not necessarily help cultivating households to spread the risk of drought, though it could help them in spreading the risk of a particular crop failure or risk of a price fall. This is because drought affects animal husbandry too, often compelling farmers to sell their cattle.

Rural industry of course helped to some extent by diversifying the economy at the village level and reducing the pressure on land, and providing alternative employment to marginal cultivators and agricultural labour even in droughts. Even animal husbandry had better chances to develop where both irrigation and rural industry had developed.

SOCIAL STRUCTURE

An important dimension of the rural economy is its caste structure. The caste which controls or owns the bulk of land also dominates the village. This may or may not be linked with numerical majority. An important question which arises here is whether the role of traditional peasant castes—which normally owned or operated the bulk of land—changes over village types. In other words, do other communities begin to emerge as equally important at higher levels of rural development, breaking the monopoly of dominant castes in the process? The second question which arises is whether the role of scheduled castes and tribes also undergoes improvement or change at higher levels of development. Thirdly, is their evidence of bondage of depressed communities or weaker sections, and whether it undergoes a change at different levels of development. We may recall here Krishna Bharadwaj's concept of interlocked markets, and how through a hold over more than one market—labour, capital, and output, certain classes consolidate their power of exploitation over other classes.[4] Though we cannot give definitive answers on the basis of hard quantitative data particularly to the third question, an exposure to field conditions and informal talks, supported also by data to some extent, has helped us in making atleast a broad assessment.

For analysing the social structure of the villages surveyed, we have classified castes into the following: Peasant castes, 'backward castes', scheduled castes and tribes, Brahmins and Vyashyas (trading community), Muslims and 'Others'. It is, however, the first three categories which generally account for the bulk of village population. It was only in two villages—one in Bijapur (Nandyal) and the other in Coimbatore (Sholamadevi) that Muslims were both numerically and economically dominant. Peasant castes are traditional cultivating communities, such as Lingayats in Karnataka, Reddis and Kammas in Andhra Pradesh and, Gounders and Naidus in Tamil Nadu. Vokkaligas, though a peasant caste, are officially classified as a backward community in Karnataka; but we did not have to classify them in either category since Bijapur district did not consist of this community. Largely, we relied on official lists of backward castes, SC's and ST's in respective states in classifying them; but there did not always exist perfect correspondence between claims of respondents and official lists. In cases of doubt, we relied on the informed judgement of our Investigators. The 'backward castes' also include certain artisan communities, though all artisans do not necessarily belong to these communities. In Vadakalur, a handloom village, the bulk of households belonged to 'Devanga' community, who were mostly weavers. However, they claimed to be a trading community—a category among Chettiars.

Our data showed clearly that even where peasant castes were not necessarily the most numerous among cultivators, they were almost invariably dominant among large holdings (4 hectares and above). In quite a few instances, they formed 100 per cent or nearly so among the largest two or three size groups of holdings. This was so even where backward and artisan communities were numerically dominant. The proportion of peasant castes among cultivators, particularly among large cultivators, seemed to be almost invariably higher than their proportion among all households. On the other hand, the proportion of backward and arisan communities was larger than their overall proportion, in the case of agricultural labour, animal husbandry and allied activities, artisans and casual non-agricultural labour. On the whole, they certainly seemed to be in an economically lower position than peasant castes.

The proportion of peasant castes or of backward castes are not correlated significantly to levels of development. That is, though there is variation in their proportion across villages, it cannot be said to be associated strongly with village types. But the prominence of backward castes was unmistakale atleast in a few villages with rural industry as noted in our village profiles. This prominence was not only numerical but also in economic terms. The dissipation of dominance of traditional castes and rise of backward castes was particularly noticeable in Korrapadu and Beluguppa villages in Anantapur; Sulibhavi in Bijapur; and Kalangal and Sirukinar in Coimbatore. There was a distinct trend in these villages of the rise of backward castes with growing diversification of the rural economy. In a few other villages also, peasant caste had lost their dominance overtime, but their place was taken by Muslims in two villages as mentioned, and by Devangas in Vadakalur. Both Muslims and Devangas are occupationally diversified communities, prominent in cultivation, industry and trade as well. Though we could not at this stage find statistical significance in differences over village types, a reduced dominance of peasant castes and greater dominance of backward castes, Muslims and Devangas was clearly discernible in more developed and diversified villages.

There was also a regional variation in the dominance of different castes, as can be seen from Table 5.2 here. Whereas peasant castes were dominant both in Bijapur and Coimbatore, backward castes dominated in Anantapur. But even in Anantapur, the proportion of peasant castes among large cultivators was more than their overall proportion, and as such enjoyed economic dominance.

The scheduled castes and tribes were not only a numerical minority in every village (only 16.6 per cent on the whole) but economically also in a vulnerable position. What is even more poignant, unlike backward castes, they could not improve their economic status even with higher levels of development and diversification of the villages concerned. They are not only

TABLE 5.2: **Average proportions of peasant castes, economically backward castes, and scheduled caste and tribe households among household categories**

	In the villages of			
	Anantapur	Bijapur	Coimbatore	All three districts
Proportion of peasant castes among (per cent)—				
(i) Marginal cultivators	4.3	37.2	45.0	28.9
(ii) All cultivators	24.1	52.0	61.2	45.8
(iii) Agri. Labour	6.4	45.7	29.1	27.1
(iv) Artisans	Nil	23.1	5.3	9.5
(v) All housholds	15.8	46.2	43.0	35.0
Proportion of backward castes among (per cent)—				
(i) Marginal cultivators	53.2	13.6	8.8	25.2
(ii) All cultivators	43.6	17.3	4.1	21.6
(iii) Agri. Labour	54.9	15.0	8.0	26.0
(iv) Artisans	84.1	37.8	45.4	55.7
(v) All households	48.2	19.2	9.6	25.7
Proportion of SCs & STs among (per cent)—				
(i) Marginal cultivators	33.1	17.2	8.7	19.8
(ii) All cultivators	23.9	9.7	4.3	12.6
(iii) Agri. labour	29.4	23.9	40.4	31.2
(iv) Artisans	2.1	10.9	2.8	5.3
(v) All households	23.0	11.6	15.2	16.6

Note : (as per cent of total households in respective categories)

normally concentrated among agricultural labour and at best among marginal cultivators, but this concentration—particularly among labour—tends to *increase* with higher levels of development. This comes out clearly from Equations 19 to 21. With the introduction of irrigation and animal husbandry their proportion declines among cultivators and increases among labourers. Animal husbandry, however, has a somewhat beneficial impact, as it tends to increase their proportion among cultivators and decrease it among labourers. There was a regional variation in the status of this social groups also. They had a comparatively better share among cultivating households—sometime even in middle holding—both in Anantapur and Bijapur, but much less so compared to their overall proportion in Coimbatore, where they were almost completely a labour class. Our field visits also gave a strong impression that the social distance between this group and others also was observed more in this district. We have already discussed this in our village profile of Kokkampalayam. This was more typical than exceptional.

Other communties, Brahmins, Christians etc. were numerically even smaller than scheduled castes and tribes, and were to be found more in large villages in particularly 'soft' occupations—government services, book keepers and managers and so on. Though here and there, they were to be found among cultivators, they did not appear to be a landed class.

Coming now to the third question posed in the opening para of this section, we may note that credit can be used as an instrument of dominance in rural society. It may be used to ensure timely availability of labour, to ensure that marketable surplus is routed through the creditor, and/or to simply ensure political support. The provision of institutional finance (from banks, co-operatives and government) has the potential to break the dominance of the rural elite, but only if directed to the poor who need credit. Otherwise, it may only replenish credit funds of the elite and reinforce their dominance. It is, therefore, useful to analyse sources of credit in different categories of households. Table 5.3 here presents this picture district-wise and for cultivators as a whole and for all households together. They are not to be treated as estimated for districts concerned, since our sample was not of adequate size for the purpose. They are only average estimates for the villages in the concerned districts. We have not presented similar details in the table for weaker sections like marginal cultivators and labour and also for aritsans, since loans outstanding in their case turned out to be practically negligible. Only a few households from these categories were indebted.

It is quite possible that there has been some under-reporting of loans taken by the weaker sections, particularly credit purchases from traders (grocers etc.) and kind loans and advance wages received from farmers. But our strong impression is that even if these loans are allowed, indebtedness on the part of the weak has been marginal. Our insistent probing into their memory, only brought forth replies like—'who will give loans to poor people like us now?' Some labourers frankly said that when approached for loans, the farmers gave them some work instead and preferred to give

TABLE 5.3 : **Loans outstanding and their sources**

District and household category	Loans outstanding per household Rs.	Their distribution : source-wise in per cent				
		Institutional	Farmers	Traders	Money Lenders	Others including relatives
Aanatapur villages :						
Cultivators	2330	15.6	36.4	42.2	4.5	1.3
All households	1425	16.7	41.1	34.2	4.3	3.6
Bijapur villages :						
Cultivators	547	67.1	Nil	Nil	6.6	26.3
All households	441	87.7	Nil	0.3	5.7	6.6
Coimbatore villages :						
Cultivators	742	8.7	78.1	2.5	Nil	10.7
All households	412	7.8	71.9	1.7	5.6	18.1
All villages :						
Cultivators	1206	30.5	38.2	8.4	3.7	12.8
All households	759	51.0	37.7	12.1	3.5	9.4

Note : Unlike other tables in this chapter, this is based on the sample survey of households and not the census survey.

wages rather than loans for the same. We had definite impressions that traditional bondage through credit has been breaking, and the weak are often asked to fend for themselves. But in the few instances, where they did get credit, it was mostly from middle and large farmers, particularly in Anantapur and Coimbatore. In two villages of Bijapur (Kambagi and Nandyal), however, a few agricultural labourers obtained loans from institutional sources for purchase of cattle, and that was reported their only source.

Indebtedness generally extended from small cultivators with more than one hectare right upto big farmers. The latter borrowed not only from institutional sources but also from other big farmers. As the table shows, institutional finance dominated only in Karnataka (Bijapur) villages, and it was only marginal in the other two districts. Their place was taken by farmers and traders in Anantapur, and by farmers in Coimbatore. Some of these money lending farmers were also traders.

There was a specific reason for the low proportion of institutional finance at least in Coimbatore villages. During the reference year of our survey and earlier, farmers' agitations were very active under Narayanswamy Naidu, and one of the demands was to write off institutional loans. Loan repayments had come to stand-still, and so were loan disbursements. This naturally increased the role of big farmers as the source of credit to middle and smaller farmers.

It may look surprising that even artisans showed no appreciable indebtedness. This was because most of them get raw material from master-weavers or traders and handed over the finished product to them. They were more in the nature of artisan-labourers on piece rates, rather than entrepreneurs on their own right. In times of need, they got advance payment for work. Such advances were strictly limited, for fear that it may enable them to come out of the grip of their masters. Where the artisans were organised in the form of a co-operative, it was the society which got institutional finance and not the individual artisans. The bondage relationship was much more conspicuous in the case of rural industry than in agriculture. There was a similar relationship in animal husbandry too. Artisans had formed themselves into co-operatives in Sulibhavi, Beluguppa and Vadakalur, and had relief from such bondage. But there were other artisans particularly in the first two villages, who were outside the co-operative framework. Their lot was comparatively unenviable. Being bonded to master-weavers and traders, they were unable to come into co-operatives.

FOCUS ON LAND DISTRIBUTION

We have relied here on the analysis of distribution of land for understanding agrarian class structure. Land is still the most sought rural asset, the control on which gives political, social and economic power. It can serve as a base for expansion of the household economy atleast in allied spheres like animal husbandry and sometimes even in industry. The landless still suffer from several disadvantages and are dependent on the propertied classes for employment and credit, unless they are on an assured income from a salaried job.

Yet, land by itself has not been considered as a satisfactory criterion for discerning class formation even in a rural society. This is because land is extremely heterogeneous, and categorisation of holdings in terms of size-classses are not comparable across different regions. Moreover, a direct criterion in terms of employment status—employers and employees—can lead to identification of two classes. The fact that often cultivators both hire in and hire out has been noted here, and the solution has been sought by Patnaik in terms of net status.[5] She has taken note of differentiation even within net employing and net employed class. At the top there is the landlord class which only hires in but does not hire out any labour, and at the bottom there are pure labourers who only hire out but do not hire in any labour. The in-between households are demarcated by an imaginary dividing line where hiring in just equals hiring out. Employing this approach, Barbara Harriss has used the ratio E=Hired in÷Hired out labour, to generate continuous values and identify five social classes demarcated in terms of different levels of the ratio. She found poor correlation between the size of holding and employment status as indicated by E ratio (viz. 0.183, which however was statistically significant for 261 cases).[6]

Her departure from the conventional approach based on distribution of land has indeed a strong theoretical backing, since after all the distinction between the employees owning the means of production and the employees is crucial to an understanding of the relations of production, which in turn are crucial in understanding the class formation in rural society. We do not intend to question this theoretical basis. We submit, however, that the baselessness of the practice to rely on land distribution, is by no means very clear as yet. Her own correlations show that E ratio had a very weak correlations with income (viz. 0.0894), while the correlation between land cultivated and income was much higher (viz. 0.4745 and statistically significant.

Our data also confirmed that a reliance on employment status for discerning class formation could lead to quite a few difficult complications, and could distort even the picture regarding income distribution. Listing out cultivating households who hired out more labour than they hired in, we found that they ranged across almost all the holding size-classes.* And this was not because such large holders who hired out more labour had infertile or useless land. Some of them received more income from cultivation than from labour. Yet they hired out labour on net basis. The two classes—cultivating labourers with labour as main source of income and 'cultivating labourers' who hired out more labour on a net basis—were not necessarily identical. The former, about which we have discussed above, was a better indicator of their proletarian status. Surely, Harriss and her colleagues too must have come across the same complication in their field work.

One of the reasons why this complication arises is because of certain recent trends which have merged in the wake of modernisation and commercialisation of agriculture. Quite a few farm families, through the use of tractors either by owning or hiring in, have reduced the need to hire in labour. At the same time, particularly larger families have hired out their own labour services along with bullocks, bullock carts, tractors and other modern devices. In the old days, bullocks and carts were operated by attached labourers. They are now increasingly operated by members of the farm family themselves, and they do not feel it below their dignity to hire out even their labour along so as to ensure their proper use. We found that there was no reluctance to such hiring out even on smaller holdings than their own, so long as those hiring in are not considered as belonging to a lower caste. This emergence of elite cultivating labour is an unmistakable trend, and poses an important difficulty in class analysis of rural society using strictly employment status.

At the other end, we had quite a few instances of even marginal cultivators who hired in more than they hired out. They were mostly small families, sometimes without adult

* This was found to be so particularly in Bijapur villages of Mughalkhod and Mulsavalgi where such net hiring out was reported even from the largest size-class of holdings. Among middle holdings this phenomenon was not at all uncommon particularly in Sulibhavi, and Kambagi in Bijapur, and Rayalacheruvu, Goridindla & Beluguppa of Anantapur. In Coimbatore villages, however, it was confined mainly to small and middle holdings. It had no particularly strong relation to irrigation.

males, or with adult males who happened to be either old or followed another occupation as a main source of income.

One more difficulty with relying on net employment status or E ratio to study agrarian structure is that *both* hiring in and hiring out increase with higher levels of development, in which case it need not be as sensitive an indicator as the proportions of landless labour and cultivating labourers (discussed above under occupational structure), or a concentration ratio indicating land distribution.

We found, therefore, that the conventional approach was both useful and practicable. Apart from considering the role of proletarian cultivators (whose main source of income is labour) as done earlier, we shall see how concentration in land changes across village types, since it gives clues to changing agrarian structure.

Gini co-efficient is one of the measures of concentration, which can be applied to distribution of land among households. We have calculated three sets of Gini co-efficients for each village; Gini (i), inclusive of agricultural labour households who have no land, but excluding other non-cultivating households; this co-efficient is derived on the basis of operated land standardised for irrigation differences; Gini (ii), derived from only cultivating households, i.e. excluding agricultural labour households, on the basis of standardised operated land; Gini (iii) as in (ii) above, but derived on the basis of nonstandardised operated land. It may be noted that Gini (i) would give a higher value than Gini (ii), and is a more appropriate measure of concentration in land since it takes into account the landless too and more adequately reflects the power of large cultivators. Gini (ii), is a measure of concentration within cultivators. It can be compared with Gini (iii) to see what difference introduction of irrigation makes to the measure of concentration. These ratios have been presented in Table 5.4 below. It may be noted that Ginis (ii) and (iii) did not differ greatly, the correlation co-efficient between them being +0.89. Their averages taking all the villages together were also close to each other. In our analysis, we have used, therefore, only the first two Ginis. The values of these ratios as also other aspects of land distribution in different types of villages and also averages for each district are presented below in Table 5.5.

TABLE 5.4 : Concentration ratios (Gini co-efficients) for operated land

Village	Including agri. labour households	Excluding agri. labour	Excluding agri. labour (for non-standardised land)
	(Land standardised for irrigation)		
	(i)	(ii)	(iii)
Rayalacheruvu	0.833	0.576	0.550
Korrapadu	0.754	0.610	0.639
Goridindla	0.620	0.480	0.471
Chinnamushturu	0.786	0.582	0.578
Beluguppa	0.844	0.618	0.613
Mughalkhod	0.633	0.443	0.465
Nandyal	0.465	0.309	0.382
Mulsavalgi	0.614	0.468	0.478
Kambagi	0.535	0.454	0.469
Sulibhavi	0.723	0.503	0.497
Sholmadevi	0.881	0.445	0.466
Kokkamapalayam	0.728	0.471	0.510
Kalangal	0.808	0.495	0.466
Sirukinar	0.628	0.386	0.437
Vadakalur	0.776	0.382	0.361
Average	0.709	0.481	0.492

The Gini ratios including landless labour ranged from 0.465 in Nandyal to 0.881 in Sholmadevi, both being irrigated villages having no large holdings. The latter had a higher proportion of landless labour, and the largest holdings within the village (though they were not larger compared to other villages) had a higher share in land. The introduction of irrigation by itself made no significant impact on Gini ratios—with or without labour (see Equations 24 and 25).

However, rural industry had the effect of *increasing* Gini ratios calculated inclusive of landless labour, since rural industry villages also had higher proportion of landless labour as noted earlier. Animal husbandry had no particular impact on any set of Gini ratios. Though as between village types variation in Gini ratios showed no particular pattern (except for rural industry's impact on them), as between districts there

TABLE 5.5 : **Features of land distribution**

Village types	Average size of holding in hectares		Gini co-efficient for operated land*		Share (%) in operated land (standardised)*, of		% of net sown area irrigated, among		
	Standard-ised*	Non-standardised	Including agri. labour	Excluding agri. labour	Marginal holdings**	Large holdings@	Marginal holdings**	Large holdings@	All holdings
	(1)	(2)	(3)	(4)	(5)	(6)	(7)	(8)	(9)
As per village types:									
Dry-a	6.26	5.22	0.58	0.45	2.2	74.5	11.7	7.7	7.3
-b	7.33	6.14	0.66	0.51	0.9	82.3	28.9	13.7	13.9
-c	4.48	4.11	0.73	0.46	5.6	66.0	16.1	16.2	17.4
-d	5.55	4.99	0.81	0.52	0.9	73.8	Nil	2.0	2.6
Wet-a	6.07	3.37	0.60	0.44	4.9	73.5	64.4	37.8	47.0
-b	7.14	4.29	0.68	0.50	5.6	81.3	59.5	46.4	48.0
-c	4.29	2.26	0.75	0.45	5.6	65.0	54.9	66.3	62.5
-d	5.36	3.14	0.83	0.52	19.6	72.8	55.0	75.5	68.7
Location-wise :									
Anantapur	6.4	4.9	0.77	0.58	3.6	84.1	25.5	24.5	25.1
Bijapur	6.0	4.5	0.60	0.44	3.4	71.5	37.6	20.5	24.2
Coimbatore	4.5	2.9	0.77	0.44	11.0	62.4	44.4	54.7	51.0
All villages	5.6	4.0	0.71	0.49	6.0	72.7	35.8	33.2	33.4

* Standardised for irrigation (1 irrig. hect. = 3 dry hectares) **With less than one hectare;
@ with more than 4 hectares.

Note : Village type values are derived in columns (1) to (4) and (6) from regression equations 22 to 25 and 27 respectively; and in columns (5) and (7) to (15) from averages of villages in respective types.

TABLE : 5.5 (*contd.*)

Village types	Leased in land as % of operated land, among			Leased out land as % of owned land, among		
	Marginal holdings**	Large holdings@	All holdings	Marginal holdings**	Large holdings	All holdings
	(10)	(11)	(12)	(13)	(14)	(15)
As per village types :						
Dry-a	4.7	4.6	5.1	Nil	0.3	0.1
-b	6.7	2.4	2.6	Nil	2.5	2.6
-c	7.7	3.9	3.7	2.6	1.1	1.4
-d	Nil	5.9	5.3	6.2	2.3	1.4
Wet-a	1.8	3.6	1.7	Nil	2.6	0.5
-b	1.9	2.7	3.2	Nil	Nil	0.5
-c	13.6	7.4	7.8	0.2	1.3	3.6
-d	67.0	36.2	28.5	14.9	Nil	3.8
Location-wise :						
Anantapur	6.1	5.5	5.3	6.2	2.2	1.6
Bijapur	2.0	2.7	2.6	3.8	1.3	0.2
Coimbatore	32.1	20.7	14.3	5.5	2.0	1.6
All villages	13.4	9.6	7.1	5.2	1.8	1.1

** and @—see page 120

was a significant difference. Bijapur villages had lower concentration ratios, with or without landless labour. Anantapur and Coimbatore villages had on the whole the same level of concentration, when ratios were calculated including labour. When excluded, concentration within cultivators was found to be higher in Anantapur than in Coimbatore.

Since Gini ratios reflect the degree of relative concentration within villages, no idea is obtained about the share of larger or marginal holdings. Taking this separately, none of the three variables—irrigation, animal husbandry and rural industry—seemed to make a significant impact on them (see Equations 26 and 27). On the whole, the share of marginal holdings (with 1 hectare and less) was quite small, being a mere 6 per cent taking all the villages together, and that of large holdings (with 3 hectares and more) quite large being 73 per cent on the whole. The variation between village types in this respect was not statistically significant. However, Coimbatore had on the whole a larger share of land under large holdings (11 per cent) and smaller share of land under large holdings (o2 per cent) than the other two districts. This was in terms of land standardised for irrigation differences.

The role of irrigation in reducing concentration seemed very limited on the whole, atleast so among the villages surveyed. In Anantapur district, the proportion of irrigated area was practically the same as between marginal and large holdings (25.5 per cent and 24.5 per cent respectively), while it was actually smaller in marginal holdings (44 per cent) than in large (55 per cent) holdings in Coimbatore district. It was only in Bijapur that the irrigated proportion was higher in marginal holdings (38 per cent) than in the large (20 per cent). Taking all the villages together, marginal holdings had 36 per cent irrigation and large holdings had a little less at 33 per cent. Unless irrigation is specially designed to serve mainly the small farmers, its introduction in an already inegalitarian rural structure is not likely to make it egalitarian.

It may be noted, that introduction of irrigation tended to reduce only the average size of non-standardised holdings (see Equation 23) but not of standardised holding (see Equation 22). Irrigation leads to a more intensive cultivation, requiring a higher man-land ratio. This tends to cause a reduction in the size of holdings particularly among middle and large size groups, but the tendency is not real enough to cause a reduction in standardised holding, nor adequate enough to significantly improve the share of marginal holdings, or reduce the overall share of larger and middle holdings. As such, the impact of this process in making the rural structure more egalitarian has not been impressive enough.

Rather unexpectedly, rural industry tended to decrease the average size of standardised holding (but not non-standardised), an effect which even irrigation did not have. This was so, inspite of the fact that rural industry tended to increase Gini ratio (inclusive of landless labour). One would have expected that by inducing more labour into industry, the presssure on land would be eased, increasing the size of holding in the process. The decrease in size would have been occasioned by the fact that rural industry also induces immigration into such villages, and the relatively better-off among artisans tend to buy some land as security. Though cultivating labourers also tend to sell or lease out land, the demand for land may well exceed supply. Such a reduction in the size of land could hardly have made the agrarian structure more egalitarian.

The average size of holding is often tried to be increased through leasing in, informally if not always openly and on the basis of mutual trust. Inspite of a ban on leasing in Karnataka and restrictions on the same elsewhere, it has continued but only marginally. Only 7.4 per cent of operated land was leased in and 1.1 per cent leased out on the whole, for all the 15 villages together (see the last 6 columns of Table 5.5). However, as the level of development rises, the proportion of leased in land increases—rising from 5.1 per cent in Dry-a village to 28.5 per cent in Wet-d village. While generally both marginal and large cultivators lease in more than they lease out, in Bijapur villages marginal cultivators leased out more than they leased in and large cultivators leased in more than they leased out. However, leasing was very marginal in Bijapur villages—lowest among the three districts. The leasing in of both marginal and large cultivators was more in the nature of making adjustments in terms of viability, access etc, rather than one of semi-feudal traditional tenancy.

The Leasing was normally on crop-sharing basis, inputs being invested by the tenant himself along with labour.

We have probed into three dimensions of rural structure in this chapter—occupational, social and agrarian. What does it all add up to? The overall trend with rising levels of development did appear to make the rural structures more inegalitarian, both by isolating some weaker sections particularly the scheduled castes and tribes from the ownership of productive assets—involving proletarianisation within, and also by inducing immigration of outside labour. This process takes time, and is better captured in cross-section comparison of villages at differential stages of development. The impact of rural industry in this sounded to be more marked than that of irrigation, while animal husbandry played a rather insignificant role except in diversifying the sources of income. However, rural industry also tended to break the dominance of traditional peasant castes, and bring other economically backward castes into prominence. This trend was discernible atleast in a few villages, if not all.

There was also evidence of traditional bondage relationships having loosened, with the poor having to fend for themselves in the absence of traditional patronage. This was true of agriculture, even in relatively least developed villages. Agriculture here too was inegalitarian, but could not nevertheless be considered as feudal. Such bondages and patronage were to be found more in rural industry than in agriculture. However, environment did play a depressive role on the agriculture of dry villages particularly in Bijapur. Whereas large landholders in Anantapur and Coimbatore district seemed both economically and politically strong and more enterprising, those in Bijapur seemed diffident, less vocal, and less interested in wider public life. However, official intervention has brought about a beneficial impact and enabled even Bijapur to achieve high growth rates in agricultural production, as we have noted in the profile of this district. The soil conservation programmes, dry land farming improvement plans, and the thrust of institutional finance have had some effect. Comparatively, such an institutional intervention particularly in the field of finance seemed less prominent in Anantapur and Coimbatore.

It was interesting to observe that the importance of land

in shaping the rural class structure is by no means lessened with a diversification of the rural economy even through rural industry. Leading cultivators were also the leading industrialists of the village. Rural industry made the society more polarised even in terms of land distribution. Landless artisans were a new proletariat added to the rural society. In a sense, irrigation augmented the supply of land and had the potential to make the distribution of land more egalitarian, while rural industry seemed to add to the demand side. A piece of land as security was prized even by artisans living in villages. This made ownership of land no less a key factor than in wet villages. On the whole the contrast in terms of polarisation of class structure seemed more prominent between a village with well developed industry and a dry village without industry, than between simply a dry and a wet village.

References

1. Mimeographed copies of village-wise detailed tables have been provided to the Central Water Commission along with our Report (Vol. II) in 1982.
2. V.M. Rao speaks of 'forced diversification' operating in villages with a high proportion of scheduled caste and tribe population, where he found a relatively significant proportion of workers in non-agricultural occupations. See his, *Rural Development and the Village*, Sterling, 1980, p. 41.
3. Krishna Bharadwaj—*Production Conditions in Indian Agriculture: A Study Based on Farm Management Surveys*, Cambridge University Press, 1974, esp. p. 3.
4. See Utsa Patnaik, 'Class Differentiation within Peasantry: An Approach to Analysis of Indian Data', *Economic and Political Weekly*. December 1976.
5. Barbara Harriss, with Chapmen *et. al*, *Exchange Relations and Poverty in Dry Land Agriculture*, Concept Publishing Company, New Delhi, 1984, Ch. 2, esp. p. 27.

APPENDIX

Equation number	Dependent variable	Intercept	Regression co-efficient of dummy variables			R^2
			Wet (=1)	Animal husbandry (=1)	Rural industry (=1)	
(1)	(2)	(3)	(4)	(5)	(6)	(7)
1.	Cultivating h.hs as per cent of All h.hs	75.72 (13.6)	—6.08 (1.02)	—7.69 (1.27)	—26.8 (4.51)	0.68
2.	Mainly cultivating h.hs as per cent of All h.hs	57.76 (10.41)	—2.29 (0.39)	—10.19 (1.69)	—21.86 (8.70)	0.60
3.	Cultivating agri. labour h.hs as per cent of All h.hs	12.34 (8.41)	—1.41 (0.90)	1.79 (1.13)	—8.62 (5.51)	0.76
4.	Non-cultivating agri. labour h.hs as per cent of All h.hs	13.52 (3.08)	9.72 (2.08)	5.01 (1.05)	8.46 (1.81)	0.46
5.	Cultivating Artisans h.hs as per cent of All h.hs	3.23 (3.19)	—2.10 (1.94)	0.46 (0.42)	1.17 (1.09)	0.31
6.	Non-cultivating Artisans h.hs as per cent of All h.hs	6.12 (2.12)	—5.23 (1.69)	—3.43 (1.09)	9.30 (3.02)	0.54
7.	Cultivating traders as per cent of All h.hs	1.00 (2.63)	—0.39 (0.45)	0.07 (0.18)	0.76 (1.87)	0.27
8.	Non-cultivating traders as per cent of All h.hs	2.26 (2.11)	—0.22 (0.19)	0.87 (0.75)	2.02 (1.76)	0.24

(1)	(2)	(3)	(4)	(5)	(6)	(7)
9.	White collar and salaried h.hs as per cent of All h.hs	0.03 (0.02)	0.99 (0.61)	2.01 (1.21)	3.84 (2.36)	0.40
10.	Cultivating h.hs with labour as minor source of income as per cent of All h.hs	24.91 (6.56)	—1.93 (0.48)	—1.77 (0.43)	—16.32 (4.03)	0.61
11.	Cultivating h.hs with animal husbandry as major source as per cent of All h.hs	—0.17 (0.19)	0.75 (0.75)	0.97 (0.96)	0.40 (0.41)	0.14
12.	Non-cultivating h.hs with animal husbandry as major source as per cent of All h.hs	—2.35 (0.95)	2.61 (0.99)	3.25 (1.22)	2.59 (0.99)	0.25
13.	Cultivating h.hs with with animal husbandry as minor source of income as per cent of All h.hs	1.55 (0.78)	0.59 (0.28)	6.89 (3.19)	—1.74 (0.82)	0.51
14.	Non-cultivating h.hs with animal husbandry as minor source as per cent of All h.hs	0.85 (2.07)	0.09 (0.21)	1.09 (2.44)	—0.87 (1.98)	0.49
15.	Per cent of h.hs having only one source of income	54.1 (11.48)	3.8 (0.75)	—11.2 (2.19)	9.5 (1.90)	0.46
16.	Per cent of cultivating h.hs having only one source of income	43.7 (7.27)	2.90 (0.45)	—13.0 (1.99)	1.27 (0.20)	0.28
17.	Per cent marginal cultig. h.hs* having only one source of income	10.13 (1.75)	7.00 (1.14)	—5.12 (0.82)	5.80 (0.94)	0.21
18.	Per cent of Agri. labour h.hs having only one source of income	84.5 (13.39)	+3.87 (0.58)	—9.63 (1.40)	—0.95 (0.14)	0.17
19.	Per cent of SCs & STs among all cultivators	16.20 (4.06)	—10.61 (2.49)	+13.44 (3.10)	—8.74 (2.05)	0.65

Appendix (Contd.)

(1)	(2)	(3)	(4)	(5)	(6)	(7)
20.	Ratios of per cent of SCs and STs among cultivators, to their overall per cent	1.05 (5.85)	—0.35 (1.85)	0.17 (0.90)	—0.56 (2.92)	0.56
21.	Ratio of per cent of SCs & STs among agri. labour, to their overall per cent	2.15 (4.03)	—0.25 (0.44)	—1.09 (1.88)	1.08 (1.91)	0.41
22.	Average size of holding in hectares (standardised)*	6.26 (6.78)	—0.19 (0.19)	1.07 (1.07)	—1.78 (1.81)	0.30
23.	Average size of holding in hectares (non-standardised)	5.22 (6.98)	—1.85 (2.33)	0.88 (1.09)	—1.15 (1.44)	0.45
24.	Gini co-efficient for concentration in operated area, inclusive of agri. labour h.hs	0.585 (12.81)	0.023 (0.47)	0.082 (1.66)	0.151 (3.10)	0.53
25.	Gini co-efficient for concentration in operated area, excluding agri. labour	0.455 (10.17)	—0.010 (0.21)	0.064 (1.33)	0.011 (0.22)	0.14
26.	Share (per cent) of Marginal holdings in operated area (standardised)**	—0.80 (0.18)	5.90 (1.27)	3.19 (0.67)	5.17 (1.11)	0.24
27.	Share (per cent) of large holdings (4 hect. & more) in operated area (standardised)*	74.5 (7.44)	—1.01 (0.09)	7.78 (0.72)	—8.47 (0.79)	0.10

Notes: The Number of observations in each equation is 15 (villages). The intercept corresponds to the value in a dry village with no animal husbandry and rural industry. Figures in brackets are 't' values; their cut off points for statistical significance here are: 3.055 at 1 per cent, 2.179 at 5 per cent and 1.782 at 10 per cent.
h.hs—households

*i.e. those with one hectare and below.
**Standardised for irrigation, by taking 1 irrigated hectare as 3 dry hectares.

6

QUALITY OF RURAL LIFE

INTRODUCTION

EVERYTHING cannot be assessed merely in terms of physical production or GNP. An important criticism of using such an approach is that it ignores quality of life and intangibles that do not get reflected in production but nevertheless make life worth living. Mahbub ul Haq has of course quipped that the concern in advanced countries is about the quality of life, whereas in our part of the world we are concerned with life itself.[1] This is a valid critique of an elitist concern for quality of life, at the cost of concern for basic things needed for living like food. But the underdeveloped countries have also to worry about quality of life that affect living itself. Housing, sanitation and health care are a matter of concern to the poor, as much as or even more than it is for the non-poor. It is wrong to believe that the poor do not aspire for better things in life and are content with just two meals a day, though they may at the same time be facing some scarcity of food and undernutrition. It may be more realistic to view semi-starvation or dire undernutrition as a phenomenon to be mainly found in certain bad years like those affected by drought, and in certain difficult days in normal years (when employment is not available continuously as in lean seasons), rather than as an invariable and rigidly given fact. Their capacity to meet any emergency or any out-of-routine expenditure is extremely low. However, the major characteristics of the poor in normal days seem to be their inability to acquire food items that could improve their diet (like oils, pulses, and fish), poor housing, insanitary conditions of living, illiteracy or semi-literacy and poor clothing, rather than starvation as such. Such conditions affect their health, productivity and time available for remunerative work. They have, therefore, a direct bearing on their level of earnings and living as well. A characteristic of the poor is the amount of hard work they have to put in to acquire the minimum necessary things like fuel and drinking water, let alone elementary schooling, medical care and so on. Their grim struggle to acquire basic necessities, even if no direct monetary cost is involved, leaves little leisure and pleasure in their life. The lot of women and children, particularly, seems to be even more unenviable. Women have to hire out their labour, and also attend to other grinding chores at home. The need for a concern for the quality of life of the poor is, therefore, no less important than the need to make adequate food and employment available to them.

An important question here is whether production-oriented strategies like introduction of irrigation, animal husbandry and rural industry also have the effect of simultaneously improving the quality of life. We have discussed infrastructure and sanitation villagewise in Chapter IV above. We may bring out here some conclusions drawn from these profiles, related to quality of life.

Irrigation by itself had no impact on the rural quality of life; nor had animal husbandry. This was so even regarding the quality of life in the village as a whole, let alone the access of the poor to it. In fact, some of the irrigated villages like Sholamadevi seemed more vulnerable to Cholera and gastro-enteritis than dry villages.

Rural industry, however, had a more discernible effect, at least in improving the overall infrastructure, particularly as the villages with rural industry happened to be large. When rural industry was combined with irrigation and animal husbandry, the level of development of infrastructure seemed better still. But even this impact was not adequate enough. Sanitary conditions particularly, though better in Coimbatore villages on the whole, were hardly satisfactory anywhere. The size of the village and presence of rural industry made no noteworthy impact on toilet facilities except that toilet habits in such cases seemed 'urbanised' in the sense that people used road sides rather than fields for the purpose!

Infrastructure does not keep pace with growth in the size of the village or even its material production, often leading to a more active role for external agents like traders trying to compensate for the inadequate access and infrastructure, at a cost of course to the village concerned. Even where village cost of infrastruture has developed, its benefits do not automatically go to the poor. However, they seem to have somewhat better access than the poor in less developed villages. There was a difference in the environment in which the poor lived in a developed village like Kalangal and the environment in which the Bijapur poor lived, though it cannot all be reduced to cold figures. This difference, however, was not necessarily reflected in all the dimensions of life. In terms of sanitation and access to medical care, drinking water, schooling and transport, the poor in Coimbatore seemed to be better off than their counterparts in other districts. Whatvever benefits of development that have reached the poor in Coimbatore, have obviously taken a long time. It may be recalled that Coimbatore has a longer history of development of modern industry and agriculture, than the other two districts. Even if certain villages in Anantapur and Bijapur may have had as much industry as Coimbatore villages, the fact that Coimbatore region as such was more developed since long, has made an impact on its villages. They have, therefore, a higher level of development than villages with industry in the other two districts.

SIZE OF VILLAGE AND HOUSEHOLDS

Let us now come to specific indicators of quality of life, which are quantifiable. Some of these indicators are more in the nature of proxies than exact measures of quality of life. Table 6.1 below presents these indicators across village types and also district-wise.

An important dimension of rural economy is the size of villages, which is also a rough indicator of quality of life therein. The importance of size as a determinant of viability of villages particularly for the diversification of rural economy, has been stressed by Prof. V.K.R.V. Rao since quite some time.[2]

Table 6.1 shows how the size of villages in terms of the number of households and also total population varies across village types.

As expected, the diversified villages particularly those having industry are larger. The concerned regression equations (Equations 1 and 2 in the Appendix to this chapter) showed that industry had a statistically significant positive impact both on the number of households and population. The impact of animal husbandry, though positive, was not statistically significant. Together, the two considerably increased the size of villages. Coimbatore villages are significantly larger, since they are also more diversified. Whether diversification leads to large size or vice versa, is debatable; probably, the direction of causation is both ways and mutually reinforcing. It is likely that presence of rural industry in a village, located in such a way as to serve surrounding villages conveniently, would eventually increase its size.

Interestingly, irrigation showed no such impact on the size of village. The regression equations actually showed a negative and statistically significant impact both on population and the number of households, given other things. It is only when rural industry is present in a wet village, that its size is larger; but a wet village, by itself, does not automatically attract or discourage industry. There was no strong correlation either way. Such a result here is not necessarily accidental or peculiar, because in another study based on Tumkur district in Karnataka also, wet villages were found to be smaller than others.[3] One possible explanation which we may offer here—which may need further corroboration—is that irrigation involves more intensive operation of agriculture and requires more compact area; spatially, they comprise a smaller area. This could restrict the size of an irrigated village in terms of the number of households and population too, unless the presence of industry allows an alternative basis for habitation.

Though presence of rural industry has a positive impact on the size of a village, it tends to promote smaller families, as judged from the statistically significant negative impact on the average size of household (Equation 3). Neither irrigation nor animal husbandry had a significant impact by themselves. A village with rural industry has also a higher proportion of adult population (Equation 4) and smaller proportion of children. This is consistent with smaller families here. The greater level of female employment in such villages may even be associated with lower fertility rates. However, the data collected by us were not adequate enough to prove this. It may also be observed that Coimbatore villages conspicuously stood apart with higher proportion of adults and smaller proportion of children in their households. This would show that even within the Indian context higher levels of development go with smaller number of children.

Housing

The situation regarding housing is quantified here in terms of four main indicators—the proportion of households living in own houses, those living in poorly constructed houses (houses or huts using no or insignificant amount of bricks), houses with less than 100 sq. ft. of living area (including kitchen space), and also proportion of houses electrified. A summary view of this across village types and districts is presented in Table 6.1. The equations presented in the Appendix to this chapter present the impact across different household categories also.

The proportion of households living in own houses is a peculiar indicator. Across categories of households within a village or a town, it can broadly indicate economic status, but it is not a very reliable indicator in this respect and has to be treated with caution. Across villages and towns, this proportion generally tends to decline with increasing level of industry and urbanisation. In our sample, however, the proportion declined only slightly with the introduction of rural industry and irrigation, but the decline was not statistically significant (see Equation 5). In fact, the proportion was higher on the whole in Coimbatore than in the other two districts. Across size-classes, however, almost all the large cultivators lived in their own houses. But even in the case of small farmers, the proportion was around 95 per cent. Among agricultural labourers too, the proportion was around 90 per cent generally, but was particularly low in Mughalkhod (W-a). Understandably, the salaried and white collar class had the lowest proportion

TABLE 6.1 : A few dimensions of rural quality of life across village types

Village types	No. of house-holds	Pupula-tion	Average size of h.h	Adults as per cent of total popula-tion	Households with				Illiterates (per cent) among adults	Semi literates among adult literates (per cent)	School-going children** (per cent)
					Own houses (per cent)	Poorly construc-ted houses (per cent)	House less than 100 sq. ft. in area (per cent)	Houses electri-fied (per cent)			
*Village type-wise**											
Dry - a	397	2268	5.8	54.5	91.5	7.0	7.9	5.3	87.9	27.6	18.6
- b	526	3039	5.8	51.2	93.2	8.5	4.2	6.2	98.6	17.0	26.6
- c	828	4269	5.1	61.0	88.3	8.3	5.3	23.3	64.7	27.4	40.2
- d	957	5040	5.1	57.8	90.0	9.8	1.6	24.2	75.4	20.8	48.8
Wet - a	223	1214	5.8	52.7	87.5	16.5	12.0	8.2	80.2	38.6	11.6
- b	352	1985	5.8	49.4	89.5	18.0	8.3	9.1	90.9	28.0	19.6
- c	654	3216	5.1	59.2	84.6	17.8	9.4	26.2	57.0	38.4	33.2
- d	783	3986	5.0	56.8	86.3	19.3	5.7	27.1	67.7	31.8	41.8
Location-wise											
Anantapur	561	3108	5.5	54.6	75.7	14.0	6.0	15.2	82.5	10.1	34.6
Bijapur	480	2916	6.1	51.5	83.5	8.1	7.5	9.2	84.3	40.9	20.0
Coimbatore	751	3432	4.6	61.5	91.4	15.8	7.3	25.5	74.6	34.3	38.0
All villages	597	3152	5.3	55.9	83.5	12.6	7.0	16.7	80.4	28.4	30.9

*Derived from Regression Equations 1 to 11.

**As per cent of all children in the age group of above 5 up to 16 years.

of households living in their own houses, though they did not belong to the weaker sections.

The quality of housing is a more reliable indication of economic status. The poor quality of housing as defined by us should normally characterise the core-poor, the poorer among the poor. The proportion of poorly constructed houses declined as the size of holding increased. The more interesting point, however, is that even among marginal farms (less than 1 hectare) the proportion was not very large, being around 11 per cent on the average. But it was around 21 per cent among agricultural labourers. There was a variation in this, which was not significantly associated with either industry or irrigation in the case of cultivating households (see Equations 6-a and 6-b). In fact, in irrigated villages like Korrapadu, the proportion of poorly constructed houses is larger among marginal farmers and agricultural labour, than in a dry and least diversified village like Chinnamushturu. This proportion was smaller for these classes also in dry villages with industry like Sulibhavi and Vadakalur. Interestingly, its proportion was higher among large farmers in Goridindla (D-b) and Mughalkhod (W-a), than in other villages. Even otherwise, there did exist poorly constructed houses even among large farm households in quite a few villages, even though their proportion was small. But in such cases, the houses were not very small. The relatively less well-to-do among the larger farmers had simple houses, particularly in less developed villages. Economic status even among large farmers may not be similar, depending on the quality of land and its management; but this does not mean that they could be considered on the same footing as marginal farmers, let alone landless labourers.

It is noteworthy that while irrigation has not reduced (or increased) the proportion of poorly constructed houses among cultivating households, the proportion was actually higher (which was statistically significant, as seen from Equations 6-c, d, e and f) in irrigated villages among agricultural labour and artisan households; this has been reflected in the proportion in the case of non-cultivating households as a whole and also all households taken together. Industry and animal husbandry had no significant effect either way.

Proportion of households with less than 100 sq. ft. of area was expected to characterise the core-poor like the preceding indicator. Sometimes, these two indicators may very well deviate; in quite a few cases, houses larger than this area were poorly constructed, and better built houses occasionally had less than 100 sq. ft. area. Most of the rural houses were in the size-group of 100 to 500 sq. ft and their proportion declined as the size of holding increased. However, not a negligible proportion of even large farmers had houses with 100-500 sq. ft area. But the smaller houses (less than 100 sq. ft) were, to be found mainly in the case of small farmers, landless labourers, rentiers and others and, sometimes even among the traders—most of whom, it may be noted, were petty sellers.

Like the preceding indicator, this proportion of households living in small houses too had higher values in wet villages. However, in terms of statistical significance, none of the three variables had a significant impact on it in respect of any class (see Equations 7-a to f), except that rural industry tended to decrease this proportion in the case of all cultivating households taken together. On the whole, this proportion was marginal, being only 7 per cent for all household categories and villages together, compared to nearly 13 per cent in the case of poorly constructed houses. There was not much variation as between the district averages in the former proportion; but in the case of poorly constructed houses, the proportion was lower in Bijapur (8 per cent), than in the other two districts (14 per cent in Anantapur and 16 per cent in Coimbatore). Paradoxically, the proportion of the poor, as indicated at least by the proportion of poorly constructed houses, was actually higher in Coimbatore, inspite of its lower proportion of the poor in terms of income. The housing conditions of the richer were, however, better in Coimbatore than in the other two districts.

Coimbatore fared much better in the proportion of houses electrified. It had highest percentage in this respect (25.5 per cent), followed by Anantapur (15.2 per cent) and Bijapur (9.2 per cent). In three villages of Bijapur, electricity was hardly used for domestic lighting though used for irrigation. Taking all the households together, the introduction of irrigation by itself did not improve the proportion of houses electrified, but rural industry improved it by over 18 percentage points partly owing to the size of such villages (see Equation 8-f). It is interesting that it is in rural industry villages that this proportion improved significantly among almost all classes, including marginal farmers, agricultural labour and artisans, though the increase was not equitable (see Equations 8-a to e). The intercept values were not statistically significant, which means that in the dry and least diversified villages the proportion of houses electrified could be taken as good as zero. In rural industry villages, however (ignoring irrigation), the proportion improved by over 27 and by 15 percentage points among cultivating and non-cultivating households respectively. Artisans also gained by over 20 percentage points, but interestingly their gain was smaller than that of cultivating households. The marginal farmers and agricultural labour households gained by nearly 17 and 5 percentage points respectively. The overall proportion was conspicuously high among cultivating households and low among agricultural labour households. In Sholmadevi, however, the latter had an impressive proportion of houses electrified, viz. 18 per cent.

While introduction of animal husbandry had no impact on this proportion, irrigation had a significant positive impact on cultivating households including marginal cultivators and a negative impact (though not significant) on non-cultivating households including agricultural labour and artisans.

On the whole, irrigation seems to have had a dubious impact on the quality of housing, particularly of non-cultivating households. Either it had no significant impact (as in the case of proportion of small houses, and houses electrified) or, it was actually associated with a significant worsening (as in the case of proportion of poorly constructed houses). Even in the case of cultivators, an improvement was restricted to the proportion of houses electrified; in the other two indicators it had no significant impact.

Literacy and schooling

Literacy and the proportion of school-going children are other non-monetary indicators of level of development. We have defined a literate as a person with ability to read and write at least a letter in any language at the time of interview, irrespective of whether he/she had gone to school at any time in the past. This definition was employed consciously and strictly; ablility to sign one's name and to read (even if unable to write) a letter was not considered as adequate for this purpose. Among literates, those who have not even finished primary education (upto 7th standard) have been taken as a separate category. We have called them as semi-literates, for want of a better them. It is possible that some of them may be pundits in their right, though lacking in formal education. But such people can be regarded as exceptional these days. The proportions of illiterates and semi-literates among adult literates (above 18 years) have been presented in summary form across village types and districts in Table 6.1. (Also see Eqs. 9a-f and 10).

Illiteracy and semi-literacy were very high among smaller farmers, and other weaker sections like agricultural labour. Occasionally, illiteracy reached even 100 per cent in such categories in villages like Chinnamushturu and Kambagi (both D-a). However, illiteracy tended to decline in villages with rural industry, not only taking the villages as a whole but also to some extent among weaker sections, though not equitably enough (see Equations 9-a to e). The decline was particularly marked in the case of cultivating households including marginal farmers, but not so (even if statistically significant) among agricultural households. Among artisans, the decline was not even statistically significant. Neither irrigation nor animal husbandry had any significant impact on illiteracy.

Illiteracy was higher among non-cultivating households than among the cultivating. On the whole, the cultivating households had 76 per cent illiteracy (84 per cent in Bijapur, 80 per cent in Anantapur and 64 per cent in Coimbatore) and non-cultivating households had 84 per cent (86 per cent in Bijapur, 85 per cent in Anantapur and 83 per cent in Coimbatore). Here again, the level of development is seen to be affecting mainly the cultivating households for it was in their case that the variation between districts was better reflected. If white collar and salaried class was isolated, the level of illiteracy among non-cultivating households would have looked far worse but for the fact that the white collar class was only a small proportion in the total.

We may note that proportion of illiteracy here was on the higher side as compared to the picture thrown up by the Population Census, inspite of the fact that proportions here have been calculated as per cent to adults only, and not to total population. Though the definition adopted by us is formally the definition employed in the Census enumeration too, it is our strong impression that it has not been strictly employed in the latter. Those who may have had some schooling decades ago may have been automatically taken as literates in Census enumeration, irrespective of present ability to read and write. Again in our case, ability to *both* read and write was a necessary condition, which may not have been strictly employed by census enumerators. Our estimates, we feel, depict more realistically the actual literacy status. If it is so, there is absolutely no case for any complacency on this front. We are really far behind the rest of world.

This picture is not likely to be reversed effectively in the near furture, if the proportion of school-going children is a guide. The goal of 100 per cent coverage is far from being realised. Only 31 per cent of children in the age group of above 5 to 16 went to school, taking all the 15 villages together. Even in the more developed Coimbatore, the proportion was only 38 per cent, followed by Anantapur with 35 per cent and Bijapur with a mere 20 per cent.

Interestingly, introduction of irrigation had the effect of actually reducing the proportion of school-going children, taking all the households together and also in the case of non-cultivating households, irrigation involves more intensive work and it could have the effect of withdrawing children from schools. But this effect was felt in the case of non-cultivating households, rather than directly on the cultivating households. There was no such adverse effect even in the case of marginal farmers; there was no significant positive effect on them either (see Equations 11-a to e). Surprisingly, the negative effect of irrigation on this proportion was not statistically significant in the case of agricultural labour or artisans taken singly. The effect was felt only when all non-cultivating households were combined. Whether irrigation directly had the effect of withdrawing children from school is debatable. It may just as well have been due to the wet villages not having as good access to schools as the other (and larger) villages.

Villages with animal husbandry had actually a higher proportion of school-going children on the whole, particularly in the case of cultivating households. This cannot be interpreted as an effect of animal husbandry as such. It is the more developed larger villages which had animal husbandry, which also incidentally had better school-going facilities and therefore, a higher proportion of school-going children.

Rural industry had a remarkably positive effect on the proportion of school-going children. Paradoxically, it did not have a significant impact in this respect on artisans (see Equation 11-d). On the whole, artisans had a high proportion of school-going children, and it did not vary significantly as between the different types of villages.

The conclusion of the chapter is not particularly flattering to our rural development strategies, and particularly to our irrigation programmes. Production-oriented rural development does not improve the quality of rural life automatically. Irrigation seemed to have even had a negative impact particularly on the proportion of poorly constructed houses and the proportion of school-going children. On the whole, rural industry seemed to have had a qualitatively better impact and also a wider spread of its benefits even among weaker sections than irrigation. Possibly, irrigation could in the long run promote industry both in villages and towns nearby, as it did in Coimbatore. By itself, however, irrigation did not seem to have such a potential. Here again, it needs to be noted that even rural industry by itself may not have a strong potential. It is the large size of villages, in which alone rural industry thrives, that is responsible for a better infrastructure and a better quality of life. But even in their case, we have a long way to go. We cannot be content merely with the fact that large size of villages or presence of industry can raise the level by so much. The base level itself is hardly satisfactory. Also, whatever effect industry and size of village had, did not lift that level high enough. Programmes oriented to directly improving the quality of the life of rural poor, have to be initiated along side or even in the absence of production oriented rural development schemes.

Improving village infrastructure—particularly drinking water facility and sanitation—should naturally receive a priority in such schemes. But the role of improving school attendance and quality of village school education should never be undermined. On the contrary, it should be considered as central. Improvement in literacy and educational level can produce an awareness among the poor of their own economic, social and political position and should enable them to identify causes of their poverty. The process of eradication of poverty starts not when funds are thrown on development schemes planned and implemented by officials, but when the poor start making an intelligent diagnosis of their ills and make concerted efforts to overcome them. Schooling and literacy can play a very helpful role in this process, if only planned and operated in that spirit.

References

1. Mahbub ul Haq, *The Poverty Curtain*, 1976.
2. Cf. 'Neglected Factors in Integrated Rural Development', Convocation Address at IARI, New Delhi 1977.
3. V.M. Rao, *Rural Development and the Village* Sterling, 1980 pp. 29-30.

APPENDIX

Equation number	Dependent variable	Intercept	Regression co-efficients of dummy variables			R^2
			Wet (=1)	Animal husbandry (=1)	Rural industry (=1)	
(1)	(2)	(3)	(4)	(5)	(6)	(7)
1.	Population	2268 (4.69)	—1054 (2.05)	771 (1.47)	2001 (3.89)	0.64
2.	Number of households	397 (6.17)	—174 (2.54)	129 (1.85)	431 (6.29)	0.81
3.	Average size of household	5.84 (17.6)	—0.02 (0.47)	—0.03 (0.10)	—0.75 (2.13)	0.29
4.	Per cent of adults in total population	54.5 (23.2)	—1.84 (0.74)	—3.15 (1.24)	6.52 (2.60)	0.45
5.	Per cent of h.hs with owned houses	91.5 (21.91)	—3.66 (0.82)	1.65 (0.36)	—3.19 (0.72)	0.11
6.	Proportion (per cent) of poorly constructed houses, among—					
	(a) marginal cultig. h.hs	8.00 (1.30)	1.84 (0.28)	5.65 (0.85)	—1.22 (0.19)	0.07
	(b) all cultig. h.hs	5.84 (1.89)	3.48 (1.05)	1.37 (0.41)	—3.15 (0.96)	0.16
	(c) agri. labour h.hs	14.66 (2.36)	13.51 (2.04)	—0.12 (0.02)	1.94 (0.29)	0.28

(d) artisans*	5.95	20.57	—3.72	2.43	0.45
	(0.85)	(2.70)	(0.49)	(0.32)	
(e) all non-cultig. h.hs	11.77	14.88	—1.85	1.34	0.30
	(1.79)	(2.12)	(0.26)	(0.19)	
(f) all households	7.02	9.33	1.48	1.25	0.29
	(1.62)	(2.01)	(0.32)	(0.27)	
7. Proportion (per cent) of houses with less than 100 sq. ft. area among—					
(a) marginal cultig. h.hs.	9.76	3.45	—4.85	—5.10	0.20
	(2.32)	(0.77)	(1.06)	(1.14)	
b) all cultig. h.hs	6.33	2.63	—2.57	—4.76	0.35
	(2.87)	(1.12)	(1.07)	(2.02)	
(c) agri. labour h.hs	17.08	2.48	—8.38	—3.16	0.20
	(3.45)	(0.47)	(1.56)	(0.60)	
(d) artisans*	5.65	6.05	—3.67	—0.08	0.17
	(1.26)	(1.25)	(0.76)	(0.02)	
(e) all non-cultig. h.hs	13.69	4.10	—6.79	—3.75	0.20
	(2.97)	(0.83)	(1.36)	(0.76)	
(f) all households	7.90	4.09	—3.68	—2.60	0.24
	(2.74)	(1.33)	(1.18)	(0.85)	
8. Proportion (per cent) of houses electrified, among—					
(a) marginal cultig. h.hs.	—4.87	12.2	5.92	16.62	0.50
	(0.77)	(1.82)	(0.87)	(2.48)	

* Since Nandyal had no artisans, the equations concerning artisans have only 14 observations (one less than other equations). The cut-off points of 't' values for statistical significance here are: 3.106 at 1 per cent, 2.201 at 5 per cent and 1.796 at 10 per cent.

APPENDIX (*contd.*)

(1)	(2)	(3)	(4)	(5)	(6)	(7)
	(b) all cultig. h.hs	0.02	14.8	7.90	27.34	0.62
		(0.00)	(1.91)	(1.00)	(2.23)	
	(c) agri. labour h.hs	—1.59	2.89	2.15	4.69	0.43
		(0.80)	(1.37)	(1.00)	(2.23)	
	(d) artisans*	11.32	—11.49	—10.81	20.44	0.40
		(1.18)	(1.10)	(1.04)	(1.96)	
	(e) all non-cultig. h.hs	5.56	—4.18	—0.96	14.78	0.46
		(1.18)	(0.83)	(0.19)	(2.94)	
	(f) all households	5.32	2.91	0.93	18.03	0.53
		(1.08)	(0.56)	(0.18)	(3.44)	
9.	Proportion (per cent) of illiterates among adults, among—					
	(a) marginal cultig. h.hs	97.12	—6.43	1.09	—19.95	0.71
		(24.97)	(1.55)	(0.26)	(4.81)	
	(b) all cultig. h.hs	89.67	—2.26	—0.49	—22.69	0.87
		(36.34)	(0.86)	(0.18)	(8.63)	
	(c) agri. labour h.hs	96.53	—2.43	2.87	—5.93	0.59
		(56.33)	(1.33)	(1.54)	(3.24)	
	(d) artisans*	79.06	1.67	9.67	—4.79	0.28
		(14.26)	(0.28)	(1.62)	(0.80)	
	(e) all non-cultig. h.hs	87.74	2.98	5.06	—12.18	0.59
		(22.12)	(0.86)	(1.44)	(3.53)	
	(f) all households	87.9	—7.68	10.72	—23.24	0.39
		(8.98)	(0.74)	(1.01)	(2.23)	

10. Proportion (per cent) of semi-literates among adult literates (All households)	27.63 (3.40)	11.00 (1.20)	—10.60 (0.02)	—0.15	0.21
11. Proportion** (per cent) of school-going children among—					
(a) marginal cultig. h.hs	5.77 (1.06)	0.41 (0.07)	12.27 (2.09)	26.49 (4.59)	0.69
(b) all cultig. h.hs.	18.51 (4.31)	—3.38 (0.74)	10.23 (2.20)	28.81 (6.29)	0.80
(c) agri. labour h.hs	8.61 (2.75)	—4.50 (1.35)	5.91 (1.74)	12.00 (3.59)	0.60
(d) artisans*	34.15 (4.66)	—0.42 (0.05)	3.38 (0.43)	5.59 (0.71)	0.06
(e) all non-cultig. h.hs	18.65 (5.98)	—11.82 (3.56)	7.34 (2.17)	17.97 (5.41)	0.79
(f) all households	18.60 (3.13)	—7.05 (1.97)	8.02 (1.82)	22.18 (5.56)	0.79

* See footnote for Eq. 6 (d).

**Taking into account children in the age group of above 5 upto 16 years.

Notes: The number of observations in each equation is 15 (villages). The intercept corresponds to the value in a dry village with no animal husbandry and rural industry. Figures in brackets are 't' values; their cut off points for statistical significance here are: 3.055 at 1 per cent, 2.179 at 5 per cent and 1.782 at 10 per cent.

7

COMMERCIALISATION OF AGRICULTURE

THE PROBLEM

A STUDY of spatial contrasts in the magnitude of commercialisation of agriculture and the circumstances which determine it can be of considerable interest. The structural aspects of agriculture associated with various levels of commercialisation can offer several insights into the process of commercialisation. Spatial variation in this respect arises not only across countries but also within a country and even within a state. Of particular interest are the differences between dry or drought-prone regions and the wet or assured rainfall regions.

In an interesting historical account of the erstwhile Madras Presidency, Washbrook has noted how commercialisation of rice cultivation had developed in wet districts since long and, how there was a broad based market access and a relatively prosperous peasantry in the delta regions. In contrast, the agrarian structure was much more unequal, market access narrowbased and usurer's role and exploitation much more dominant in the dry zone. In this zone, peasantry was very poor, marketing was more out of distress than out of surplus, and trading concentrated in a few hands.[1] Are wet regions then necessarily more commercialised ? A possible factor in favour of commercialisation of dry regions is the greater proportion of land in larger holdings there, resulting in a larger marketable surplus and hence sales. But when holdings were standardised for irrigation difference, no significant difference in this respect was observed between dry and wet villages as noted above in Chapter 5. Introduction of cash crops like cotton and groundnut which are grown mostly in rainfed areas also could—and they did—promote commercialisation in such regions.

There exists stratification of different magnitudes even in wet regions and agrarian structure is not necessarily egalitarian. Rice growing regions of Assam seem to be less commercialised due to the heavy hangover of feudal social structure, than the rice growing regions of Tamil Nadu.[2] Even within Tamil Nadu, rice is marketed more in Coimbatore than in Tanjavur.[3] But here the difference arises because rice is grown in Coimbatore relatively more for exchange and millets are purchased by such farmers for consumption. Coimbatore is much more a multi-crop economy inclusive of millets, than Tanjavur.

Commercialisation of wet regions receives a further impetus when technological advance takes place, which increases not only the overall productivity of land but also raise it particularly in those holdings (large) which even earlier had a larger share in the product market. Introduction of commercial crops like sugarcane and tobacco would be further contributing factors, which also link agriculture more closely with industry.

Since commercialising factors exist both in wet and dry regions, it is difficult to assert *a priori* that all wet regions would essentially have a more commercialised agriculture than dry regions. Moreover, the industrial environment in which they are placed can also be a major contributory factor. They also need not be associated with identical features related to agrarian structure. It would be useful to have a look at the village level pictures representing diverse conditions, and see to what extent and under what circumstances commercialisation of agriculture varies across space and with what agrarian features it is associated; what factors could have influenced the variation therein and how this is reflected in different size-classes of holdings.

Commercialisation means market involvement, which need not necessarily be equally advantageous to all. Quite apart from the advantage derived from physical quantity of marketed surplus, the price at which it is sold need not be uniform for all. It is generally believed that small farmers are particularly at a disadvantage in this respect, and there is also some evidence available in support of this view.[4] We therefore, intend here to check how far differences in realised prices affect different size-classes of holdings and different types of villages.

Commercialisation of agriculture here is as reflected by the proportion of sale of farm produce in total farm production. This is only gross sale, and is not net of repurchases for consumption. If it is so netted, farmers' involvement in the product market and hence commercialisation would be underestimated.[5] Both sales and production of different crops have been aggregated in value terms, at realised prices. This issue is discussed further in the next section. Receipts in kind were also included in production; they were, however, quite marginal in magnitude. Sales include disposals under procurement levy, but do not include payments and gifts in kind. For the purpose of this chapter and the next, sales and production relate only to those arising out of cultivation, and hence exclude those arising out of dairy or animal husbandry and other activities.

Valuation of output

Output from agriculture is hardly homogeneous. Different farmers adopt different cropping patterns even within a village. Output cannot be measured in terms of physical units at an aggregate level of the farm household. Our main interest is in the farm economy of the household, rather than in individual crops. There is no dearth of information on productivity of different crops in physical units, both for rainfed and irrigated crops separately, since this is being collected district-wise in a systematic way by official agencies. The main contribution from a study like this it gives an idea of differences in productivity as between different size-classes of farm holdings. We may, however, stress here that the nature of peasant decision making is such that they do not necessarily intend to maximise productivity of each crop separately. When more than one crop is grown, the total productivity of all crops together is tried to be raised. Where double cropping is possible, it is the productivity per hectare of net sown area which may be tried to be maximised, and not just productivity per hectare of gross sown area. But this is another issue. The level of development and prosperity of a cultivating household is determined by cropping pattern, cropping intensity, productivity of crops per hectare, and—last and certainly not the least—by the price levels of different crops. The valuation of output of a household should reflect all these elements, which determines income, given the cost of cultivation. The question of income and cost of cultivation may be deferred to the next chapter.

Output can be valued either at actually realised prices (through sales) or, at some uniform or notional price which may well be different from prices actually realised by individual farmers. The difference arises because farmers hardly receive the same price. Prices differ both within a village as between different farmers and across villages. This depends not merely on the quality of the product, but also on the time and place of sale, access to market and the bargaining position of the concerned parties in the market. We have valued output at both prices separately—realised (differential) prices and uniform prices at the village level.

Both of these sets have analytical significance. It is the actually realised prices which determine the actual income of farmers, and not notional prices. As such we have used the valuation of output at realised prices for the purpose of computation of income and also for analysing the relation between output and sales. However, we need the valuation of output at a uniform price for comparison with the valuation at realised prices. Apart from the fact that differences in output at a uniform price reflect differences on account of physical factors like productivity, crop pattern and cropping intensity which have their own significance, a comparison between the two sets of valuation can indicate the role played by price differences on different size-classes of farmers. From this we can know if any particular set of farmers are placed at a disadvantage in the market for agricultural goods. Though such a comparison is plagued by quality differences in products, we may remember that the alleged quality differences and farmers' ignorance about it is itself a major source of their exploitation. Anyway, it was not possible for us to grade their products and distinguish price differences on account of quality differences from those on acconnt of imperfect market conditions.

The realised prices are defined here for the purpose of valuation as the prices actually received by respective farmers in their sale transaction. In the valuation according to realised prices, the same prices have been used for the valuation of unsold production (self-consumption, payments in kind etc.). When a farmer did not sell any part of his output of a crop, the price realised by a farmer in the same village having a holding nearest in size, was used in the former case also. The uniform price used here for an alternative valuation is the average of prices for the concerned crop realised by all farmers in the concerned villages. Though there are other possibilities of a uniform price, viz., district level average or average for all the three districts, we have not used them (unless otherwise specified). Our uniform price is at the village level, and the across village differences are not averaged.* We could have run the risk of allowing a much greater role for quality differences, if we had used district averages or averages for all three districts for valuation. Quality differences in respect of a given crop are more likely across villages than within. We shall, however, separately indicate the extent of difference made by across-village differences on the valuation of output at the village level.

The Appendix to this chapter presents details holding size-wise for each of the selected villages, on gross value of agricultural output and sale of output.

Differential prices : Extent and pattern

We may first take up the question of whether there is any significant difference between the two sets of valuation of agricultural output discussed above. Column 6 in the Appendix table below presents the ratios of valuation at realised prices as a percentage over the valuation at village average price, for different size-classes of holdings. For the village as a whole, the ratio should be 100 per cent, since the question of divergence arises only at the level of individual farmers or size-classes of holdings. In fact, however, the ratio at the village level diverged a little, the range being 112.9 to 90.6 across the 15 villages.

* It may be noted that studies in the Economics of Farm Management initiated since the fifties also use village level uniform prices. They do not present alternative sets of valuation.

This was because village average prices were not weighted for differences in quantity sold. To correct the distortions produced as a result, the ratios at size-class of holdings were standardised by dividing them by village level ratios, the quotients being expressed as percentages. Only these standardised ratios are presented in the Appendix table below.

Unfortunately, our elaborate exercise here did not yield expected patterns, though it did show that considerable differences existed between the two sets to valuations. There was no significant pattern in any village in the sense of smoothly increasing or decreasing ratios related to size of holding. There were very fluctuating trends. This meant that it was difficult on the basis of our data to corroborate any hypothesis on the lines that price advantage increased with the size of holding. There was no such relation in a continuous sense at least. However, if we concentrate on marginal holdings (the smallest size-class, with less than 1 hectare of operated area), they were more often at a disadvantage, as seen from ratios being less than 100 in their case in 8 villages. Of these 4 were relatively dry and 4 irrigated. In one of the remaining 7 villages (dry), the ratio was 100 (actually 100.1) and in 6 villages it was higher in the case of this size-class. The latter belonged all to Coimbatore, except for Nandyal of Bijapur where the range between large and small farms was smaller than in other Bijapur or Anantapur villages. On the whole, small farmers were relatively at a disadvantage in Anantapur and Bijapur and large farmers at an advantage in this respect. As we shall see shortly, their agriculture is less commercialised than in Coimbatore. It is in less commercialised and interior villages that the disadvantage of small farmers was highest; here it is the large farmers who can afford to take their produce to good markets.

We also tried to see from the primary data if the quantum of product sold gave a relative price advantage in respect of individual crops. However, we found no consistent pictures in this respect. Between a farmer selling a small quantity and another selling a large quantity of a particular crop, there was no consistent difference in price secured. At times, small quantities had the advantage of being transported easily though bullock-carts, whereas large quantities posed transport problems. Contrary to popular impressions it would not be quite true to assert that small sales are confined to respective villages alone. Even small farmers and agricultural labourers tended to keep bullock-carts in more commercialised villages having good market access as in Coimbatore, which could be hired to transport small quantities to the market, apart from their own produce.

We also explored the question of whether particular villages as a whole suffered a price disadvantage. For this purpose, another set of valuation of agricultural output using district average prices of respective crops was computed, and the value of agricultural output at village level prices was expressed as a percentage over the value at the concerned district average prices for each of the 15 villages. This valuation was done only at the village level and not at the level of holdings. The results are presented in Table 7.1. It was

TABLE 7.1 : **Village price levels relative to corresponding district averages, for farm produce (Ratios in per cent)**

Village types	Wet villages		Dry villages	
(a)	M'khod (B)	83.5	C'mushturu (A)	98.1
	N'yal (B)	101.1	Kambagi (B)	93.4
(b)	K'padu (A)	101.7	G'dindla (A)	102.5
			M'valgi (B)	100.6
(c)	R'cheruvu (A)	99.3	S'bhavi (B)	109.9
	K'palayam (C)	107.9	S'kinar (C)	94.8
			V'kalur (C)	101.9
(d)	S'devi (C)	98.7	B'guppa (A)	97.8
	K'gal (C)	106.2		

(A—Anantapur, B—Bijapur and C—Coimbatore villages)

interesting to find that there was no difference between wet and dry villages in this respect though within them there were significant differences. The average ratios turned out to be almost the same close to 100 both for the wet and dry villages. The prices realised by village as a whole are determined by a number of factors like access to villages, quality of products sold and the level of development and diversification of the village. It is difficult to generalise in terms of one factor alone. However, the least developed type—dry and least diversified villages—fared worse, though in terms of access they were not worse off. Their essential difficulty seemed to be that they were least commercialised as we shall soon see. Among the two least diversified wet villages, Mughalkhod was worse off (it received lowest prices amongst all 15), which could have been due to its bad access. Taking the two most diversified wet villages, one had a ratio of a little less than 100 (viz. 98.7), while the other had a significantly higher ratio (viz. 106.2). The latter village—Kalangal—is near Coimbatore, more industrialised and has very good access. Taking wet villages with rural industry, Rayalacheruvu actually has better access and yet the other village—Kokkampalayam—fared better. This was mainly because of the better prices it got for its important crop of tobacco. Other Coimbatore villages did not receive equally good prices for this crop, since some large farmers of Kokkampalayam participated in trading and cultivated superior varieties.

Since it is the realised prices which determine actual incomes, we have used the valuation based on them in what follows. In any case, we have already an idea of what difference it makes if the output is valued at uniform village level prices in the case of each size-class of holding.

Factors behind commercialisation

The necessary details on the magnitude of commercialisation can be seen from the Appendix (table) to this chapter. The proportion of sales to agricultural produce which indicates commercialisation, can be seen from the table for different size-classes in each village (col. 8). The degree of concentration in sales among size-classes is indicated by column 7 which presents the share of each class in the total farm sale of respective villages. The role of foodgrains in the picture is shown by columns 9 to 10 in the table, which respectively give size-classwise details of the proportion of foodgrains production in total farm produce and the proportion of sales to foodgrains production. A summary view of the ratio of sales to total farm produce in different villages is presented below in Table 7.2.

It is interesting to note here that commercialisation of agriculture is not just marginal. In 12 out of 15 villages, over half of the farm produce was sold; and in 8, the proportion was above 60 per cent. The average value (not weighted)

TABLE 7.2 : **Proportion (per cent) of sales to farm produce and village ranking accordingly**

Village types	Wet villages		Dry Villages	
(a)	M'khod (B) N'yal (B)	64.4 (7) 50.9 (12)	C'turu (A) K'bagi (B)	38.9 (14) 28.4 (15)
(b)	K'padu (A)	53.5 (10)	G'dla (A) M'valgi (B)	52.2 (11) 62.5 (8)
(c)	R'ruvu (A) K'lyam (C)	69.2 (6) 88.5 (1)	S'bhavi (B) S'kinar (C) V'kalur(C)	46.0 (13) 76.4 (4) 82.8 (3)
(d)	S'devi (C) K'ngal (C)	72.5 (5) 86.5 (2)	B'guppa (A)	58.1 (9)

Note : A, B and C as in Table 7.1. Figures in brackets are ranks as per the proportion of sales.

for all the 15 villages turned out to be as high as 62 per cent, though the range extended from 28.4 to 88.5 per cent. If either marketable surplus or sales net of repurchases had been taken instead of gross sales, such a proportion would have naturally looked smaller;[6] but this would not have indicated the involvement of a large section of cultivators who produce for exchange and also repurchase. The high proportion of sales makes it difficult to characterise our agriculture as subsistence agriculture. As we shall shortly see, this is so even in the case of small farmers. The bulk of agriculture is commercialised and produces for exchange.

We may easily see from the table that irrigation is not a very strong or an exclusive factor behind commercialisation at the village level. Since irrigation increases productivity and hence marketable surplus too, it should have been a strong factor in commercialisation. Indeed, the average proportion of sales in wet villages was 69.4 per cent, while in dry villages it was 55.7 per cent. Though on the whole, irrigated villages were more commercialised than dry villages, there was a considerable fluctuation in ranking cutting across these two broad types. The co-efficient of correlation between proportion of sales and proportion of irrigation across the 15 villages was only 0.49, which was significant 10 per cent level. The regression equation with dummy independent variables for irrigation (wet), animal husbandry (AH) and industry (Ind) and with proportion of sales as dependent variable (Y) turned out to be (15 villages as observations):

$$Y = 43.2 + 11.9\ \text{Wet} + 4.2\ \text{AH} + 21.8\ \text{Ind.}$$
$$(6.83)\ (1.77)\qquad (0.61)\qquad (3.22)\qquad\qquad R^2 = 0.57$$

It can be seen from this that the rural industry alone was significant, while the dummy for irrigation just missed being significant at 10 per cent level. Animal husbandry was hardly significant. Irrigation by itself was not a strong commercialiser. Even within the two broad types—wet and dry—rankings in terms of commercialisation were not smoothly related to the level of diversification as they cut across the types. For example, the most commercialised was not the most diversified village. However, both of the least developed villages (D-a) were also the least commercialised. Diversification, particularly through rural industry, is expected to increase the level of commercialisation, if it reduces the number of cultivators depending on agriculture, increasing the marketable surplus of cultivating households in the process. Animal husbandry does not have such an effect, but industry—within the village or in the region in which it is located—can have this effect. It is significant in this connection that among our 15 villages, the more commercialised also had a lower proportion of cultivating households, the correlation being —0.60, which is statistically significant.

It is the larger villages, which are on the whole diversified and also have lower proportion of cultivating households and more commercialised. The size of a village is a rough indicator of its market access as well, and favours commercialisation*. The location of a village—whether it is on the main road or in the interior—is not by itself a major factor. In fact, no selected village was so very isolated as to be almost a self contained economy. The development of the market in the region as a whole is more important than the location of villages, provided that the location does not make the village

* Co-efficient of correlation between village size (no. of households) and percentage of sales to farm produce was 0.46 (significant at 10 per cent level).

extremely isolated. Development of regional market provides a more meaningful market access than a nominally good location could. In this sense, Coimbatore district has a more developed regional market. It is not incidental that all its villages—wet or dry—were highly commercialised, occupying the first 5 ranks and all registering well over 70 per cent sales. The averageproportion of sales in Coimbatore villages was 81.3 per cent, Anantapur villages following rather far behind with 54.4 per cent and Bijapur villages with 50.4 per cent. However, even in the latter, commercialisation was not marginal inspite of their being relatively backward (except the two villages under D-a types).

Regional development apart, the strongest factor affecting the commercialisation of agriculture across villages, is the value of farm produce per cultivating household, the co-efficient of correlation across villages being 0.67. This is not surprising because higher marketable surplus results under such conditions. Though concentration in land tends to increase both farm produce per cultivating household and marketable surplus, share of large holdings in area did not by itself emerge as an important positive factor behind differences in the levels of commercialisation; because concentration in land among cultivators existed generally both in more and less commercialised villages. What made the crucial differences is that commercialisation of agriculture stimulated higher production, both in agricultural and non-agricultural activities, particularly as seen across villages. This is a point of significance with implications for welfare. If commercialisation of agriculture takes place under force or bondage, it cannot stimulate agricultural development or production. But more genuine commercialisation can do so and thus increase welfare. If, for example, milk production is commercialised under bondage, much of it may be simply sold depriving the producing household of its own intake of milk and milk products and even a fair return from sale. But if commercialisation increases production, household's own intake need not fall and its income also would increase. Commercialisation, at least at the present stage of development, is much more of the latter kind, as corroborated by the survey referred. Such a commercialisation cannot take place unless there is prospect of gaining higher income for household through market involvement.

There is a qualification to the correlation between commercialisation and farm produce per cultivating household. If commercialisation is measured in terms of gross sales as a proportion of output (without netting for repurchases), even small farmers were almost as commercialised as large farmers, and the above correlation need not hold very strongly across households within a village. But this is not because the small farmers are compulsively involved in the market under conditions of bondage. Their market involvement was more to maximise their purchasing power, with which they could purchase what they liked—mainly foodgrains. In rice growing villages, small growers sold rice and purchased jowar—an activity which maximised their purchasing power available to meet their needs. By and large, such calculations get submerged in intervillage camparisons, except when the village consists mostly of small and medium holders who are also highly commercialised as it happened in Vadakalur village in Coimbatore district. Barring such exceptions, the role of per household production as an important factor in commercialisation—influencing it and also influenced by it—clearly emerges. It may be noted that if commercialisation were to be measured in terms of *net* sales instead of gross sales, such a correlation would emerge even in intravillage situation across households.

The crop pattern was also a relavant factor in affecting commercialisation. The proportion of foodgrains had a negative influence, the co-efficient of correlation between the same and proportion of agricultural output sold being —0.58 across villages, which was statistically significant. But production of foodgrains like paddy and wheat also helped commercialisation in irrigated areas, while dry non-foodgrain crops like groundnut helped the commercialisation of even dry villages. It was because of commercial crops in dry villages that the correlation between irrigation and commercialisation turned out to be not quite strong. Vadakalur and Sirukinar—both dry villages in Coimbatore—were highly commercialised because, apart from regional effect, both produced commercial crops in dry as well as whatever little wet lands they had. The same factor explained why some wet villages like

Nandyal were less commercialised. Food crops like jowar and maize dominated here even under irrigation.

Structural attributes of commercialisation

We may now study a few structural attributes of more commercialised villages. An interesting aspect of the level of commercialisation is its high positive association with non-cultivating or landless agricultural labour. The correlation between the two across villages was 0.56 (significant at 5 per cent level). This is not surprising in view of the strong positive correlation (viz. 0.80) between landless labour and per household agricultural produce. It is interesting that the correlation between the proportion of landless labour and per household farm produce was stronger than the one between the former and proportion of irrigated area (viz. 0.66). It is not just a question of irrigation attracting a greater supply of labour. Landless labour has been a very important factor in stepping up production and it is through this process that commercialisation of agriculture has advanced. Commercialisation in turn also tends to promote proletarianisation. It was this factor which made the agrarian structure of more commercialised villages more inequitous, rather than a higher concentration among cultivators themselves.

Interestingly here, the more commercialised is a village, the less it would have cultivating agricultural labourers.* Under higher levels of commercialisation, cultivators hire in—rather than hire out—labour and there is a cheap source of landless labour. Under a commercialised setting, wage levels are higher. While the line of viability also may come down to include smaller holdings under commercialisation through irrigation and/or cash crops (reducing in the process the number of cultivators dependent on wage income), very small cultivators may actually find it more remunerative to opt for agricultural labour rather than be bogged down to disadvantageously small scale cultivation. They may be induced to lease

* The co-efficients of correlation between proportion of sales on the one hand and the proportion of cultivating households with labour as main source of income and those with labour as a secondary source of income on the other, turned out to be —0.50 and —0.62 across the 15 villages.

out or even sell their land. This situation can arise in rainfed areas too, but they may have to move out of such villages altogether to opt for more remunerative labour. In commercialised villages, they do not have to. The latter is therefore, a more favourable situation for cultivating labour to be less and non-cultivating labour to be more. The fact, however, remains that even in villages with medium commercialisation, cultivating labour continues to form a large proportion unless there is a significant rural industry.

It would be interesting to see if more commercialised villages have a higher proportion of trading households. The proportion of households engaged in trading varied between 1.8 per cent (in Nandyal with low level of commercialisation) and 10.8 per cent (in Sholamadevi which is more commercialised). It cannot, however, be said that more commercialised villages had a higher proportion of traders. In fact, the correlation was weak and non-significant. The proportion of trading households, however, was positively and significantly related to the size of village (in terms of total number households in the village). This would mean that it is more linked with the development of the village economy and size of population rather than with the volume of sales from agriculture alone, most of which in any case would go outside the village. In fact, village traders were engaged more in bringing outside produce and selling within villages and meeting local wants, than in the sale of local product outside. It was not the village traders themselves who were instrumental in the sale of farm produce, which was done by the farmers themselves or by agents of big traders from outside. A large proportion of local village traders were only petty sellers with nominal or no establishments. The proportion of cultivating traders among trading households varied from zero in Nandyal to 73.9 per cent in Mulsavalgi—a dairy village. This again had no correlation with the level of commercialisation in agriculture. The cultivating traders are not necessarily traders in agricultural produce (other than their own), nor are they essentially from large farmers' class. There was no significant correlation between the proportion of cultivating traders and the share of large farmers in total area of farm sale.

The fact that the bulk of village traders are petty sellers

with or without establishments and handle mostly urban goods for sale in the villages has been observed by V.M. Rao too in his field work in Tumkur. He speaks of an asymmetry in market functionaries—those in in-coming channel handling urban goods being more numerous than those in the outgoing channel. As he says, 'the markets bringing in urban goods may be expected to seek functionaries, with a wider rural spread and capable of reaching out to the rural people. The markets drawing out the agricultural produce would tend to rely more on the rural elite having the requisite local experience, capacity and hold over the farmers and their produce. Compared to these two, the markets moving out the non-agricultural rural produce are likely to be relatively weak and unorganised'.[7] It is thus clear that the need for a greater number of market functionaries arises when the size of village, its development level in general—and hence purchasing power —are higher, and not just because more agricultural produce has to be sold from such a village. The latter is handled in any case by a—literally—privileged few. It is because the commercialised village also is generally a larger and developed village, it may have more market functionaries.

Even if the proportion of cultivating traders among traders need not necessarily increase with commercialisation of agriculture, there is unmistakable presence of a few rich cultivators in the outgoing channel handling local produce. Naturally their power cannot be assessed by their number, but by the turnover they handle. There were quite a few households in Coimbatore villages who handled a good proportion of agricultural sale, not only of their farm produce, but also of others, and obtained bulk of their income from trading.* They were to be seen in Rayalacheruvu too from Anantapur, the most commercialised among our villages outside Coimbatore. In fact, they were, more properly traders than cultivators. Yet, as Barbara Harriss, has observed in the context of Coimbatore itself, they were active in the Farmers Association in Tamil Nadu as its Members, and effectively frustrated farmers' agita-

* Some of them neglected agriculture and reported crop failures, and yet their total income was comfortably high bulk of which came from trading, as for instance in the case of large farmers in Vadakalur.

tions against commission Agents in Regulated Markets and similar attempts to reform the market system.[8] They were associated with merchants' associations too. Leading traders even if having their farms and houses in villages had wider contacts, and wielded political influence. Harriss has observed that they were larger than average both as traders and farmers.

It would be useful to summarise main points of general interest which have emerged here. Though higher commercialisation by itself does not suggest a higher level of development, we have evidence at least in the regions covered here to indicate that it is so here. This comes out clearly in the cross-section comparison of villages and also districts concerned. Within villages, small farmers too were as much commercialised as the large, in terms of gross sales. But this did not seem to be under duress or just to repay debts. It was more genuine, to exchange cash crops or superior food crops for more basic or staple foodgrains.

Commercialisation was hardly marginal. On the whole over 62 per cent of agricultural output was marketed, the proportion being much higher in Coimbatore. It is not surprising that this district was the breeding ground for farmers' agitations on price and related issues.

What makes commercialisation appear here as a progressive force associated with development of the forces of production, is the fact that it is the farm produce per household which was the most important positive factor determining the level of commercialisation. The two important factors which have positively influenced the level of per household produce were a cheap supply of labour in the form of landless labour and irrigation. They in turn determined commercialisation. It could also very well be that under a commercialised setting it was more remunerative for very small cultivators to be non-cultivating labourers. Commercialisation has, therefore, been a proletarianising force; making the agrarian structure more inequitous. While commercialisation may tend to weed out nonviable holdings from cultivation, they need not at the same time increase the share of large holdings. Small holdings above some line of viability may very well thrive under commercialisation without having to depend much on wage labour as a source of livelihood. This also could have been an important factor in reducing the proportion of cultivating labour.

There were also dry villages which were more commercialised and wet villages less commercialised. Proportion of foodgrains production, size of the village and the fact of being a part of a developed region and its level of commercialisation, explain the deviations from the expected pattern. Cultivation of cash crops in rainfed conditions or in villages with moderate irrigation have improved the cash economy of such villages and also of small farmers in several villages.

The question of whether market involvement or commercialisation has been depressive and immiserising could be discussed more definitively only in the light of findings from the next two chapters. It is, therefore, taken up in the concluding chapter. At this stage, we can only say that a mere increase in the proportion of non-cultivating labourers occurring with commercialisation, is not a sufficient evidence to conclusively answer this question.

References

1. Cf David Washbrook, 'Country Politics : Madras 1880 to 1930', *Modern Asian Studies*, Vol. 7, Part 3, July 1973, pp. 475-531.
2. Cf Narendar Pani, "Production Conditions in Rice Economy" Ph. D. Dissertation, University of Mysore, 1984 (unpublished).
3. This is seen from Farm Management Studies data. A similar difference arises between the Punjab and West Bengal in respect of rice. For a review of such regional differences, see M. V. Nadkarni, *Marketable Surplus and Market Dependence in a Millet Region*, Allied, New Delhi, 1980, Ch. 1, pp. 29-35.
4. See, for example, Suman Sarkar, 'Marketing of Foodgrains: An Analysis of Village survey data for West Bengal and Bihar', *Economic and Political Weekly*, Review of Agriculture, Sept. 26, 1981.
5. Neither Marketable surplus nor net marketed surplus would suit this purpose. K.N. Kabra also supports the view that commercialisation of agriculture can be indicated by sales. See his, 'Marketed Surplus or self provisioning of food: Questions concerning Contexts and Concepts' Working Paper. IIPA, New Delhi, 1981 (Mimeo).
6. For the same reason, the estimate of monetisation in the Indian economy indicated by Madalgi could be on the lower side than what it really is. See S.S. Madalgi, *Trends in Monetisation in the Indian Economy*, RBI Staff Occasional Papers, Vol. 1(1), June 1976, pp. 46-72.

7. V.M. Rao, 'Barriers in Rural Development', *Economic and Political Weekly*, 2 July 1983, pp. 1187-8, Rao considers this asymmetry as an instance of depressive market penetration into villages. It may, however, be also noted that even retail traders in agricultural produce—whether in urban areas or the rural—are, by their very nature, even more widespread, and not necessarily richer than retail traders in urban goods.
8. Barbara Harriss, *State and Market*, New Delhi, Concept Publishing Company, 1984, pp. 297-8.

APPENDIX

GROSS VALUE OF AGRICULTURAL OUTPUT (GVAO) AND ITS SALE (VALUED AT REALISED PRICES)—HOLDING SIZE-WISE

Size class of holding	GVAO at realised prices (Rs)				GVAO at realised prices as per cent over GVAO at village average price	Share (per cent) of the size-class in total (per cent) agri. sale	Sale as per cent of agri. produce	Per cent of foodgrains in total agri. production	Sale as per cent of production in foodgrains
	Per cultivating household	Per hect. of operated area	Per hect. of gross sown area	Per hect. of net sown area					
1	2	3	4	5	6	7	8	9	10
				Rayalacheruvu					
1	988	1,691	3,530	3,801	91.9	3.8	32.7	86.8	25.4
2	3,175	2,335	1,799	2,629	100.1	10.4	63.0	22.1	35.7
3	5,120	1,744	1,744	2,163	92.6	22.1	81.2	6.8	Nil
4	8,294	1,883	1,784	2,457	119.7	12.6	65.2	41.0	41.5
5	21,048	2,505	2,476	2,962	105.4	24.3	85.4	22.1	46.6
6	12,540	885	1,998	2,580	103.9	3.7	78.0	22.0	Nil
7	99,955	2,904	2,862	3,135	102.4	23.1	79.6	22.8	41.6
All	5,463	2,145	2,259	2,859	100.0	100.0	69.2	25.9	34.2

				Korrapadu					
1	2,520	3,111	3,111	3,889	98.8	13.4	49.6	37.9	33.4
2	2,167	1,568	2,195	2,512	106.3	6.4	43.3	33.7	Nil
3	4,677	2,008	2,933	3,619	96.7	19.3	71.7	10.2	Nil
4	3,943	885	1,717	2,245	93.2	4.7	51.4	23.9	Nil
5	8,088	982	1,427	1,462	102.3	10.7	53.5	24.1	20.6
6	14,860	1,222	1,426	1,573	97.5	17.3	50.0	21.5	25.1
7	99,308	2,300	2,703	3,548	104.7	28.2	51.9	42.2	31.6
All	8,448	1,794	2,265	2,711	100.0	100.0	53.5	29.6	24.4
				Goridindla					
1	1,527	2,314	2,151	2,314	95.2	3.7	66.6	23.6	Nil
2	447	441	441	441	98.1	Negl.	Negl.	82.1	Nil
3	782	371	536	536	99.5	6.9	30.7	50.5	Nil
4	3,128	772	1,123	1,166	104.6	19.4	54.7	39.1	41.9
5	2,040	282	916	959	99.0	4.2	21.6	73.5	13.3
6	9,905	796	1,483	1,795	97.7	25.3	54.6	29.3	12.4
7	29,136	1,049	1,589	1,795	102.6	40.5	66.6	43.8	53.9
All	3,018	691	1,126	1,213	100.0	100.0	52.2	42.9	28.9
				Chinnamushturu					
1	304	500	500	500	98.7	5.3	54.3	16.5	Nil
2	950	704	704	1,018	100.3	3.6	45.6	45.0	Nil
3	393	167	486	486	100.0	Negl.	Negl.	74.6	Nil
4	1,520	326	417	417	101.9	10.4	39.8	28.7	Nil
5	1,987	258	491	491	99.1	8.3	25.2	49.9	Nil
6	9,108	643	813	813	99.7	52.1	48.3	70.0	50.2
7	8,973	302	526	529	102.1	20.6	31.8	45.8	Nil
All	2,237	385	597	598	100.0	100.0	38.9	54.6	27.6

Appendix (Contd.)

1	2	3	4	5	6	7	8	9	10
				Beluguppa					
1	1,100	1,811	1,811	1,811	97.3	2.9	77.3	Nil	Nil
2	1,205	850	992	992	99.2	4.6	70.8	Nil	Nil
3	2,664	1,012	1,196	1,196	97.0	12.2	70.0	6.6	Nil
4	3,523	790	870	870	99.0	9.5	64.8	14.5	Nil
5	8,247	1,058	1,061	1,105	98.8	16.2	46.1	20.4	Nil
6	13,845	868	1,036	1,077	107.2	28.9	53.3	20.4	Nil
7	23,850	694	856	856	107.5	25.7	63.3	9.3	11.3
All	5,866	871	996	1,016	100.0	100.0	58.1	14.7	1.7
				Mughalkhod					
1	1,924	3,035	2,741	3,473	94.4	10.5	67.8	31.0	Nil
2	1,794	1,265	1,155	1,398	106.4	3.1	33.6	90.7	32.8
3	3,715	1,439	1,631	2,096	104.4	13.8	55.9	61.1	33.1
4	8,081	1,814	1,947	2,576	99.3	25.5	74.0	46.9	51,8
5	14,130	1,774	2,554	2,554	97.9	29.0	81.0	32.0	47.5
6	29,767	2,228	2,371	3,675	98.2	14.6	47.3	28.3	35.8
7	41,520	1,465	2,563	2,563	95.8	3.5	72.7	27.9	13.8
All	5,579	1,808	2,059	2,566	100.0	100.0	64.4	42.5	37.7
				Mulsavalgi					
1	1,571	2,212	1,409	2,212	97.7	0.2	5.5	97.9	12.7
2	1,569	1,107	914	1,107	94.8	1.0	11.0	87.5	Nil
3	2,475	905	889	905	103.7	19.9	80.2	23.2	23.6
4	2,289	510	375	510	95.7	5.2	41.3	77.5	30.4
5	2,327	265	260	272	101.4	8.5	45.8	72.8	29.3
9	11,181	806	824	870	106.3	43.4	71.6	33.6	26.0
7	19,565	386	425	447	83.1	21.8	72.2	40.0	43.2
All	4,112	560	550	597	100.0	100.0	62.5	45.9	26.2

				Nandyal					
1	1,919	2,370	1,422	2,370	110.9	4.8	55.6	76.2	46.5
2	2,950	1,969	1,234	1,969	108.1	16.9	41.0	66.9	22.2
3	3,387	1,216	837	1,216	88.5	13.0	31.2	78.9	23.2
4	6,345	1,305	1,353	1,392	94.3	29.4	59.4	48.6	29.0
5	5,593	805	715	805	103.3	23.4	60.8	65.8	49.6
6	15,211	963	963	963	100.0	12.5	74.1	30.9	27.1
7						—	—	—	—
All	4,265	1,187	980	1,203	100.0	100.0	50.9	61.9	31.0
				Kambagi					
1	814	2,143	1,147	2,143	100.1	2.2	4.4	93.1	Nil
2	885	582	624	624	97.0	4.7	25.4	56.9	Nil
3	2,094	766	811	880	94.5	6.0	10.0	73.0	7.9
4	1,770	372	407	514	104.7	4.8	13.1	86.3	13.9
5	3,835	557	578	842	107.8	40.9	40.4	52.5	33.6
6	2,652	170	131	181	97.4	16.6	33.8	64.4	14.2
7	11,169	496	461	627	90.3	24.8	65.1	51.0	44.5
All	2,328	414	339	501	100.0	100.0	28.4	66.9	16.4
				Sulibhavi					
1	294	518	606	606	102.7	0.2	2.0	99.2	Nil
2	598	422	454	454	100.6	2.2	12.6	81.2	Nil
3	1,318	542	542	542	93.1	19.3	49.3	44.4	Nil
4	2,443	503	503	503	100.2	14.2	65.6	25.0	Nil
5	4,055	435	435	541	104.2	27.5	42.7	62.1	14.9
6	9,314	476	469	515	105.8	21.6	46.5	49.8	57.9
7	41,377	831	818	831	101.0	15.0	79.8	50.0	47.6
All	1,773	491	496	540	100.0	100.0	46.6	54.8	9.0

Appendix (Contd.)

1	2	3	4	5	6	7	8	9	10
				Sholmadevi					
1	7,657	24,462	18,361	32,036	101.0	43.8	79.7	25.4	27.3
2	20,007	12,887	6,109	12,887	102.8	13.9	56.0	62.6	32.1
3	69,800	23,741	8,107	23,741	96.4	29.9	68.8	81.7	63.2
4	64,568	15,729	7,630	16,022	91.1	12.4	84.8	50.9	47.8
All	14,870	19,878	9,617	21,585	100.0	100.0	72.5	52.5	48.0
				Kokkampalayam					
1	3,783	6,413	3,841	6,523	112.4	6.3	90.7	1.0	Nil
2	2,911	1,816	1,538	2,457	101.0	3.1	59.6	43.8	40.1
3	3,387	1,546	2,731	4,314	91.4	5.3	75.0	38.5	43.5
4	12,897	3,184	2,709	4,107	108.8	11.5	87.1	28.7	76.3
5	20,814	2,532	3,486	4,304	89.2	18.7	85.5	25.9	58.9
6	25,664	2,113	2,775	4,580	86.4	12.1	81.0	24.0	54.8
7	3,42,467	12,214	24,691	40,746	116.8	43.0	98.2	4.5	69.0
All	13,352	3,537	4,335	6,480	100.0	100.0	88.5	17.8	58.1
				Kalangal					
1	397	646	451	651	106.2	Negl.	Negl.	91.7	Nil
2	685	501	501	501	95.5	1.3	56.9	52.6	33.3
3	7,349	2,291	1,871	2,792	109.0	18.2	73.4	79.3	75.5
4	10,760	2,310	1,915	2,690	93.5	18.2	89.8	87.0	92.2
5	7,320	892	904	904	88.3	4.6	58.1	92.9	62.5
6	33,883	2,636	2,408	2,711	100.0	25.4	93.1	43.4	67.0
7	1,80,900	7,314	10,270	11,170	92.1	32.2	99.5	7.9	94.8
All	9,405	2,373	2,181	2,400	100.0	100.0	86.5	52.6	76.3

				Sirukinar					
1	1,114	1,833	1,255	2,091	90.5	1.3	51.5	54.0	29.9
2	680	494	700	763	90.2	0.1	1.8	43.6	Nil
3	7,590	3,257	5,761	6,378	106.4	44.4	88.4	9.4	1.8
4	8,053	1,711	2,524	2,891	119.7	24.4	84.8	13.6	30.9
5	4,870	647	940	1,240	104.3	12.4	77.3	34.9	50.1
6	12,184	905	1,783	2,188	70.6	16.3	55.7	40.6	65.5
7	7,535	233	4,651	4,651	141.4	1.1	89.8	13.5	36.4
All	5,815	1,355	2,182	2,651	100.0	100.0	76.4	22.1	42.8
				Vadakalur					
1	3,309	6,110	4,915	6,147	117.9	31.6	89.6	50.6	92.8
2	2,681	1,656	1,974	1,974	85.5	24.9	86.4	7.3	Nil
3	5,195	1,823	1,664	1,893	96.1	30.9	72.9	14.5	36.6
4	6,320	1,300	1,435	1,505	102.0	10.8	90.2	3.8	Nil
5	5,800	955	932	963	84.5	1.8	76.8	16.7	Nil
All	3,791	2,081	2,080	2,276	100.0	100.0	82.8	22.3	69.9

Note: For size-classes of holdings see Table 1.2.

8

IMPACT OF IRRIGATION ON OUTPUT, COST AND INCOME FROM AGRICULTURE

CONCEPTUAL ISSUES

In this chapter also, our attention is focussed on agriculture as in the last. We shall bring in other sources of income including income from animal husbandry, in the next chapter. Here we propose to analyse the variation in land use, output and productivity, cost structure and net income after deducting costs, both across size-classes of holdings and villages. The main interest here is to analyse the impact of irrigation on all these factors. As discussed earlier, output has been valued in terms of realised prices and aggregated for crops. Receipts in kind, arising out of crop-sharing arrangements were included in output, while those received as part of wages in kind were included in other sources of income (wages). The former receipts, as reported, were quite marginal in magnitude. Even if some under-reporting is conceded here (which could arise even in the case of output), we have no reason to believe that receipts in kind on account of crop-sharing are anything more than marginal. Costs incurred in connection with crop sharing were also included under the costs. Generally, when land is leased out, costs in the nature of annual overheads and investment in durable assets are incurred by the owner. When land is leased in, costs incurred on such land are in the nature of labour and material costs of a current nature. Where ownership only formally belongs to others as in the case of city-dwelling close relatives, even costs in the nature of capital investment and annual overheads may be incurred by the actual operators.

We have included only paid-out costs in our calculations. The imputed cost of family and animal labour is not included. Only paid out costs on hired as well as animal labour have been included. Cost of farm produced inputs like manure and seed, however, were included in costs, but being part of gross value of output, they were taken into account in output also. If they are deducted on cost account, they have to be added on output account. Apart from farm produced inputs, the major material inputs include purchased manure, fertiliser, insecticides and seed. The annual overheads, which consititute another cost item, include repairs and maintenance of farm capital, expenses on attached or contract labour (annual mostly), cost of animal feed and treatment, electricity charges, land revenue, interest paid on loans etc. Whenever feasible, costs incurred on animal feed and attached labour attributable to animal husbandry were separated, on the basis of number of non-draught animal stock. Only where such data were deficient, these costs were included under crop cultivation, which could have occasionally resulted in a marginal over-estimation of cost of cultivation. It may be noted that imputed rent on own land and depreciation of capital are not included in costs. As such our cost concept corresponds to cost A of Farm Management Studies.

Village-wise and holding size-wise details on gross value of agricultural output (GVAO) per cultivating household, per hectare respectively of operated area, gross sown area and net sown area have already been presented above in the Appendix to the preceding chapter. Each of these measures of productivity have significance. It is the product per cultivating household which determines the income of the household and its marketed surplus. While maximising productivity per unit of land is important, it does not give an idea of whether the holding is viable in the sense of providing a minimum level of living after deduction of atleast paid-out costs. A tiny holding may have the highest productivity, and yet it may not provide him two meals a day round the year.

Productivity in relation to land raises the question of which land is to be included. The whole of operated area may hardly be cultivated and there could be a certain pattern in land remaining uncultivated. For this reason, we cannot take only cultivated land into account for computing productivity, since we should also know that there could be an opportunity cost of high productivity of cultivated land if it is associated also with a high proportion of cultivated land. A large holding may not be productive enough in terms of its overall holding, and yet the farmer may still be winning prizes in yield performance competitions! Moreover, as noted earlier, productivity per hectare of gross sown area may not be high, but it may be impressive in terms of net sown area because of high intensity of (double) cropping. There has been a considerable amount of controversy in the wake of Farm Management Studies about whether productivity tends to decline or increase with an increase in the size of holding. We can see here in what exact context, it shows a pattern if at all.

Impact on uncultivated land

In a study of well irrigation in Kolar, a drought-prone district in Southern Karnataka, it was found that farmers relatively neglected dry parts of holdings, concentrating their labour and other inputs on irrigated parts.[1] This opportunity cost of irrigation can be reflected directly in terms of some dry land being left idle, either in the form of a fairly high proportion of current fallows, or in the form of fallows of longer duration and culturable waste. The proportion of such idle land was not insignificant in the surveyed villages, indicating underutilisation of the most sought after asset—land. Taking all 15 villages and all holdings together, current fallows amounted to 9.4 per cent of operated land, and other fallows and culturable wastes togethar another 4.9 per cent, adding upto 14.3 per cent. Table 8.1 here presents this picture villagewise and districtwise, and also separately for marginal and large holdings, and all holdings together. It also presents similar details on cropping intensity.

The extent of this idle land was particularly high in Coimbatore, almost offsetting its higher cropping intensity. The tendency to some extent at least was to concentrate on irrigated parts of the holding, and leave marginal lands uncultivated. There was also the problem of water logging in irrigated areas,

TABLE 8.1 : **Features of land use**

Village types	Current fallows as per cent operated land			Other fallows and cultivable waste as per cent of operated land			Cropping intensity (per cent)		
	Marginal holdings*	Large holdings@	All holdings	Marginal holdings*	Large holdings@	All holdings	Marginal holdings*	Large holdings@	All holdings
	1	2	3	4	5	6	7	8	9
As per village types:									
Dry-a	Nil	2.7	4.1	Nil	1.1	0.6	108	104	104
-b	6.0	11.2	10.8	Nil	1.9	2.4	115	109	109
-c	4.3	8.2	8.8	0.4	9.4	8.1	108	111	111
-d	4.7	1.6	1.8	0.8	1.4	1.2	100	101	101
Wet-a	3.1	9.6	6.8	1.3	15.2	11.7	128	115	115
-b	5.7	14.1	12.9	5.5	2.3	3.6	137	121	121
-c	28.4	23.9	26.0	4.3	12.2	9.9	141	150	150
-d	Nil	10.5	4.4	Nil	10.3	3.5	150	170	170
Locationwise:									
Anantapur	17.1	12.7	11.2	3.0	2.8	2.4	119	114	113
Bijapur	3.1	5.4	4.6	1.1	4.1	2.5	116	110	110
Coimbatore	4.5	16.2	12.5	2.0	14.9	9.7	134	146	130
All villages	8.2	11.4	9.4	2.0	7.3	4.9	123	123	118

* With less than one hectare.
@ With more than 4 hectares.
Note : Values here are simple averages of villages under respective types.

as a result of which large tracts of land were rendered useless, unless reclaimed. This was particularly true of Kokkampalayam. Irrigation thus was found to have an indirect cost of leading to neglect of land—both dry (by having to concentrate on wet land) and wet (through over irrigation and water logging). This was particularly pronounced on larger holdings, as can be seen from the table. Paradoxically, a higher level of development of agriculture did not involve a fuller use of culturable area, though it involved a more intensive use of sown area. This must have constrained a fuller development of employment and production opportunities in agriculture and a proper spread of benefits of development to a larger section of rural people. It seemed as if the large farmers emulated the dog in the manger in this respect. They prefer to keep it idle, instead of leasing it out to a tenant who may not be loyal enough. It could well be that this negative effect of irrigation is also a result of paucity of resources including credit, the availability of which may not keep pace with the size of holding. Independently also, size of holding can be an important factor behind idle land, since large holders have other earning opportunities outside agriculture, leading to a neglect of less fertile lands.

To know how far irrigation and the size of holding affect this, we fitted linear regression equations on sample data, taking size-classes as observations and pooling across villages of given districts (omitting, naturally the average value for all cultivators). Separate regressions were fitted for the three districts, since there could be a significant element of regional effect on the proportions of uncultivated area. Our variables are:

$Y=$ Proportion of uncultivated land (current and other fallows including culturable waste) as per cent to total operated area;

$X_1=$ Proportion of net irrigated area as per cent of net sown area; and

$X_2=$ Average size of operated area in hectares.

Our results were as follows:

Anantapur (N=35) : $Y=18.96^{*}+0.25^{**}X_1+0.23X_2^{ns}$ ... Eq (1)

$$\qquad (3.58) \quad (2.09) \qquad (0.75)$$

$R^2=0.135$ $\bar{R}^2=0.054$

$r_{yx1}=0.346^{**}$; $r_{yx_2}=0.132^{ns}$; $r_{x1x_2}=0.023^{ns}$

Bijapur (N=34) : $Y=3.16^{ns}+0.17X_1^{*}-0.23X_2^{ns}$ ... Eq (2)

(0.98) (3.15) (1.48)

$R^2=0.261$ $\bar{R}^2=0.189$

$r_{yx1}=0.457^{*}$; $r_{yx_2}=0.159^{ns}$; $r_{x_1x_2}=0.145^{ns}$

Coimbatore (N=30) : $Y=11.85^{ns}+0.01X_1^{ns}+2.02X_2$ ... Eq (3)

(1.61) (0.05) (4.55)

$R^2=0.438$ $\bar{R}^2=0.376$

$r\ _{x_1}=0.0861$; $r_{yx_2}=0.662^{*}$; $r_{x_1x_2}=0.120^{ns}$

Note : *, **indicate significance levels at 1 and 5 per cent levels respectively; ns—not significant; N is number of observations in respective districts. Figures in parentheses are *t* values.

$\bar{R}^2$ is R^2 standardised for differences in the number of observations and independent variables, so that they are comparable between equations. Notation *r* is co-efficient of correlation between variables indicated in the subscripts.

Though the extent of variation in the dependent variable (*Y*) explained by our independent variables is not high (except in Coimbatore where it is satisfactorily high), the equations give some interesting results. Proportion of irrigation turned out to be a significant positive factor both in Anantapur and Bijapur villages. If the proportion of irrigation were to be raised by let us say 10 percentage points, it had the effect of increasing the proportion of uncultivated land by 2.5 and 1.7 percentage points respectively in the two districts. However, the size of holding had no significant effect in these districts. In Coimbatore, the proportion of irrigation had no such effect, but there was a very significant positive relation between uncultivated land and size of holding here. The relevant policy measure to reduce the problem of uncultivated land seems to be to step up resources available in the hands of farmers corresponding to the development of irrigation potential in Anantapur and Bijapur villages, but to more effectively impose ceilings and reduce the number of large holdings in Coimbatore. A proper land use policy including penalty for neglect of land should be an essential part of irrigation projects. Lands of those habitually keeping them idle should be transferred to the more needy. This should be done in addition to a proper implementation of land reforms—particularly in irrigated areas.

Impact on cropping intensity

A similar issue arises in the case of cropping intensity. The expected increase in double cropping need not take place as a result of irrigation, which keeps down the productivity per hectare of net sown area—if not per hectare of gross sown area. It is necessary to see to what extent irrigation succeeds in increasing cropping intensity, and how far scale of cultivation operates as a helpful or inhibiting factor behind this. Gross sown area of a holding can be accepted as an indicator of scale of cultivation, but not total operated area part of which may remain uncultivated as we have seen.

A regression analysis was carried out with the following variables on the sample data, taking size-classes of holdings as observations, as done above.

Y=Cropping intensity (i.e. Gross sown areas as percentage over net sown area)
X_1=Proportion (per cent) of net irrigated to sown area
X_2=Average gross sown area per household (hectares)

Since the regression co-efficient for X_2 turned out to be statistically not significant and since its inclusion in multiple regression hardly improved the $\bar{R}_2$, these results have not been presented here. It is nevertheless important to note that in *none* of three districts, scale of cultivation was a significant factor behind cropping intensity, although in one or two Coimbatore villages it actually tended to increase with the size of holding (in Kalangal particularly). Even simple correlation between Y and X_2 also turned out to be low and statistically not significant in all the three districts. The correlation between X_1 and X_2 was also similarly low. The relation between Y and X_1 emerged as follows:

Anantapur : $Y = 99.85^* + 0.35X_1^*$ . . .Eq (4)
$(57.50)\ (8.82)$
$\bar{R}^2 = 0.702 \# \bar{R}^2 = 0.684$

Bijapur : $Y = 115.30^{*} + 8.18X_1^{***}$ . . . Eq (5)
$\quad (20.78) \quad (1.78)$
$R^2 = 0.090 \quad \bar{R}^2 = 0.033$

Coimbatore : $Y = 95.62^{*} + 0.80X_1^{*}$ . . . Eq (6)
$\quad (6.18) \quad (3.28)$
$R^2 = 0.278 \quad \bar{R}^2 = 0.226$

Note : As in Eqs. (1) to (3) above *** Significant at 10 per cent.

Though irrigation turned out to be a significant factor behind cropping intensity in all the three districts, it explained the highest variation in Anantapur (70 per cent as indicated by R^2). Though Coimbatore villages had the highest level of cropping intensity, irrigation explained only 28 per cent of variation therein; however, the regression-co-efficient had the highest value here. In Bijapur, hardly one per cent of variation in Y was explained, and the regression-co-efficient had also the lowest value here. Irrigation as yet has been a weak influence in Bijapur, and not as strong as it should have been in Anantapur considering its not high enough regression-co-efficient. On the whole, if a dry holding were to be fully (i.e. 100 per cent) irrigated, it increases cropping intensity by only 18 percentage points in Bijapur, 35 percentage points in Anantapur and 80 percentage points in Coimbatore. An interesting point about Bijapur is that even if irrigation were to be completely absent, there would still be double cropping—the intercept indicating the cropping intensity in such a case to be 115 per cent. This is not the case both in Anantapur and Coimbatore.

Though scale of cultivation did not emerge as significant in our regression analysis, we cannot rule out size of holding as an important factor behind cropping intensity. The lack of significance of this variable was due to the fact that different villages exhibited different patterns in this relationship. We can see atleast three patterns. The holding-size-wise data indicated a U-pattern (cropping intensity first declining and then again increasing, as size of holding increased) in Rayalacheruvu, Goridindla, Mughalkhod and Mulsavalgi; an inverse pattern (declining cropping intensity with increasing size of holding) in Korrapadu, Nandyal and Kambagi; and almost a constancy at an insignificant level of intensity in the two dry villages of Chinnamushturu and Beluguppa.

Irrigation alone does not explain these patterns though its role is not ruled out. The villages with U-pattern were relatively more developed in agriculture; in exploiting this, the small farmers had the advantage of family labour which they employed more intensively on their farms and the large farmers had the advantage of better access to capital and credit with which they hired more labourers. Apart from (or because of?) the fact that middle farmers did not have this advantage, their attention had to be devoted also to rural industry and or animal husbandry. Compared to agriculture, these two activities can have (though not always) a quicker turnover and the waiting period for recovery of capital invested seemed less. This could have led to a relative neglect of agriculture in middle holdings. The inverse pattern in Nandyal and Kambagi was closely associated with a similar pattern in the proportion of irrigated land. But this seems to be more an apparent than a real factor. The large farmers have not shown enough dynamism here in developing their own sources of irrigation like wells, which the smaller farmers here had shown. There was a striking difference between the more developed and commercialised villages and the less developed, as far as large farmers were concerned. Though small farmers may be working more intensively, here, it did not have the strength to transform the whole village into a more developed commercialised set-up.

It is conceded that our measure of cropping intensity which is also a standard or commonly used measure—does not allow for the fact that annual or commercial crops remain standing throughout the year, involving another dimension of intensive land use; this is not captured by our measure since technically it does not involve double cropping or sowing more than once. Our measure of cropping intensity could, however, indicate the employment potential in agiculture, and it is disappointing that irrigation did not show the expected impact on this measure. There are obviously other factors which inhibit double cropping, apart from the quality and availability of irrigation itself for double cropping. The same factor—resource constraint—which puts a break on the scale of cultivation as noted in the preceding section, could be operative here too.

Impact on gross output, cost and income per hectare

Once we know the impact of irrigation on uncultivated land and cropping intensity, we can concentrate on gross output; cost of cultivation and net income per hectare of gross sown area. Given the output or income per hectare of gross sown area, the same per hectare of net sown area can be derived by using cropping intensity as a multiplier. Our notion of gross sown area in this chapter is not standardised for irrigation differences. That would not have made a meaningful analysis of the impact of irrigation possible. The sizeclass-wise details regarding cost of cultivation, its composition and income are presented in the appendix to this chapter. A summary view can be obtained from Table 8.2 below, which presents details for different village types in terms of per hectare of gross sown area.

On the whole, we have a poor picture of levels of productivity and income from agriculture, considering the fact that taking all the size-classes and all villages together, the value of agricultural produce per hectare is a mere Rs. 2138, and income after deduction of paid out costs only Rs. 1113. In terms of output cost ratio, it may not sound bad, being 209 per cent. However, the absolute levels of production and income are rather quite low. There is indeed a lot of variation both across different districts, across village-types and also across size-classes. Coimbatore fares better than the other two, whose farmers invest more (in terms of paid out costs) and also obtain more production per hectare. Bijapur fares worst in both respects—expenditure on costs as well as output. On the whole, Coimbatore farmers get Rs. 4079 of gross output and Rs. 2200 of income compared to Bijapur farmers who get only Rs. 885 output and Rs. 442 income. The difference is partly because of the dominance of high value crops in Coimbatore like paddy, tobacco and groundnut, and the dominance of low value and low-productivity crops like jowar and bajra in Bijapur. Apart from the higher level of irrigation in Coimbatore which itself has stimulated high value and high productivity crops there, factors like higher level of regional development and higher resource availability with the farmers enabling them to invest more, would also have helped them to achieve higher levels of production. Interestingly, the output cost ratio itself is not very dismal in Bijapur, and comes close to Coimbatore. In this respect, the three districts are fairly close to each other, though there is variation in this ratio both between village types and size-classes.

As expected, the difference between wet and dry villages in respect of output, cost and income is quite significant. The gross output per hectare in wet villages was Rs. 3385, which was 3.2 times* higher than in dry villages. Paid costs per hectare were also higher, but by only 2.3 times, resulting in a more significant difference in income. Whereas farmers on the whole could get Rs. 406 as income per hectare in dry villages, they got Rs. 1939 in wet villages, a difference by nearly a factor of 5. We wish to emphasise, however, that though the relative difference is significant, the absolute achievement per hectare even in wet areas has not been impressive enough.

Interestingly, the presence of rural industry seems to have an impact even on income from cultivation. The production and income levels per hectare in such villages were significantly higher than in those without it, both in wet and dry villages. This could be due to the fact that rural industry villages are larger, have better contacts and infrastructure, and better access to resources and extension services. The effect of rural industry however, is not as strong and consistent as 'irrigation' and could be considered as supplementary, though important.

The question of marginal farmers—many of whom are cultivating labourers—being less efficient, is complex and not amenable to a universal generalisation. It was interesting to find different patterns in wet and dry villages as can be seen from Table 8.2 here. A comparison between marginal farmers and large holdings shows that, the former have obtained more output and income in dry villages, and less of it in wet villages. Even the output/cost ratios are on the whole higher for

* Incidentally, this would justify our earlier formula for standardisation of area, treating 1 hectare of irrigated area as equal to 3 hectares of dry area.

TABLE 8.2 : **Output (O), Cost (C) and Income (I) from cultivation per hectare of gross sown area (in Rs.)**

(Averages for village types)

Village types	Among marginal holdings (below 1 hectare)				Large holdings (above 10 hectares)				All holdings			
	O	C	I	O/C per cent	O	C	I	O/C per cent	O	C	I	O/C per cent
Dry - a	574	539	35	106	483	385	98	125	468	350	118	134
- b	1780	631	1149	282	1081	514	567	210	838	420	418	200
- c	2259	854	1405	265	1930	1290	640	150	1586	1043	543	152
- d	1811	879	932	206	946	416	530	127	996	450	546	221
Dry all	1662	723	939	230	902	685	217	132	1046	640	406	163
Wet - a	2082	828	1254	251	1969	662	1307	298	1520	650	870	234
- b	3111	847	2264	367	2064	992	1072	209	2265	1080	1185	210
- c	3686	1720	1966	214	8082	1731	6351	467	3297	1359	1938	243
- d	9406	3960	5446	238	6339	1335	5004	475	5899	2510	3389	235
Wet all	4780	1981	2799	241	4666	1168	3498	399	3385	1446	1939	234
Anantapur	2221	913	1308	243	1529	801	728	191	1449	754	695	192
Bijapur	1465	700	765	209	999	401	598	249	885	443	442	200
Coimbatore	5765	2317	3448	249	7763	1929	5834	402	4079	1879	2200	217
All villages	3150	1310	1840	240	3430	1044	2386	329	2138	1025	1113	209

Note : (i) Output is gross value of all agricultural output at realised prices, and costs are paid out costs. I=O—C

(ii) Since there were no holdings above 10 hectares in two villages of Coimbatore, the average for this district in respect of large holdings is only for the remaining 3 villages.

marginal farmers in dry villages and lower for them in wet villages. While marginal farmers obtained a net income of Rs. 939 per hectare of GSA, the large farmers could get only Rs. 217 in dry villages; on the other hand, in wet villages, they obtained respectively Rs. 2793 and Rs. 3498. It is interesting that though irrigation is often supposed to go in favour of small farmers (on the ground that small farms are more irrigated) it tends to absolutely as well as relatively increase the income of large farmers. It is clear that marginal farmers too gain in absolute terms significantly enough, but they are more than overtaken by large farmers. One explanation, hypothetically, is that when irrigation is introduced, the supply of inputs and credit seems to go more in favour of large farmers to the relative neglect of the small. It is paradoxical to observe however, that the level of inputs in the case to marginal farmers is higher than in large holdings, both in dry and—particularly so—in wet villages. While the marginal farmers have stepped up inputs considerably in wet villages, the increase in output is not commensurate with this. Are large holdings more efficient in wet villages ? Do they tend to treat agriculture more seriously as a business only when there is an improvement in the forces of production like irrigation, technological advance or opening of new profitable opportunities in the crop pattern made possible by new markets ? It is difficult to decide the question of which type of farmers—marginal or large—are inherently more efficient. Objective circumstances, related to technology, market and their bias to scale of cultivation, determine this efficiency. If this is the case, the very question of inherent efficiency unrelated to the objective circumstances around, would appear meaningless. Inclusion of imputed cost of family labour, would have reduced the net income of marginal farmers on account of cultivation in dry areas and would make them appear less efficient (by business standards). There is a stronger tendency to hire in labour even among small farms in wet areas, however. Paid-out costs on hired labour are included in costs, but not the imputed cost of family labour.

It would be necessary to estimate the impact of irrigation more accurately, so that we can even assess the impact at different levels of irrigation. We tried two models for this purpose, taking size-classes of holdings as observations and pooling them across villages for each district separately as in the equations above. One was to treat the Gross Value of Agricultural Output (GVAO) per hectare of GSA (in Rs) as dependent variable (Y), as determined by three independent variables : paid out costs per hectare of GSA in Rs (X_1), proportion (in per cent) of gross sown area irrigated (X_2); and average size of gross sown area in the size class in hectares (X_3), the last indicating the scale effect. However, irrigation itself can influence the level of expenditure on inputs, and hence the paid-out costs, apart from exercising a direct influence on output. In this exercise, though X_1 emerged as significant in all the three districts, X_2 was statistically significant only in the Bijapur, but not in Anantapur and Coimbatore. Similary, X_3 was significant only in Coimbatore. Even after conceding the limitations of irrigation, it could not have been expected as non-significant in determining GVAO per hectare, and that too in Coimbatore. This surprising result could be due to high inter-correlations particularly between X_1 and X_2, which are presented below :

	Anantapur (N=35)		*Bijapur (N=34)*		*Coimbatore (N=30)*	
	X_1	X_2	X_1	X_2	X_1	X_2
X_2	0.743	1.000	0.830	1.000	0.536	1.000
X_3	0.101	0.048	–0.324	–0.226	–0.018	0.165

We tried, therefore, an alternative model directly estimating the impact of irrigation separately on GVAO and costs, and then compute the difference between the two as income at different levels of irrigation. In other words, Y was taken as a function of X_2 and X_3, and also separately X_1 as a function of X_2 and X_3, and then estimated X_1 was deducted from estimated Y at different levels of X_2, given X_3. There were two further variants of this model. The equation $Y=f(X_2)$ was tried both in linear and quadratic form, the latter to find out if there are diminishing increasing returns to increase in the level of irrigation, with X_3 given. The quadratic form was confined only to X_2, since an exercise in respect of cost of cultivation showed that a quadratic relation did not arise there. The exercise showed that X_3 did not emerge as significant in influencing Y and X_1 in Anantapur and Bijapur and its inclusion in the equations hardly increased the value of R^2. Similarly quadratic forms did not emerge as significant for Coimbatore. These equations are not, therefore, presented here. The equations which we ultimately found useful were:

Anantapur:

$$Y=938^{*}+17.83X^{*}_{2} \quad \ldots \bar{R}^2=0.406 \text{ (Eq. 7)}$$
(6.151) (5.090)

$$Y=716^{*}+51.04X^{*}_{2}-0.41X_{2}^{2*} \quad \ldots \bar{R}^2=0.539 \text{ (Eq. 8)}$$
(4.740) (4.763) (3.236)

$$X_1=450^{*}+10.19X^{*}_{2} \quad \ldots \bar{R}^2=0.525 \text{ (Eq. 9)}$$
(6.472) (6.380)

Bijapur:

$$Y=427^{*}+15.17X^{*}_{2} \quad \ldots \bar{R}^2=0.688 \text{ (Eq. 10)}$$
(4.523) (8.768)

$$Y=558^{*}+1.180X_{2}^{ns}+0.13X_{2}^{2***} \quad \ldots \bar{R}^2=0.706 \text{ (Eq. 11)}$$
(4.690) (0.226) (1.721)

$$X_1=285^{*}+4.74X^{*}_{2} \quad \ldots \bar{R}^2=0.670 \text{ (Eq. 12)}$$
(9.276) (8.430)

Coimbatore:

$$Y=-1886^{ns}+74.45X_{2}^{**}+382.59X_{3}^{***}$$
(0.915) (2.385) (1.937) $\ldots \bar{R}^2=0.216$ (Eq. 13)

$$Y=-589^{ns}+84.40X_{2}^{**} \quad \ldots \bar{R}^2=0.139 \text{ (Eq. 14)}$$
(0.289) (2.616)

$$X_1=156+26.41X^{*}_{2} \quad \ldots \bar{R}^2=0.236 \text{ (Eq. 15)}$$
(0.314) (3.359)

(Notations as in earlier equations in this chapter)

Irrigation emerged as a significant factor behind agricultural output per hectare in this model. The scale-effect or the size of GSA per holding has a significant co-efficient only in Coimbatore (sig. at 10 per cent level) showing a positive sign. Given irrigation, an increase in the scale of cultivation had no significant effect on the output per hectare in Anantapur and Bijapur, but increased it by Rs. 383 with every increase of one hectare in GSA in Coimbatore. No such relation was noticed, however, in any of the three districts including Coimbatore in respect of paid out costs per hectare. That is, the level of costs did not necessarily increase with the scale of cultivation. The increase in output per hectare in the case of large holdings does not, therefore, seem to be associated with a higher level of paid-out costs or inputs. This corroborates our observation made above with respect of Table 8.2 when the performance of large holdings was compared with small holdings. Since the positive effect of scale on output is witnessed also in Coimbatore where agriculture is more commercialised, its association with a greater efficiency of larger holdings should not be surprising. The term 'efficiency' here is used in a narrow sense, and not in terms of total resource use. It is pertinent to recall that uncultivated land also tended to increase in this district with the size of holding. It indicates that instead of using all or most of the available land, farmers are selective and confine their cultivation to probably the best portions of this land, leaving other land fallow. This probably enabled them to increase output and reduce costs per hectare. How far this practice, even if profitable from a private or personal view point, is also socially desirable is another question.

Though we estimated the impact of different levels of irrigation using both linear and quadratic equations in the case of Anantapur and Bijapur, the quadratic form was relied upon in their case since it gave better results. Estimates for Coimbatore use only linear equations, since the quadratic form was not significant. The results are presented in Table 8.3 here* at a few hypothetical levels of irrigation. For visual clarity, the results are also presented in the form of a chart.** Hopefully, the table and the chart should be of interest to irrigation administration and credit agencies, since we can estimate the required finance for paid-out costs at different levels of irrigation in different districts and the expected

* The note below the Table 8.3 indicates the equations used for respective estimates. It may be added here that these estimates (equations actually used in estimates) ignore the scale effect, which was only marginally significant (at 10 per cent level) in Coimbatore, and not significant in the other two districts.

** Since the magnitudes involved in Coimbatore were much larger, logarithmic scale was applied to output and cost for the district in the chart (see page 196 for the chart).

TABLE 8.3 : **Impact at different levels of irrigation (as estimated from equations)**

Level of irrigation in GSA (per cent)	Linear			Quadratic	
	GVAO	Costs	Income	GVAO	Income
	per hectare of gross sown area				
(1)	(2)	(3)	(4)	(5)	(6)
			Anantapur		
0	938	450	488	716	266
10	1116	552	564	1185	633
20	1294	654	640	1573	919
30	1472	756	716	1878	1122
40	1650	858	792	2102	1244
50	1829	960	869	2243	1283
60	2007	1061	948	2302	1241
70	2185	1163	1022	2280	1117
80	2364	1265	1099	2175	910
90	2542	1367	1175	1989	622
100	2721	1469	1252	1720	251
			Bijapur		
0	427	285	142	558	273
10	579	332	247	589	257
20	730	380	350	646	266
30	882	427	455	729	302
40	1034	475	559	838	363
50	1185	522	663	973	451
60	1337	569	768	1134	565
70	1489	617	872	1321	704
80	1641	664	977	1534	870
90	1792	712	1080	1773	1061
100	1944	759	1185	2038	1279
			Coimbatore		
0	NS	NS	NS	NS—Constant (intercept) not significant statistically, and hence taken as zero.	
10	844	264	580		
20	1688	528	1160		
32	2100	845	1255		
50	4220	1320	2900		
100	8440	2640	5800		

Note: Results estimated from Equations (7) and (9) in linear and (8) and (9) in quadratic case for Anantapur. Corresponding Equations for Bijapur are (10) and (12), and (11) and (12). In the case of Coimbatore, only linear form was used based on Equations (14) and (15). Columns (4) and (6) were obtained by deducting estimated costs (column 3) from estimated output (columns 2 and 5 as the case may be). Since costs column is common to linear and quadratic case (only linear equations were used for them), it is not repeated again under quadratic form.

return (allowing for increase in inflation after 1978-79). Caution is needed, however, since situation differs from district to district and it is difficult to generalise about the magnitude of the effect of irrigation. The table could only serve as a very rough guide. Interestingly, there are decreasing returns to irrigation in Anantapur, increasing returns in Bijapur and constant returns in Coimbatore. Because of decreasing returns, the highest point in the level of output is reached in Anantapur at the level of 60 per cent (see the chart), after which output per hectare of GSA starts declining in absolute terms. Extending irrigation beyond 50 per cent of sown area in Anantapur holdings, would be counter-productive since beyond this point paid out costs increase more than addition made to output through irrigation. In other words, income declines absolutely. Though, Bijapur showed increased returns, the level of productivity is quite low. Even at 100 per cent irrigation, the output per hectare of GSA in Bijapur is lower than what it is at 40 per cent irrigation in Anantapur and 32 per cent in Coimbatore (See Table 8.3).* The problem of Bijapur cannot be solved by merely increasing the level of irrigation. There has to be an upward shift in the function itself, which means technological change involving the cultivation of better yielding crops. There is however a constraint on shifting to high value crops like paddy and sugarcane, since the soils are not suitable for irrigation.

Impact on income per household

The interest in output or income per hectare is mainly because it helps to increase the income of households, given the size of land. The former by itself gives no indication of the level of income of households. We have, therefore, taken direct note of income level of households, as derived from crop cultivation. While the details are presented in the Appendix tables, a summary view can be had from Table 8.4 here.

As anticipated, cultivators in Coimbatore turned out to be the richest, the poorest being in Bijapur, considering the income from cultivation alone. The difference is by more

* That is, taking quadratic forms in both Bijapur and Anantapur.

TABLE 8.4 : **Output (O) and Income (I) from agriculture per cultivating household (Rs.)**

(Averages for village types)

Village type	Among marginal farms (below 1 hectare)		Large farms (above 10) hectares)		All cultivators	
	O	I	O	I	O	I
Dry - a	559	202	7,975	2,098	2,282	683
- b	1,549	922	17,691	8,762	3,560	1,620
- c	1,572	985	16,854	8,087	3,793	1,201
- d	1,110	566	18,848	10,945	5,866	3,212
Dry - all	1,255	721	14,841	5,099	3,616	1,428
We t- a	1,921	1,100	28,833	19,170	4,922	2,706
- b	2,520	1,833	57,084	30,134	8,448	4,421
- c	2,385	1,378	1,20,154	95,032	9,408	50,620
- d	4,029	2,295	1,07,391	85,932	12,138	6,858
Wet - all	2,398	1,626	75,939	56,477	8,769	17,829
Anantapur	1,288	818	32,148	22,202	5,006	2,424
Bijapur	1,307	661	19,497	11,210	3,611	1,756
Coimbatore	3,252	1,950	1,00,437*	82,547*	9,447	5,305
All villages	1,949	1,143	50,694	38,653	6,021	3,162

Note: Output is gross value of all agricultural output at realised prices, and income is the same net of all paid out costs.

*Since there were no holdings above 10 hectares in two villages of Coimbatore, this is an average of the remaining 3 villages.

than a factor of 2. Taking all the 15 villages, average income from cultivation per household was not more than Rs. 3162 in a year, which was rather very low. There were, however, significant variations in this across village types and the size-classes. The difference between size-classes was much more conspicuous than between village types. But the latter difference was also quite high. The difference between the income of a marginal farmer (below 1 hectare) and large farmer (about 10 hectares) in a least developed dry village (D-a type) was by a factor of over 10, but in the most developed village type (W-d) the difference between the two size-classes was by a factor of nearly 38 ! This does not mean that there has been no improvement in the income of marginal farmers in wet villages. In fact, a marginal farmer household in a W-d type village has an income of a Rs. 2295, which is more than the income of a large farm household in D-a type of village, viz. Rs. 2098.

Both animal husbandry and rural industry made a positive and strong indirect impact on income from cultivation as observed earlier. However, here again, the impact was more in favour of large farmer who gained substantially more than marginal farmers.

There were only two instances of negative income or loss from cultivation. One related to the marginal farmers in a dry and least diversified village (viz. Chinnamushturu in Anantapur). Another instance was diametrically opposite on the social scale. It related to the size-class of 6 to 10 hectares in a dry village with rural industry (viz. Vadakalur in Coimbatore) which incidentally was the largest size-class in the concerned village. The heads of households were actually rich traders, for whom cultivation provided a secondary source of income. Though their expenditure on paid out costs per hectare compared favourably with others, their output was not commensurate with it. This was reported to be mainly because of the loss of groundnut crop due to pests. The menance of pests was indeed significant and has played havoc in many cases, particularly in cash crops. However, it is also likely that the fact of their being much involved in business other than cultivation, would have led to the neglect of agriculture. While in the marginal farmers' case, they are forced to rely on other sources of income like wage labour, in the large farmers' case there was no such compulsion. Possibly, outcome from cultivation under dry conditions is even less secure and profitable than from trading, deserving, therefore, only lower priority in the assessment of these trader-cultivators.

References

1. Kamble N.D. Abdul Aziz *et al.*—'Economics of Well Irrigation', Part IV in M.V. Nadkarni, V.M. Rao *et al.*, *Impact of Irrigation—Canal, Well and Tank*, Himalaya, Bombay, 1979.

APPENDIX-I

COST OF CULTIVATION AND INCOME FROM AGRICULTURE

Size class	Total cost* per hect. of gross sown area (Rs)	Per cent to total cost*			Income from cultivation			Gross output as per cent over total cost
		Material cost (current)	Human and animal labour	Annual overheads	Per culti. h.hold	Per hect. of gross sown area	Per hect. of net sown area	
1	2	3	4	5	6	7	8	9
				Rayalacheruvu				
1	1,947	41.3	33.6	25.1	443	1,583	1,704	182
2	889	47.7	26.1	26.2	1,607	910	1,331	203
3	1,081	47.7	37.0	15.3	2,068	663	874	168
4	1.348	49.1	24.3	26·6	2,029	436	601	133
5	1,235	47.5	21.2	31.2	10,554	1,241	1,485	201
6	1,424	34.2	27.0	38.8	3,602	574	741	140
7	1,181	51.4	19.7	28.9	58,685	1,681	1,841	243
All	1.226	45.3	29.9	24.8	2,498	1,033	1,307	184
				Korrapadu				
1	847	50.4	35.5	14.1	1,833	2,264	2,830	367
2	1,205	62.0	25.9	12.1	978	990	1,016	182
3	1,720	67.9	26.4	5.6	1,934	1,213	1,497	171
4	945	54.4	29.5	16.1	1,774	772	1,010	182
5	763	53.7	32.8	13.5	3,766	664	681	188
6	719	55.8	25.6	18.6	7,385	709	782	199
7	1,264	63.4	15.5	21.1	52,883	1,439	1,890	214
All	1,080	60.9	22.0	17.0	4,421	1,185	1,418	210

* Paid out costs only (i.e. excluding imputed costs of own human and animal labour).

				Goridindla				
1	380	79.2	5.5	15.3	1,257	1,771	1,905	566
2	156	44.4	44.2	11.4	288	285	285	283
3	349	46.9	4.4	48.7	273	187	187	154
4	404	49.3	27.1	23.7	2,002	719	746	278
5	392	64.9	28.9	6.3	1,168	524	549	234
6	681	48.5	35.9	15.6	5,356	802	971	218
7	682	46.5	27.3	26.2	16,635	907	1,025	233
All	497	49.6	25.4	24.9	1,685	629	677	227
				Chinnamushturu				
1	512	73.3	23.9	2.8	—8	—12	—12	98
2	449	56.0	36.7	7.3	344	255	255	157
3	269	18.1	35.4	46.5	176	217	217	181
4	358	74.5	14.4	11.1	214	59	59	117
5	348	39.5	13.6	46.9	581	143	143	142
6	758	35.9	20.1	44.0	619	55	55	108
7	470	43.6	25.1	31.3	962	56	57	112
All	516	43.8	21.0	35.2	302	81	81	116
				Beluguppa				
1	879	56.1	31.1	12.8	566	932	932	206
2	700	73.0	23.4	3.6	355	292	292	142
3	529	71.1	22.9	6.0	1,485	567	667	226
4	326	65.5	27.3	8.2	2,202	544	544	267
5	494	53.5	41.0	5.5	4,405	567	590	215
6	510	52.3	21.6	26.1	7,031	526	547	204
7	323	69.7	24.1	6.2	14,859	533	533	266
All	450	60.0	27.0	13.0	3,212	546	556	221

Appendix (Contd.)

1	2	3	4	5	6	7	8	9
				Mughalkhod				
1	918	37.4	6.9	45.7	1,279	1,823	2,309	299
2	660	50.2	29.3	20.4	769	495	599	175
3	732	48.7	32.5	18.8	1,842	809	1,039	199
4	582	47.2	22.4	30.4	5,666	1,365	1,806	335
5	842	53.8	20.5	25.7	9,475	1,712	1,712	304
6	778	70.5	19.3	10.1	19,995	1,593	2,468	305
7	738	45.0	35.1	19.9	29,567	1,825	1,825	348
All	749	53.3	23.2	23.4	3,548	1,310	1,631	275
				Mulsavalgi				
1	883	14.2	45.2	40.6	587	526	826	160
2	515	26.3	42.7	31.0	685	399	483	178
3	450	26.1	58.8	15.1	1,223	439	447	198
4	322	22.1	66.7	11.2	323	53	72	117
5	255	18.4	61.9	19.7	48	5	6	102
6	437	27.2	47.2	25.6	5,244	387	408	189
7	255	19.5	34.1	46.4	7,815	170	179	167
All	342	23.2	50.8	26.0	1,553	208	226	161
				Nandyal				
1	739	28.5	37.3	34.2	922	683	1,138	193
2	668	34.8	34.4	30.8	1,353	566	903	185
3	522	39.8	14.9	45.3	1,274	315	458	161
4	600	33.8	34.2	32.0	3,531	753	775	226
5	495	27.2	51.7	21.0	1,718	220	247	144
6	460	27.4	57.8	14.8	7,949	503	503	210
All	552	32.8	36.6	30.6	1,865	428	526	178

				Kambagi				
1	567	37.8	28.0	34.2	412	580	1,084	198
2	223	19.7	41.1	39.2	569	401	401	280
3	205	27.7	63.4	8.9	1,565	606	658	396
4	327	16.1	52.6	31.3	348	80	101	125
5	291	21.9	51.7	26.6	1,902	287	418	199
6	126	24.0	56.1	19.9	92	5	6	104
7	184	21.5	51.8	26.7	6,717	277	377	251
All	184	22.6	52.6	24.8	1,063	155	229	184
				Sulibhavi				
1	392	22.4	57.0	20.6	104	214	214	155
2	327	23.8	59.2	17.0	168	127	127	139
3	345	32.4	31.5	36.1	478	197	197	157
4	248	26.9	27.2	45.9	1,238	255	255	255
5	286	29.0	42.6	28.4	1,390	149	186	153
6	222	24.6	54.7	20.7	3,329	247	272	212
7	355	27.2	44.6	28.2	23,444	463	471	231
All	286	27.7	42.8	29.4	750	210	228	113
				Sholmadevi				
1	7,573	22.2	54.0	23.8	4,499	10,788	18,823	243
2	2,991	31.8	54.2	14.0	10,212	3,118	6,578	205
3	3,184	21.1	41.4	37.5	42,384	4,923	14,416	255
4	2,929	25.9	38.2	35.8	39,862	4,710	9,891	263
All	4,010	24.3	48.8	26.9	8,669	5,507	12,584	241

Appendix (Contd.)

1	2	3	4	5	6	7	8	9
				Kokkampalayam				
1	1,493	45.3	33.8	20.9	2,312	2,348	3,987	162
2	810	33.2	54.8	12.0	1,374	726	1,159	190
3	1,860	47.0	41.6	11.4	1,080	871	1,375	147
4	909	54.2	25.9	19.9	8,569	1,800	2,729	298
5	1,440	37.7	46.1	16.2	12,212	2,046	2,525	242
6	2,079	34.8	48.5	16.7	6,434	696	1,148	134
7	2,239	38.5	42.0	19.5	3,11,408	22,452	37,050	1,103
All	1,493	40.1	43.3	16.6	8,754	2,842	4,248	291
				Kalangal				
1	347	52.1	11.8	36.1	91	104	150	130
2	229	79.5	18.1	2.4	372	272	272	219
3	1,210	60.8	14.7	24.5	2,597	661	987	155
4	1,185	40.7	43.0	16.3	4,103	730	1,026	162
5	682	45.1	41.5	13.4	1,798	222	222	133
6	1,110	26.0	59.2	14.8	18,263	1,298	1,461	217
7	1,561	36.6	39.5	23.9	1,53,401	8,704	9,472	658
All	1,010	44.2	37.1	18.7	5,047	1,171	1,288	216
				Sirukinar				
1	519	19.3	10.7	70.0	653	736	1,226	242
2	392	32.1	49.2	18.7	300	308	336	179
3	1,880	17.2	60.9	21.9	5,114	3,881	4,296	307
4	1,482	36.2	53.1	10.6	3,325	1,042	1,194	171
5	913	34.6	51.8	13.6	142	27	36	103
6	1,288	35.5	40.3	24.2	3,382	495	607	128
7	3,296	14.1	18.5	67.3	2,195	1,355	1,355	141
All	1,588	30.8	49.8	19.4	2,549	594	1,162	178

				Vadakalur				
1	1,652	58.3	29.9	11.8	2,197	3,263	4,081	298
2	1,066	49.7	38.1	12.2	1,233	908	908	186
3	1,335	60.5	27.4	12.1	1,027	329	374	125
4	1,048	47.8	32.3	19.9	1,705	387	406	137
5	1,111	41.3	42.6	16.0	—1,115	—179	—185	84
All	1,255	55.6	31.2	13.2	1,503	825	902	166

Chart—Response of output and costs per hectare to level of irrigation.

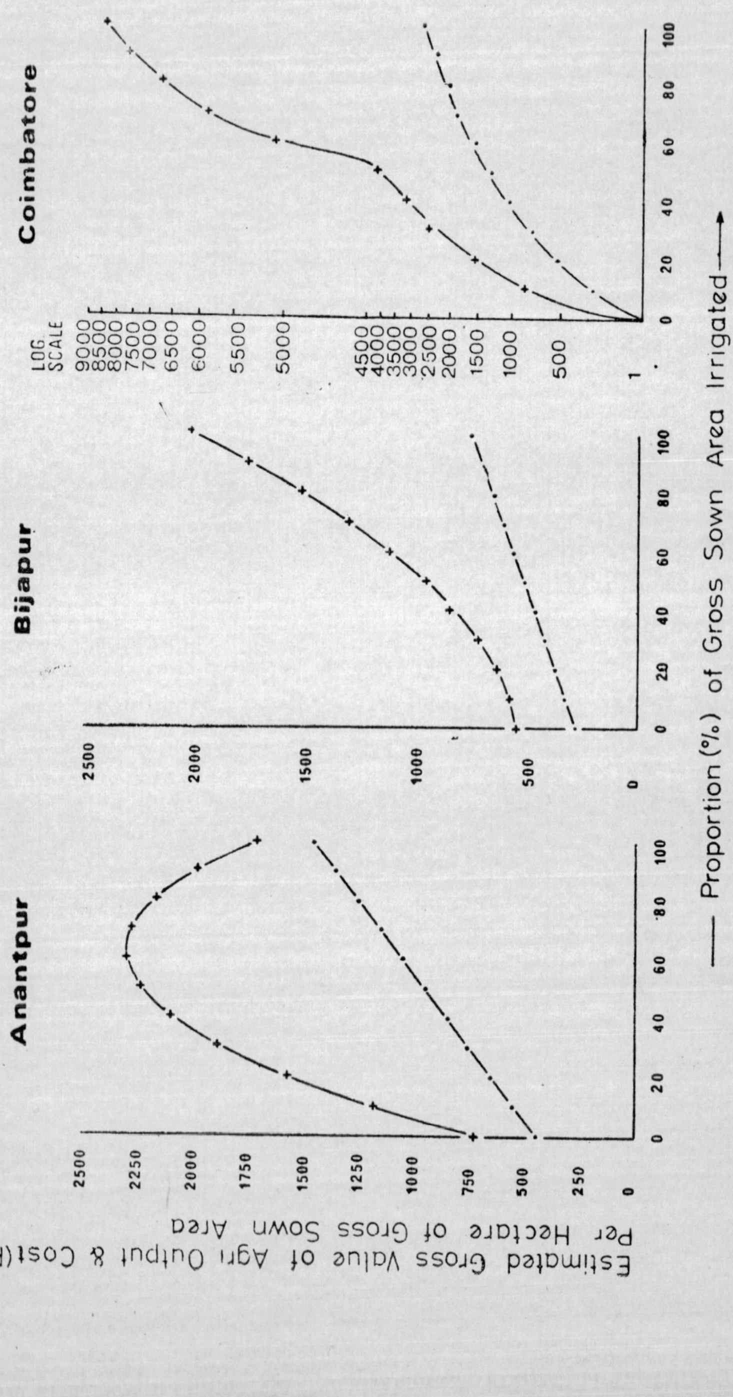

9

TOTAL INCOME OF HOUSEHOLDS

Focus on Poverty and Inequality vis-a-vis Levels of Development

In this chapter, the total income of households in the surveyed villages is estimated taking into account all other sources of income, in addition to income from cultivation. These other sources are income from animal husbandry, wage income, income from manufacturing or rural industry, salary and professional incomes, income from trading and transfer incomes like rent, help from relatives and pensions. As we shall see, income estimation has been used to assess the extent of poverty and inequality in each village and study the variation therein across village types.

In this again, we have carefully deducted only the paid-out costs from their gross receipts. Income from trading was computed first by estimating gross income as the difference between turnover at sale price and the purchase value, and then deducting other paid out costs like hired labour, rent and interest from this gross income. Imputed rent on own premises and interest on own capital was not deducted, so that the same concept of cost is employed both in agriculture and other activities. It was difficult to distinguish between receipts through hiring out labour and receipts through hiring out bullock cart etc. Hence they were combined and grouped under income from labour. Labourers have often to use their own tools, when they offer their labour. Small repairs are carried out by themselves often at no cost in cash. Such costs could not be estimated. Only costs of repair and maintenance incurred in cash were included in costs. It may be noted that our primary purpose has been—in the last chapter as well as here—the estimation of actual income enjoyed by a household, and not estimation of cost of production of economic enterprises. That is why imputed items of costs like cost of family labour, interest on own capital, and rent on own land and premises have been ignored. Therefore, incomes estimated here—whether from cultivation or other sources—are not pure profits, and include elements of wage, rent and interest too.

There is a possibility of underestimation of output particularly in animal husbandry. Milk output and self consumption—month by month—was difficult to remember; it was much easier in agriculture where harvested output could be more easily recalled. Frequent visits at least once every month are suitable for studying the economy of animal husbandry. Cash income from animal husbandry or actual sales were easier to remember for the households. Output of milk products consumed at source has also been included in income, but the margin of error on account of its underestimation is not likely to be serious. Generally bulk of the milk output is sold and only a small portion is consumed. Even if not sold in towns or cities, milk is sold to tea-shops within or around the villages. Children of farmers with milch cattle consume some milk, but our strong impression gained from informal conversations is that adults hardly consume pure milk or curds everyday, except in the form of tea. It is not uncommon to find marginal and small farmers selling practically all their milk to tea-shops and drinking tea there. The latter enjoyment is of course the privilege of male adults, though most of the work of tending and milking cattle is done by children and women. By and large, milk is treated as a superior good, the sales proceeds of which are used generally to purchase more basic goods like foodgrains, essential clothing, or saved to meet contingencies. It was only where dairying was more developed as in some of the Coimbatore villages and where income levels are higher, that consumption of milk at source was higher in absolute terms, if not relatively to output.

The total income per household for each category of households in each village is presented in the Appendix to this chapter. Table 9.1 here presents the income per household of main categories estimated for different village types, and also for the three districts. The equations from which the estimates for village types are made are presented in the Appendix to this chapter.

Four questions interest us here. First, how do main categories of households fare at different levels of rural development, represented by village types having respectively irrigation, animal husbandry and rural industry and combinations of the three? That is, which of them are able to improve their income significantly and which not? Secondly, what is the magnitude of poverty in each village, and how does it compare with levels of development and commercialisation? Do rural development and attendant commercialisation of agriculture succeed in reducing the magnitude of the proportion of the poor? Thirdly, who constitute the poor? What is the nature of such households? Fourthly, what is the degree of inequality of incomes of households, and how is it related to levels of development? It may be noted that our discussion of these questions is based on the income data (from all sources of income) on per household basis in each category of household, and not per capita income. It is possible that on a per capita basis, inequality might look slightly less, but only slightly so. It is conceded that the average size of households among the poor is smaller than among the rich. But this difference is quite small compared to differences in income.

One can even take the stand, which some economists have already taken, that considering inequality in terms of per capita income or expenditure underestimates inequality, since it is the income of the household which is crucial and size of family is adjusted to it. N. Krishnaji has argued that a higher level of mortality rate, particularly infant mortality, could have kept the size of household small in poor households.[1]

Taking the first question above, we find that the income of marginal farmers varied widely as between the least developed D-a type village (viz. Rs. 1157) and W-d type village (Rs. 5347). Due to variation within types, the regression coefficient for irrigation taken as a dummy variable was not significant in the case of marginal farmers. As a further check, correlations were computed on the basis of actual values between income of marginal farmers and proportion of irrigation within village; it turned out to be +0.54, which was significant at 5 per cent level.

On the other hand, the results derived from dummy variables were significant in the case of all cultivators taken as a whole; co-efficients of each of the three variables were significant—the strongest impact being made by rural industry, followed by irrigation. This phenomenon was already observed and explained in the last chapter in connection with the income from the cultivation. It is interesting that rural industry showed stronger impact than even irrigation on the income of cultivators. Since the impact was significant in the case of cultivators taken as a whole, and not so much in the case of marginal farmers, it is obvious that gains of development were mostly cornered by the larger farmers. Even if absolute level of income of marginal farmers may have increased somewhat, relatively to large farmers they were worse off at higher levels of development.

The income levels of agricultural labour households responded significantly to rural industry, but not to irrigation and animal husbandry. Surprisingly, the co-efficients of the latter two were even negative, though not statistically significant. Rural industry seems to give them alternatives, and improve their bargaining position. This can result in a more remunerative employment for them, both from agriculture and industry.

The income of artisans did not respond significantly to the presence of rural industry, though their number was proportionately more in such villages. Their average income was generally higher than the income of cultivators *taken as a whole*, and this did not consistently vary with levels of development. This does not mean that there was no poverty among them. As we shall soon observe, in a few villages they belonged to the poorest two or three categories. Vadakalur is the only village where they enjoyed a significantly high level of income (viz. Rs. 11,696 per household). They are effectively organised here and have been more successful in controlling trade channels both in terms of raw material and finished product. On the other hand, in Sulibhavi and Beluguppa of Bijapur and Anantapur respectively, they have not been quite successful in countering the exploitation by middle-men. All the three are major handloom centres, but the difference in income levels came out conspicuously.

The income of traders, who mostly included petty traders, did not seem to be responsive to levels of development; at least the regression co-efficients were not statistically significant. This is because when development takes place, it is either the more prosperous among farmers who take to profitable trading or outside traders take advantage of it. Non-cultivating households taken as a whole responded only to rural industry, whereas all households together (cultivators and others) responded both to irrigation and industry, but more to the latter. In sum, whereas the impact of irrigation was more confined to larger cultivators, the impact of industry was both more widespread and stronger.

More than irrigation, commercialisation of agriculture seems to have a stronger impact on the incomes of all households as a whole, and also of marginal farmers and agricultural labour. Correlation across villages between sales ratio and income of marginal farmers was 0.48; it was 0.62 with the income of agricultural labour and, 0.84 with the income of all rural households taken together. The correlation between this income and irrigation was significant only in the case of marginal farmers and not in the case of agricultural labour and all rural households taken together.

Coming to the second question posed above, we have defined the poverty line for our purpose at the level of Rs. 4360 for all the villages, which is the average of all households' income taking all the villages together. This measure helps us not only to know the proportion of households below average income, but also to know how skewed the income distribution is. Since it leads us to the last of the questions posed, at the moment we confine ourselves to the magnitude of poverty as shown by this indicator. By sheer coincidence, this poverty line comes very close to the one at the national level calculated for 1978-79. The poverty line, it may be recalled was fixed at Rs. 20 *per capita* per month at 1960-61 prices. Adjusting it upward for the rise in the cost of living (of agricultural labourers), we get the figure of Rs. 73 for 1978-79. As the average size of households in our villages

TABLE 9.1 : **Total income (Rs) per household, by main categories and village types, and poverty**

Village type	Marginal farmers (below 1 hect.)	Large farmers (above 10 hect.)	All cultivators	Agri. labourers	Artisans	Trading h.hs	All non-cultig. h.hs.	All households	Proportion of poor households (per cent)
Dry - a	1,157	3,846	994	1,897	3,235	799	2,481	2,434	88.6
- b	2,669	11,012	3,369	1,736	3,236	4,253	2,408	2,998	88.5
- c	2,768	5,713	5,313	2,753	4,290	3,611	3,186	4,454	71.0
- d	4,280	14,656	7,688	2,592	4,318	7,065	3,113	5,018	70.9
Wet - a	2,224	23,313	4,748	1,784	3,177	4,475	2,159	3,768	85.5
- b	3,736	32,959	7,123	1,623	3,205	7,929	2,086	4,332	85.4
- c	3,835	1,48,364	11,442	2,640	4,232	7,287	3,508	5,788	67.9
- d	5,347	95,312	13,817	2,479	4,260	10,741	3,435	6,352	67.8
Anantapur	2,201	37,906	4,669	1,942	3,231	4,442	2,666	3,676	85.1
Bijapur	2,067	24,753	3,408	1,812	11,051	3,137	2,283	3,094	87.4
Coimbatore	5,082	91,732	9,921	9,954	5,269	8,609	4,113	6,308	60.9
All villages	3,117	51,464	5,999	2,236	6,517	5,396	3,021	4,359	77.8

Note : Derived From Equations 1-(a) to (g) and 2 in the Appendix to this chapter, except in the case of large farmers (above 10 hectares) since a few villages did not have this class. In their case, averages for remaining villages under respective types were taken.

happened to be 5*, this gives us a figure of Rs. 4380 per household per year. We have, however, used a slightly lower figure of Rs. 4360 as the poverty line, as explained above. Adding up the proportion of all household categories below this income as per cent to the respective village totals, we get the magnitude of poverty in each village, which is presented in Table 9.2 here under the column—total poor.

The villages in this table are arranged in order of level of development under both dry and wet villages separately. The average proportion of the poor households amounted to 79.8 per cent in dry villages, and hardly lower at 75.5 per cent in wet villages. The average proportion for all the villages together was 77.8 per cent. This is a staggering level of poverty, on which neither irrigation nor animal husbandry has made a sufficiently strong impact. Curiously, villages with the highest as well as lowest poverty levels were both relatively dry, though the former was in the least diversified D-a type and the latter D-c (with industry only) type. Equation-2 in the Appendix here shows that though all the three dummy variables have negative regression co-efficients, those for irrigation and animal husbandry are not statistically significant. Only rural industry showed a statistically significant impact, with the introduction of which the proportion of the poor households tended to be lower by 17.6 percentage points. In a village which was least developed, the proportion of the poor was as high as 88.7 per cent; there was no significant reduction in this with the introduction of irrigation or animal husbandry. As a further check, a correlation co-efficient between proportion of poor households and per cent of net sown area irrigated was calculated, which turned out to be only —0.26, which was not statistically significant. It was, however, interesting to find a very strong negative correlation (viz. 0.81) between the proporation of poor households and the level of commercialisation of a village, indicated by the proportion of produce marketed.** This showed that with an

* Though it was actually 5.3, we have used the rounded off figure.

** Though commercialisation was positively correlated with the size of a village (measured in terms of the number of households—the correlation being only 0.46, significant at 10 per cent level), the latter was found to have no significant impact on the proportion of the poor. The co-efficient of correlation between the two was only —0.36, which was not statistically significant.

advance in commercialisation, which is also positively associated with rural industry (correlation co-efficient +0.66) the proportion of poor households tended to decline significantly. Commercialisation of agriculture results from a number of influences as we have seen, irrigation being only one of them. If commercialisation of agriculture can be taken as an approximate index of rural growth (if not development), it is heartening to see that it increased the incomes of poor and lifted some of them above poverty line, though it also increased the incomes of the rich even more.

It is important, however, to note that within the existing agrarian structure, even a high level of diversification and presence of significant rural industry has not succeeded in eliminating poverty. The extent of poverty that remained even in the most diversified and developed village type, Wet-d was 67.8 per cent on the average, as seen from the last column in Table 9.1. This is after a reduction of only 20.8 per cent points from the least developed Dry-a type. Coimbatore villages on the average had, of course, even lower magnitude of poverty than this, viz. 60.9 per cent, but even in this developed district poverty ranged from 78.5 to 44.3 per cent in the five suryed villages. It is no co-incidence that the village with the highest poverty in this district had also the highest value of concentration ratio (Gini) for operated land standardised for irrigation differences and calculated by including landless agricultural labour, viz. 0.881. On the other hand, the village with the lowest proportion of poverty had the lowest value of this ratio in the district, viz. 0.628. However, taking all the 15 villages together, a correlation between poverty and Gini ratio did not emerge. This is because whereas in the districts like Bijapur, lack of development and diversification was the most prominent factor behind poverty, the inequitous agrarian structure seemed to account for the staggering poverty that still remained in developed districts like Coimbatore.

An idea of who constitute the poor and the rich in each village can be obtained from the Appendix table. The non-cultivating households (with the exception of white collar professionals), the marginal farmers and the small farmers cultivating upto 2 hectares broadly constituted the poor. But there was no perfect consistency in this, since sometimes a category which was poor in most villages emerged out of the poverty line in some. Similarly, a category which is rich in most of the villages at times plunged below poverty line in some villages.

In particular, marginal farmers (below 1 hectare) emerged out of poverty only in three villages—all in Coimbatore and all with industry, two of them irrigated. It was not just because of irrigation, but because they could successfully diversify their household economy. In Kokkamapalayam it was mainly because of irrigation, and also because they could earn a sizeable amount in wages. Small farmers cultivating between 1 to 2 hectares also were poor in most of the villages, but could come out of the poverty line in three villages—once again all in Coimbatore and all with industry, two of them irrigated. Both in Kalangal and Sirukinar they were quite successful in trade, having derived most of the income through trading; it was not due to irrigation, not at least directly.

Non-cultivating agricultural labourers were consistently poor in all villages. Whatever increase in income they enjoyed in some villages, did not enable them to emerge out of poverty line. Non-cultivating households reporting animal husbandry as main occupation were also poor in all villages, except in Sirukinar of Coimbatore. This cotegory of households did not necessarily derive the main part of income from animal husbandry. They sometimes collected milk or milk products from others and sold them at a margin or on a little commission in nearby towns and villages mainly to tea-shops. They also had to depend on agricultural labour.

Though artisans also were mostly in poverty, they could come out of it only in three villages—in Kokkamapalyam and Vadakalur of Coimbatore and in Korrapadu of Anantapur. In Vadakalur particularly, they made it really good—a phenomenon already referred to. Neither in Beluguppa (Anantapur) nor in Sulibhavi (Bijapur) they could emerge out of poverty line.

Though it may look surprising, traders were not above poverty line consistently. They were above only in Korrapadu, Chinnamushturu, Nandyal, Kalangal and Vadakalur—a rather mixed group. They were a notable success only in Kalangal. Though white collar professionals including white collar employees were above poverty line, the same thing could not be said about others on regular salary (6th category among non-cultivators in our tables). The latter emerged above poverty line only in Beluguppa, Mughalkhod, Kalangal and Sirukinar—villages either with industry or irrigation or both. Non-agricultural casual labour households managed to be out of poverty only in Kalangal and Vadakalur—villages with industry. Otherwise, they were as poor or even poorer than agricultural labourers. Rentiers were a mixed category. They were mostly in the poor category except in Kalangal, Beluguppa and Mughalkhod, the former two with industry, and the last an irrigated village. They were generally old people, depending on pension, help from relatives and occasionally rent. In one or two rare cases, the group included beggars too.

Since poverty was so endemic, our attention could now be focussed on the poorest among them. Table 9.2 here indicates the poorest two categories in each village, and how they stand in relation to the income of the richest category in the respective villages. It is marginal farmers (particularly in dry villages), agricultural labourers, non-agricultural casual labour and rentiers who figures there mostly. Surprisingly, in one village (Sholmadevi) non-cultivating traders emerged as the poorest! Even when irrigation and rural industry tends to lift some sections out of poverty line, there are others who seem to be forced below it.

It may look surprising that sometimes even the cultivators above the small size category also came under the poorest. A look at the Appendix table also would show that quite often cultivators other than small and marginal farmers also came below the poverty line. It is easy to dismiss this as a case of under-reporting of output and income, if one does not recall to one's mind the state of uncertainty and insecurity in agriculture. A cultivating household may be quite rich in one year, and poor in another. Indeed our reference period was a normal year and was not marked by a drought beyond the normal level. Even so, other hazards—particularly on account of pests and diseases—are not insignificant, and adversely affected the concerned households. When cross-questioned about their output being lower than what can be considered reasonable in relation to their cultivated land, the explanation was invariably in terms of crop failures. It was

TABLE 9.2 : The poor and, the poorest two household categories relative to the richest : a) Household category; b) its income in Rs; c) Ratio of the income of the richest category over the income of the concerned category in the village

Village type and village	Total poor* per cent	Poorest			2nd Poorest			Richest
		a	b	c	a	b	c	a
1	2	3	4	5	6	7	8	9
Da—C'turu	92.6	Marginal farmers	777	8.6	Culti. with 2 to 4 hect.	1067	4.2	White collar
—K'bagi	96.8	Rentiers	780	10.3	Culti. with 10 to 20 hect.	1344	6.0	Culti. with above 50 hect.
Db—G'dla	91.4	Rentiers	1546	12.1	Non-cultig. A. husbandry	1560	12.1	-do-
—M'valgi	87.0	Cultig. with 6 to 10 hec.	1304	9.1	Agri. labour	1472	8.1	-do-
Dc—S'bhavi	89.9	Non-agril. casual labourer	1250	90.9	Marginal farmer	1332	90.9	-do-
—S'nar	44.3	Rentiers	350	37.0	-do-	1990	6.6	-do-
—V'lur	57.3	Non-cultig. A. husbandry	1270	333.3	With 2 to 4 hect.	2654	142.9	Cultig. with 6 to 10 hec. (largest size class in the village)
Dd—B'guppa	79.4	Agri. labour	2094	8.5	Artisans	2135	8.3	Cultig. with above 50 hect.

1	2	3	4	5	6	7	8	9
Wa—M'khod	79.5	Artisans	1562	24.3	Agri. labour	1808	21.3	Culti. with above 50 hect.
—N'yal	83.8	Agri. labour	1586	5.6	-do-	1701	5.3	Cultig. with 10 to 20 hect. (largest size class in the village)
Wb—K'padu	80.0	Non-cultig. A.husbandry	1700	33.3	Non-agri. casual labour	1770	32.3	Cultig. with above 50 hect.
Wc—R'ruvu	82.2	Rentiers	337	714.3	Artisans	1536	151.5	-do-
—K'palyam	71.3	Non-agri. labourers	960	333.3	Non-cultig. A.husbandry	1311	250.0	-do-
Wd—S'devi	78.5	Non-cultig. traders (petty traders)	2744	15.4	Agri. labour	2760	15.4	Cultig. with 2 to 4 hect.
—K'gal	53.3	Agri. labour	2780	55.6	Non-cultig. A.husbandry	2810	55.6	Cultig. with above 50 hect.

* i.e. households, having an annual income of less than Rs. 4360, as per cent of total number of households in respective villages. (See text for explanation of this poverty-line)

not uncommon to find farmers having lost thus being poorer than landless labourers, atleast in the year concerned. However, the fact of an important assest like land being under their control, has a significance of its own, which keeps them socially at a higher level than landless labourers.

Before we take up the last question posed above, we may note that there was no statistically significant correlation between the proportion of poverty and the proportion of income derived by village households (taken together) from different sources like cultivation, agricultural labour etc. That is, a village which derived a higher source of income from cultivation (or wage labour or any other source respectively) did not necessarily have a higher (or lower) proportion of poverty. This was because an increase in the level of development raises the average level of income more than the proportion of income derived from different sources. Thus, a village with rural industry—more than increasing the proportion of income derived from rural industry—increases the absolute level of income derived from cultivation also. We have already noted this fact in the last chapter. It had a similar impact on the quantum of wage income earned too. Promotion of industry is not then at the cost of agriculture; as a matter of fact, they promote each other. We could atleast say that the amount of diversification achieved in the rural economy so far has not been such as to significantly reduce the reliance on agriculture. There has no doubt been a fair amount variation in the proportion of income derived from cultivation across the villages. But often—though not always—a higher level of rural development has even increased the proportion of income derived from agriculture, by making agriculture more productive and profitable. We have a different but interesting case in Chinnamushturu—a dry and least developed village, and Kalangal—wet and developed villages. Both derive very small proportion of income from cultivation, the former 5.9 per cent and the latter 8.6 per cent. The former ranked high among the villages in the magnitude of poverty, having 92.6 per cent of households as poor, whereas Kalangal ranked low in this respect having 53.3 per cent of households below poverty line. When a village is dry and not well diversified, its poor households tend to go out in search of seasonal wage labour.

We come now to the issue of inequality in incomes. As remarked earlier, the very fact that a substantial proportion of households lie below the average income is a pointer to an extremely skewed distribution of incomes. However, we had taken an overall average for all the villages together as the poverty line (which corresponded also to the conventional poverty line at the national level), and from this we get no indication of within village inequality. We have two indicators of inequality within villages. One is provided in Table 9.2 itself, which presents the ratio of the income of the richest category of households over the income of the poorest category in respective villages. The higher the ratio, larger is the inequality. We have the highest degree of inequality in Rayalacheruvu of Anantapur, followed by Vadakalur and Kokkampalayam—both in Coimbatore. In Rayalacheruvu, the richest received over 700 times the income earned by the poorest. Interestingly, Vadakalur (where the ratio was 333) did not have any household with holdings above 10 hectares, and yet it had one of the highest degree of inequality indicated by this measure. Obviously, apart from land, other sources of inequality also entered the picture, though indirectly control over land could have been at the source of it. In terms of this ratio, the least inequality was in Nandyal of Bijapur, an irrigated village.

Though this measure gives a broad indication of the range of income, it does not take into account all the categories of households, but only the households at the two extreme ends. Though this information is valuable in itself, it could be misleading at times unless we have an alternative measure which takes into account all categories of households. For the type of data we have in the table—namely, income per household in different categories—the co-efficient of variation in incomes within the village was thought to be adequate enough. The values of this measure are presented in Table 9.3 here for villages classified according to village types. The higher the magnitude of this value, the higher is the magnitude of inequality or variation in incomes per household. This measure takes into account all the categories, unlike the ratios above.

An interesting, if not surprising, finding that we get here is that the proportion of the poor and inequality in incomes are

TABLE 9.3 : **Co-efficicnts of variation (per cent) in income per household of different categories within villages**

Village type	Dry villages		Wet villages	
a	C'turu	47.9	M'khod	125.4
	K'bagi	69.1	N'yal	63.9
b	G'ndla	107.7	K'padu	159.6
	M'valgi	75.1		
c	S'bhavi	267.5	R'cheruvu	282.4
	S'nar	64.7	K'lyam	298.9
	V'lur	301.4		
d	B'guppa	80.2	S'devi	113.3
			K'ngal	185.0

not positively correlated.* When the level of average income of households in a village increased, the proportion of the poor decreased, but inequality increased. The co-efficient of correlation between average income per household and the proportion of the poor was as high as —0.72 across the 15 villages, while the same between the former and inequality (i.e. CV in incomes per household within each village) was 0.62, both being statistically quite significant—at 1 and 5 per cent levels respectively. Inspite of this statistical significance, the impact on poverty was not substantial. The simple regression coefficients showed that with every hundred rupee increase in the average level of income of village households, the proportion of the poor declined by only one percentage point and CV in incomes increased by 3 percentage points.

We get a similar contrast when we study the impact of levels of development represented by dummy variables for irrigation, animal husbandry and rural industry (see Eqns. 2 & 3 in Appendix here). While the first two variables had no statistically significant impact on both poverty and inequality** rural industry villages had significantly less poverty but more inequality. It is thus clear that while rural development particularly through industry, can have some measure of success in reducing poverty, any success in reducing inequality is very doubtful.

* The direct correlation between the two was actually negative (viz. —0.25) though not statistically significant.

** The correlations in terms of actual values in respect of poverty and inequality on the one hand and proportion of irrigated area on the other, also showed no statistically significant results.

It was so with other development indicators too. We may recall that commercialisation of agriculture had a strong impact by way of reduction in poverty. But it was found to have the opposite impact of increasing inequality, the co-efficients of correlation being 0.52 (sig. at 5 per cent level). The size of village in terms of number of households, which had negative but no significant impact on poverty, had a positive and significant impact on inequality, the correlation being 0.57 (sig. at 5 per cent level). Even where a development indicator showed no impact in terms of reducing poverty, it nevertheless succeeded in increasing inequality. While diversification through rural industry was a more powerful factor than merely irrigation in reducing poverty, even this could not go far. This was because it even tended to make the agrarian structure even more inequitous. *If the process that reduces poverty does not also reduce inequality, it has severe limitations even in removing poverty itself.* Such a danger is inherent also in cluster approach to rural development (intended to increase the viability of villages and build strong rural communities), if it is pursued through mechanistic and input oriented strategies.

It may be argued that proverty that still remains in the most developed villages is due to immigration of landless labour from outside. It is true that a village is not a closed economy and even the most developed village cannot insulate itself from the ocean of poverty around it. However, all the poverty that remains in the most developed villages cannot be attributed to immigration of the poor from outside, since the proportion of immigrant households was much less than the proportion of the poor households in such villages.* Even

* In terms of the migration status of the present head of the household—usually the most elderly, the average proportion of the immigrant households in the five least poor villages (incidentally, all in Coimbatore) was only 4.6, as against as many as 60.9 per cent households being poor. It was only in a relatively newly irrigated village like Mughalkhod, the proportion of immigrant housedolds was high, being 36.3 in this village. But even here, the proportion of the poor (viz. 79.5) far exceeded immigrants. On the whole, the proportion of immigrants was marginal, but it could be higher if immigration of earlier generations is taken into account. This, however, could not be estimated. It may also be noted that usually a smaller part of immigrants were in the category of labourers, others being farmers, salaried persons, traders, artisans and animal husbandry keepers.

after allowing for immigration, the poverty that still remained was significant and reflected on the quality of the development process itself.

In a way these are disturbing results. The path of rural development is not smooth and does not necessarily hold rosy promises for the poor. There are indeed signs of hope particularly because of the positive impact of irrigation and rural industry on incomes per hectare of sown area and even to some extent per household. The mechanisms that produce this result need to be strengthened. But there is also the risk that these mechanisms accelerate inequaitly, even if they reduce absolute poverty. There seems to be no escape from this dilemma in capitalist development.

Reference

1. N. Krishnaji, Poverty and family size, *Social Scientist*, Vol. 9, No. 4, November 1980.

APPENDIX-I

REGRESSION EQUATIONS

(1)	(2)	(3)	(4)	(5)	(6)	(7)
1.	Total income (from all sources) per household (Rs)					
	a) marginal cultivators	1157 (1.10)	1067 (0.96)	1512 (1.33)	1611 (1.44)	0.31
	b) all cultivators	994 (1.09)	3754 (3.86)	2375 (2.40)	4319 (4.44)	0.80
	c) agril. labour h.hs	1897 (8.73)	—113 (0.49)	—161 (0.68)	856 (3.70)	0.57
	d) artisan h.hs	3235 (2.02)	—58.15 (0.03)	27.65 (0.02)	1055 (0.61)	0.04
	e) trading h.hs	799 (0.28)	3676 (1.19)	3454 (1.10)	2812 (0.91)	0.25
	f) all non-cultig. h.hs	2481 (4.35)	—322 (0.53)	—73 (0.12)	1349 (2.22)	0.32
	g) all households	2434 (3.65)	1334 (1.88)	564 (0.78)	2020 (2.85)	0.54
2.	Proportion (per cent) of households below poverty line	88.6 (13.37)	—3.07 (0.043)	—0.06 (0.01)	—17.6 (2.49)	0.37
3.	Co-efficient of variation (per cent) in the total income per h.hold within village	93.4 (2.45)	44.0 (1.08)	—45.7 (1.10)	100.9 (2.48)	0.45

Note: The cut-off points for statistical significance of t values (given in brackets) are 3.055 at 1 per cent, 2.179 at 5 per cent and 1.782 at 10 per cent. Since Eq. 1.d. has only 14 observations, the respective cut-off points for it are 3.106, 2.201 and 1.796.

APPENDIX-II

TOTAL INCOME PER HOUSEHOLD (RS.)—VILLAGEWISE AND HOUSEHOLD CATEGORYWISE

Household categories	Anantapur villages				
	R'vu	K'padu	G'dla	C'turu	B'ppa
Cultivating households					
1	1,897	2,384	3,672	777	2,306
2	2,872	2,799	3,488	2,344	2,955
3	6,203	3,811	1,650	1,607	3,205
4	5,229	2,571	2,939	1,964	3,807
5	12,627	14,786	2,668	3,271	6,550
6	19,384	9,343	6,882	2,858	11,616
7	2,32,845	56,575	18,709	3,153	17,696
Total culti.	6,410	6,514	3,187	1,645	5,590
non-cultivating households					
1	1,759	1,833	1,702	2,322	2,094
2	2,137	1,700	1,560	—	—
3	1,536	7,810	2,102	2,570	2,135
4	4,192	7,476	2,183	4,670	3,688
5	6,880	6,600	10,245	6,710	4,220
6	2,746	3,524	1,610	—	5,136
7	2,280	1,770	1,940	3,187	2,550
8	337	2,600	1,546	2,793	5,450
Total non-culti.	2,384	3,071	2,035	2,992	2,848
All h.holds	3,978	5,254	2,876	2,304	3,967

See Table 1.2 for description of household categories.

Household categories	Bijapur villages				
	M'hod	M'lgi	N'yal	K'gi	S'bhavi
Cultivating households					
1	2,301	2,704	1,586	2,410	1,332
2	2,119	2,859	2,712	1,676	2,629
3	3,149	3,259	2,369	2,980	2,039
4	7,845	1,606	4,648	1,915	2,468
5	11,615	1,304	2,388	4,119	4,820
6	22,572	6,610	8,969	1.344	6,574
7	38,397	11,847	—	8,030	1,18,434
Total culti.	5,075	3,341	2,920	2,661	3,042
Non-cultivating households					
1	1,808	1,472	1,701	1,616	2,461
2	4,135	3,310	—	—	3,603
3	1,562	2,691	—	2,642	4,156
4	2,135	2,375	6,145	1,996	3,033
5	3,000	3,227	—	5,713	3,930
6	6,150	1,772	—	—	3,383
7	—	3,266	—	1,549	1,250
8	5,070	2,815	—	780	1,420
Total non-cultig.	2,025	2,017	2,056	1,985	3,334
All h.holds	4,032	2,980	2,726	2,561	3,171

Household categories	Coimbatore villages				
	S'devi	K'yam	K'gal	S'nar	V'lur
Cultivating households					
1	10,045	5,396	2,936	1,990	5,045
2	11,534	2,701	10,349	4,762	2,985
3	42,384	2,035	7,320	5,481	2,654
4	41,948	10,029	13,375	5,386	3,715
5	—	13,387	8,838	4,698	3,94,959
6	—	8,526	34,883	5,489	—
7	—	3,32,700	1,55,741	13,055	—
Total culti.	13,094	10,917	12,707	4,921	7,964
Non-cultivating households					
1	2,760	2,782	2,780	3,393	3,053
2	—	1,311	2,810	9,710	1,270
3	4,320	4,628	3,510	2,193	11,696
4	2,744	3,728	26,515	3,619	6,440
5	3,875	5,100	15,168	2,120	4,960
6	3,586	2,570	9,185	7,260	3,700
7	--	960	4,500	—	4,786
8	—	—	4,600	350	3,683
Total non-cultig.	2,973	3,195	4,582	3,040	6,775
All households	5,305	7,184	7,670	4,178	7,205

10

OVERCOMING DROUGHT-PRONENESS AND POVERTY
A Conclusion

THREE theoretical perspectives were presented in the opening chapter as possible explanations for variations in the levels of regional development. While the first stressed the importance of resource endowment and natural environment of regions, the second viewed regional underdevelopment as a counterpart process of capitalist development of the central or metropolis region which exploits the periphery by involving the latter in the national market through commercialisation. The third perspective was historical and institutional, tracing regional backwardness to differential colonial policy for different regions, which produced zamindari in some and ryotwari in other regions. It was also suggested that there cannot possibly be one universal or grand theory, explaining regional backwardness in every situation in terms of a single factor.

The role of environment could not be completely negated, particularly in districts like Bijapur and Anantapur, plagued by frequent failures of rainfall. At lower levels of development, particularly when the mainstay of the economy is agriculture and forces of production are yet to develop even within agriculture, environment becomes indeed the most dominant factor behind endemic poverty and regional backwardness. At these stages the distinction between drought-prone and non-drought-prone regions is also likely to be very conspicuous. The mainstay of our economy is still agriculture, but there is fairly adequate evidence to show that differences between the two types of regions have narrowed down, sometimes rendering the remaining difference insignificant. Even in cases where the difference remained significant, the disparity had narrowed down. This was evident both in indicators of quality of life and levels of agricultural development. It showed that the constraining or inhibiting influence of environment was being steadily overcome if not fast enough to eliminate it totally. It was particularly heartening that drought-prone areas in general recorded faster rates of growth in production and yields of foodgrains, inspite of higher instability in yields and rainfall. As a result, the disparity in yields per hectare of foodgrains declined significantly.

How could this come about? Almost all the regions in the three southern states were under ryotwari system, and the institutional set up was not so oppressive here as in Zamindari areas. They could therefore respond to government efforts of initiating growth and altering adverse environment. There were of course quite a few pockets under zamindars even in these states who converted themselves into capitalist farmers by the end of fifties. In fact, this was generally the fate of land reforms. The dominance of large holdings both in number and area in drought-prone areas may also have ensured that risk aversion which characterises mainly the small holders did not become a hindrance to the growth process. However, it was not necessarily a process initiated by the large holders. Official intervention to promote growth factors also played an important role in altering the depressive status quo.

Several factors have contributed to this growth process particularly in agriculture—irrigation, fertilisers, introduction of HYVs and mechanisation. In each of this, the disparity between drought-prone and other regions is narrowing down, with quite a few of the former regions being converted to non-drought-prone status in course of time. Coimbatore district itself is an example of a beneficiary of this process. Though irrigation has been an important factor in this change, fertilisers, HYVs and mechanisation are being introduced even under rainfed conditions.

Moreover, apart from irrigation, industrialisation of the region and industries located in villages, themselves have also been a very important factor in altering the environment and overcoming dependence on drought-prone agriculture.

Agriculture, made prosperous by irrigation, can itself stimulate industrialisation both through the generation of investible surpluses seeking opportunities of making profits even outside agriculture, and also through making possible the setting up of processing industries.

However, such industrialisation has not necessarily accompanied irrigation development. For example, there are several other districts in Tamil Nadu which are more irrigated than Coimbatore and for a longer time, and yet much less industrialised. Coimbatore, however, has certain unique features, which may have favoured both commercial development of agriculture and industrialisation. The average size of holdings here is larger than in other districts of Tamil Nadu, and the dominance of large holdings is more. It has relatively more commercial crops, though a millet region. There are also communities known for entrepreneurship—Naidus, Chettiars and Devangs. There is much greater integration between agriculture and industry and even its villages are more urbanised, with better infrastructure and access. Though the district has the highest instability in rainfall among the three states and its unirrigated villages are as vulnerable to climate as similar villages in Anantapur and Bijapur, the district has overcome its drought-proneness through higher level of industrialisation and development of the tertiary sector even in its unirrigated parts. Industries here are decentralised and mostly in the small scale and rural sector. In fact villages without a fairly significant number of artisans are rare to find here.

This process of altering the natural environment either through irrigation or industry has not been an unmixed gain. The growth process even in agriculture, relying mainly on fertilisers and HYVs, has at times even interfered with or upset time-honoured practices of adjustment to drought-proneness. Thus, cultivators had evolved systems of crop combinations and rotations which enabled them to survive risks, provided them protein-rich pulses, and maintained or even improved soil fertility. Introduction of HYVs particularly under irrigation has upset these practices.

Farmers also had the time-honoured practice of storing foodgrains enough for the family for atleast two years. They had, in other words, their own buffer stock operations to face the eventuality of droughts. When patron-client relations between landlords and tenants or labourers were strong, these buffer stocks were used to avert the starvation of the latter (of course, at a cost which the latter often did not realise). This practice of private buffer stocks is now steadily breaking down even among large and middle cultivators. The dominance of cash economy has perhaps induced liquidity preference and made them prefer cash to store grains to tide over droughts. The question of such buffers arises when the farmers concerned are mostly subsistence motivated and grow mainly foodgrains. When they raise cash crops for profit, there is little scope for storing foodgrains. Even when they grow foodgrains, it is mainly for the market and the tendency is to sell all harvested output, keeping an year's requirement of the household. The intention here is not to suggest that private buffer stocks with farmers are preferable to buffer stock operations by the government. After all, the former were hardly adequate to cover all sections of the society. The latter can be on a more planned basis and also can liberate the weaker section in rural areas from the costly patronage of landlords. However, with the breakdown of private buffer system, the dependence on the government during droughts has increased, and if the government system does not cover rural areas adequately, the weaker sections would be in the blissful state of dependence only on God ! It must be noted however that though the public distribution system did not cover rural areas adequately, the institution of relief works particularly in drought years provides the purchasing power to them to avert starvation, if not to emerge out of poverty.

Besides eroding the traditional disaster survival practices, the input oriented growth strategies have involved opportunity costs even in terms of neglect of land itself. Thus there was evidence particularly in Anantapur and Bijapur that with an increase in the level of irrigation, there was a tendency for idle land (current and other fallows) to increase. This was, however, mainly because resources at the disposal of farmers did not increase commensurately with the level of irrigation. Farmers preferred to concentrate on irrigated land. There was significant idle land in Coimbatore too, but at the holdings level it was more associated with the size of holding than with irrigation, the larger holders having more of it. However, irrigation did contribute to neglect of land even in Coimbatore at a macro level. Large areas were water-logged and rendered unsuitable for cultivation. There was more emphasis on providing water and much less on land and water management. Even the farmers did not seem to bother much about it. While they were organised to fight the government for obtaining water on a regular basis, to reduce electricity dues and so on, the same organisational spirit was not forthcoming to have a more rational and equitable system of water distribution. On its part, government was more organised to provide physical inputs, than to promote co-operative endeavour among farmers for a systematic land and water use.

The magnitude of idle land in Bijapur was limited, but was significant in Anantapur and Coimbatore. Under drought-prone conditions, while farmers in Bijapur tried to use most of the land available, the farmers in the two other districts concentrated on more productive portions of land. Normal rotational fallowing is not in itself objectionable, but the tendency to neglect certain portions of land for long periods rendering it a waste in course of time without either tree cover or grass cover, is indeed undesirable particularly in the context of general scarcity of land. The large holders follow the policy of dog in the manger, neither using it themselves nor selling or leasing it out. This tendency becomes stronger at more developed levels rather than in areas like Bijapur where productivity levels are still low. The problem is serious enough to penalise holders who cause deterioration of land or keep it idle for more than a year.[1]

Irrigation of course increases cropping intensity, offsetting to some extent the negative impact in terms of land kept idle. Its impact tended to be marginal in a less developed district like Bijapur, was somewhat better in the more developed Anantapur and fairly good in the most developed Coimbatore. The potential of irrigation seemed to improve with levels of overall economic development. On the other hand, double cropping almost tended to be completely absent in both of the latter districts when irrigation was absent (as shown by intercept values). While it was still positive and significant in Bijapur even under conditions of zero irrigation. The size of holding, given irrigation, was not a significant factor in affecting cropping intensity. What interests here is the fact that the traditional cropping intensity under dry and rainfed conditions breaks down under more developed conditions, depending there solely on irrigation. If irrigation itself were to be uncertain, as it indeed is in quite a few cases, double cropping too becomes uncertain. It is unfortunate that in the very process of overcoming drought-proneness through irrigation, there is a tendency to become more vulnerable to droughts. We may recall here Prof. V.K.R.V. Rao's observation that rainfed conditions have accounted for the larger part of double cropped area in India and that the potential for a higher cropping intensity in irrigated areas remains underutilised.[2] Another poignant dimension that needs to be added to this observation is that once a farmer or a region is accustomed to double cropping under irrigated conditions, the old ways of double cropping under dry conditions are forgotten, with the result that double cropping in dry portions is practically absent in such regions.

Paradoxical though it may seem, some of the development efforts have a backlash even on the quality of life. Irrigation in the absence of rural industry seems to have this impact in certain respects like withdrawing children from schooling. Its beneficial impact on aspects like literacy, village infrastructure, sanitation did not prove to be significant. Introduction of animal husbandry on the other hand improved the proportion of school-going children both among cultivating and non-cultivating households, though some of this influence was due to the fact that villages with animal husbandry were larger and had better schooling facilities. Rural industry had a more favourable and widespread impact on all these aspects. But even with the introduction of rural industry, the magnitude of illiteracy, inadequacy of toilet facilities, the proportion of children not going to schools, houses without electricity and the like were still quite significant. Even the capacity of rural industry did not go far enough, calling for more concerted and direct efforts to improve quality of rural life. It may be noted however that though rural industry had limited impact on the quality of life within concerned villages in underdeveloped regions like Bijapur, the industrialisation or development of the region as a whole had much better impact as exemplified by Coimbatore villages. Size of the village and its access also had an important role to play in improving the quality of life—a point which Prof V.K.R.V. Rao has often stressed. But even the size of village did not lift the quality high enough.

The significance of quality of life is that unlike the improvement of the forces of production which mainly benefit the large and middle farmers, an improvement in the former is more equitably shared. It could also make people progress-oriented and forward looking. Improvement in literacy and educational levels can produce awareness among the poor of their own economic, social and political position and should enable them to identify causes of their poverty. The process of eradication of poverty starts not so much when funds are thrown on official development schemes but when the poor start making an intelligent diagnosis of their ills and make concerted efforts to overcome them. Schooling and literacy programmes can play a crucial role in this process, if only planned and operated in that spirit.

The rural structure also undergoes a few important changes as the environment is transformed through irrigation and rural industry. Animal husbandry had a weak influence in this regard. Irrigation tended to attract non-cultivating labour, which could be both through inmigration of labour from outside and also through conversion of cultivating into non-cultivating labour. Industry also had the same impact and introduced a sharper division of labour than irrigation. Both made the agrarian structure more inegalitarian, not so much by increasing concentration of land within cultivators, but by sharpening the difference between agricultural labour and cultivators. Gini ratios for concentration in holdings calculated by excluding landless labour did not change much between developed villages and the least developed. However, Gini ratios calculated by including landless labour, did increase with higher levels of development.

Yet there were certain trends which obfuscated polarisation along class lines, particularly if we try to distinguish between those who hire in and those who hire out labour on a net basis. The magnitude of hiring increased with levels of development among both, so that even small cultivators hired more in developed villages than in the least developed. There was also the emergence of elite cultivating labour—those who hired out bullocks, bullock carts and tractors along with their own labour service for operating the same. In the old days, attached labour used to operate bullocks and bullock carts of even middle size holders. The attached labour is now being slowly displaced by family labour itself. Moreover, the use of tractors has reduced the magnitude hired in labour among large holders and increased family's own self-employment. We could come across quite a few instances where those who hired out labour were richer than those who hired in on a net basis. Moreover, at higher levels of agricultural development, even marginal holders that remained identified themselves more with larger cultivators in class terms than with the landless labour.

We find this paradoxical trend even in social structure. The peasant castes dominated land in almost all villages even where they were not a numerical majority, with the exception of two Muslim majority villages. Large holdings were a virtual monopoly of peasant castes almost everywhere. Irrigation and animal husbandry hardly weakened their dominance. Rural industry, however, was more successful in this. The diversification of the rural economy particularly through rural industry seemed to increase the role of backward castes and professional (artisan) communities. The social structure in rural industry villages was generally multicaste or pluralist. Yet, scheduled castes and tribes, who were a numerical minority in every village and also relatively landless, were unable to benefit directly from either irrigation or industry except through wage labour. The proportion of these communities among cultivators actually tended to decline both with irrigation and rural industry, though it tended to increase a little with animal husbandry. On the other hand, their proportion tended to increase among landless labour with the introduction of irrigation and industry.

We get a clue from these paradoxical changes both in agrarian structure and social structure that higher levels of development may bring significant gains to the middle tiers of the society, though it increases the social distance between the lowliest and the highest. The middle tiers as they gain more from the development process identify themselves more and more with the rich. The proletarianisation process plays a prominent role mainly among the lowliest in the social structure—the scheduled castes and tribes, and not in the middle tiers.

The traditional patron-client relations have also undergone a change in their magnitude and context. What holds the landless labour under the power of rich farmers is not the extension of private credit, but the power to help them in obtaining credit from the institutional sources, or to get free house sites for them, to get relief works started in or near their village and so on, apart of course from their power to provide employment in busy seasons. Patronage does not have to be direct now and at a cost to the elite, it is through the government. It has become immensely more difficult to get credit for the landless labour and agricultural labour from private sources, while it is not easy for them to get it from institutional sources either. We found some instances of institutional credit extended to them only in Bijapur villages in Karnataka, but not in Anantapur or Coimbatore. On the whole, however, the poor while seemingly liberated from traditional patronage, are yet to find their feet. Though in agriculture proper the traditional patron-client relationships are hardly conspicuous, they are more prominent in rural industry. Artisans, unless organised on a co-operative basis, were usually under traders or master-weavers. Often their status was little different from that of labourers on piece rates. They could of course get advance payment of wages in times of need, the raw material usually provided by and belonging to the masters themselves. Where artisans were under co-operatives, they enjoyed better income and status.

Though the development process made the rural structures more inegalitarian, it did not involve deprivation or immiseration in absolute terms. This was evident both from irrigation and rural industry, particularly the latter. A comparison between marginal cultivators (with less than a hectare) and the large (with over 10 hectares) showed that the former obtained more output and income *per hectare* than the latter in dry villages, but less than them in wet villages. It was in a less developed setting where forces of production had not developed enough that the family labour of smalls farms became a major advantage. Under a more commercialised setting where there was a greater requirement of market inputs, large farmers have a relatively greater advantage. Paradoxically, the level of input use (paid out costs) per hectare was actually higher in the marginal holdings than in the large, both in dry and wet villages. While marginal farmers stepped up market inputs considerably in wet villages, the increase in output was not commensurate with this. Objective circumstances related to technology, market, their bias to scale of cultivation, determines the relative efficiency of different size-classes of cultivators. Another factor in favour of large cultivators particularly in Coimbatore was that, as noted above, they left large portions of land idle concentrating only on better portions—an option which the small holders did not have. This may have increased the output and income per hectare of cultivated land, though at a social cost of some land left idle.

These factors also meant increased inequality in agricultural incomes. The difference between the income of a marginal farm household and a large farmer in the least developed dry village was by a factor of over 10, but in the most developed wet village the difference was by a factor of nearly 38! Despite this disparity marginal farmers gained in absolute terms by increased levels of development. In fact, a marginal farmer in the most developed wet village had a higher income than a large farmer in the least developed dry village.

The nature and role of commercialisation of agriculture in the development process also needs to be noted. It was highly and positively related to levels of development of the village, measured in terms of average income per household and also in terms of presence of industry, infrastructure and size of village. Regional development apart, the strongest factor affecting commercialisation across villages was the value of farm produce per cultivating household. Commercialisation of agriculture stimulated higher production both in agricultural and non-agricultural activities, particularly as seen across villages. Commercialisation can take place even under conditions of bondage where it leads to deprivation and immiseration. But our field observations did not indicate the dominance of such commercialisation. It was more genuine, taking place under conditions where commercialisation increased the incomes of households.

Though small farmers were also involved in the market particularly in the more commercialised villages, it was not under duress or bondage. It was rather to take advantage of the market, to increase their purchasing power by selling output where they had advantage and purchasing goods which they needed. It was in more commercialised villages that even the small and marginal farmers obtained better prices for their farm produce. It increased the incomes of not only marginal cultivators but even of agricultural labour and artisans. The agricultural labourers got more employment as well as a little higher wages in more commercialised and developed villages. Whereas wage rates in less developed villages of Bijapur even for male labour were Rs. 3 per day, they could get around Rs. 6 in Coimbatore. It was not, therefore, surprising that the more commercialised villages were found to have a smaller proportion of poor households. It is the isolated and less commercialised villages which provided the dismal contrast with urban areas rather than the more commercialised ones. Commercialisation was concomitant, if not identical, with rural development. There was no evidence of its immiserising or depressive impact.

However, commercialisation increased inequality though not absolute poverty. It increased the incomes of the rich even more than the incomes of the poor. It was associated with more inegalitarian agrarian structure and a larger proportion of landless labour which was instrumental in increasing agricultural productivity. Commercialisation often enabled big cultivators to enter trading also and increase their total incomes.

However, this does not mean that commercialisation led to an increase in the number of traders. The latter was more the result of overall development of the rural economy and particularly of the size of villages. The power of traders cannot be measured positively in terms of their number. In fact most of them were petty sellers and from poor sections of the rural society. Sale of agricultural produce did not necessarily take place in villages themselves, though outside traders also played an important role in collecting local produce particularly in the case of animal husbandry and rural industry. While food-grain markets were more developed and fetched on the whole competitive prices, there was much less choice in trading outlets and hence more monopsonistic conditions in the sale of commercial crops like groundnut and tobacco. Groundnut particularly had the added disadvantage of higher instability both in prices and yields. Inspite of these problems, however, growers of commercial crops had on an average higher incomes than millet growers. There was no evidence that commercial crops were grown mostly by the large holders. Small growers too were involved.

The impact of rural industry also was the same as commercialisation of agriculture. In fact it had a stronger impact in terms of increasing the incomes even of the poor and in reducing poverty than irrigation, but it also increased inequality more than irrigation. This was because even rural industry operated in the context of unequal agrarian structure. Rural industry had several indirect effects of improving the access and infrastructure of the village and increasing its size which benefited richer peasantry more. Rural industry helped them to get increased income both from cultivation and animal husbandry. Even directly, rural industry became an extra source of income to several cultivators particularly from the richer sections. However, rural industry increased the wage levels of agriculture labour and improved general quality of life affecting all sections of the rural society, though not sufficiently enough. Rural industry had a better impact in reducing poverty where the region as a whole had widespread industrialisation of a decentralised type as in Coimbatore. Though Coimbatore had large industries too, its small scale industrial sector was also well developed and provided better linkages with the agriculture and rural sector.

Perhaps it is such industrial development that holds better prospects for rural development and advancement of forces of production, for skill formation and positive attitudes to development than merely irrigation. This may also accentuate rural inequalities, but this increased inequality within rural areas may be prefertable to a state of rural underdevelopment obtaining under conditions of industrial development confined to metropolitan areas whose only link with rural economy is by way of receiving raw material and other marketed surplus from there, but contributing little by way of providing employment and reducing poverty. Inequality in the overall economy is in all probability much more in such a metropolitan types of industrial development than under a decentrialised better dispersed and relatively small scale type of industrial development even if the latter increases inequality within rural areas. The role of rural industries is not envisaged here in terms of self-sufficiency of villages. They will have to seek markets outside their own village, and in the larger economy. They face disadvantages here no doubt, but helping them overcome these would promote rural development more than exclusive reliance on irrigation. This may not be an easy task since these disadvantages are imposed mostly by industrial monopolies. It would be in their interests if rural development takes place more through the provision of industrial inputs than through industries competing with them in textiles, footwear and so on.

In this context, irrigation would of course have to continue to play an important role in rural development. But it would also be important to see that some of its backlash effects noted above are overcome through direct, concerted action. The response of agriculture to irrigation also needs to be improved through a more efficient land and water management. A purely 'technocratic strategy'—as Nanjundappa has termed it[3]—which concentrates only on providing modern inputs would not go far enough even in the limited sphere of agricultural development, leave alone rural development in general. Unfortunately that seems to be the only choice left with administrators and technocrats. It is really the task of political leadership to organise farmers in development efforts to make use of scarce resources like land and water on a more rational and equitable basis. Such leadership is not in evidence at grass roots level. Administrators do not prove equal to such a task. In any case, irrigation has to be considered only as part of an overall strategy for rural development and cannot be wholly identified with it. This would need giving attention not only to other productive sectors of the rural economy, but also to direct measures of improving the quality of life of the poor and increase their relative advantage in the overall institutional framework. The significance of these measures arises particularly because whatever impact irrigation and even rural industry has so far made, has been no source of consolation. Even in the most developed villages the poverty that has remained is staggering enough. The development processes that increase inequality have serious limitations in eliminating poverty, though they may reduce poverty to some extent.

It is true indeed that drought-proneness unattended to can be an important reason for endemic poverty. This is poverty at lower levels of development. The institutional structures are adapted to this environment and perpetuate that poverty. Interventions to overcome drought-proneness through irrigation and industry have of course altered the environment and reduced poverty, but poverty still persists since new institutional forces arise which accentuate inequality and even produce backlash effects on traditional adaptation to environment. Poverty is like the *Vetala* tormenting King Vikramaditya. As soon as the King solves one of its problems, it is back on his neck with another. It needed tremendous patience for the king to solve this problem ultimately, a patience which may not necessarily be shared by the victims of poverty.

References

1. Kusum Nair has advocated the use of taxes to make it 'too costly to leave any portion of cultivable land idle or use it below its productive capacity'. See her "*In Defence of the Irrational Peasant—Indian Agriculture after Green Revolution*", University of Chicago Press, Chicago and London, 1979, p. 97.
2. V.K.R.V. Rao, 'New Challenges before Indian Agriculture', in Indian Society of Agricultural Economics, 'Seminar on Role of Irrigation in the Development of India's Agriculture', Bombay (delivered in 1974 as Panse Memorial Lecture at the 27th Conference of the Indian Society of Agricultural Statistics, New Delhi).
3. Cf. D.M. Nanjundappa, '*Area Planning and Rural Development*', Associated Publishing House, New Delhi, 1982, pp. 3 and 4.

AUTHOR INDEX

Abdul Az:z, 189
Ahluwalia, Montek, 20
Bharadwaj, Krishna, 5,6,109
Binswanger, Hans P., 6
Borkar, V.V., 21
Chakraborty, S., 20
Chattopadhyay, Boudhayan, 20
David, Washbrook, 146
Dandekar, V.M., 20
Deshpande, R., 43
Harriss, Barbara, 116,117
Jodha, N.S., 37,43
Kabra, K.N., 162
Krishnaji, N., 199
Kurien, C,T., 75
Lipton, Michael, 20
Madalgi, 55,62
Mencher, P., 72,73
Muthayan, K., 95
Nadkarni, M.V,, 21,43,75
Nair, Kusum, 231
Nanjundappa, D.M., 230,231
Naidu, Narayanswamy, 115
Pani, Narendar, 162
Patnaik, Utsa, 116, 125
Prasad, Pradhan, H., 20
Rao, V.K.R.V., 89,131,223,224
Rao, V.M., 125, 141, 163
Raza, Moonis, 20
Rajan, M.A.S., 75
Reddy G. Damodar, 75
Sonachalam, K.S., 72,73
Sarkar, Suman, 162
ul Haq, Mahbub, 129, 141

INDEX

Adult literacy, 138
Adverse environmental factors, 38
Afforestation, 53
Agrarian structure, 23,22,118,147, 225
Agricultural development, 38
Agricultural incomes, 227; labour households, 200; lower proportion of, 37; migration of, 100; association of, 95; land act, 1948, 63; output, valuation of, 148, gross value of, 171
Agriculture, Commercialisation of, 117, 146ff, 201, 212, 227; cost and income from, 170 ff; employment and income charge of, 1; industrialisation, commercial development of, 220; industry and infrastructure, 74; growth process, factors of, 219
Amenities and infrastructure, 82
Anantapur, 9,53,57
Andhra Tenancy Act of, 1956,56
Animal husbandry, 53,56,70,90,106, 119,124,130,138,200; bondage relationship in, 115
Artisans, 108,115,200, 226
Assured rainfall regions, 146
Banjara Welfare Association, 83
Beluguppa, 82
Bijapur, 9,58,59,60,65
Black cotton soils, 59
Bondage relationship, 115
Bovine population, 61
Boyas community, 82
Canals, 60,78; irrigation, 93: features of, 69
Capitalist development, delemma in, 213
Castes: Brahmins, 79,91; Boyas, 82; Kammas, 79; Kapu, 78; Devangas, 79,89; Kurubas, 78,79,83,89, 96; Muslims, 86,89, 91; Naidus, 74,96,200; Vysyas, 79
Central Water Commission, 24,55
Chettias, entrepreneurship of, 220,
Chinnamushturu, 81
Class structure, polarisation of, 125
Climate role, under utilization of, 36
Coimbatore, 9,68, 73,74, 131,132; crop pattern of, 67; Coimbatore Madurai Highway, 91
Commercial crops, 36,93
Commercialisation and agriculture, impact on incomes, 201; inequality of, 228; implication of, 147, 154,204; nature and role of, 227; factors behind, 153-58
Concentration, measures of, 118
Conventional poverty line, 210
Co-operative farming society, 63
Cost Concept, 171
Credit, agricultural schemes for, 77
Crop combinations and rotations, 36; cultivation of, 171; failure and poverty, 206
Cropping intensity, 35,177,178,222; economic development of, 222, impact on, 176
Cultivating artisans, impact of, 106; labourers, 117,118
Cultivation in DP areas, nature of, 37; exclusive dependency of, 13
Development levels, impact of, 211

Differential prices, extent and pattern of, 150
Diversification of household economy, impact on, 108
Drought-prone areas, 28; distribution of, 28,29; factors behind, low productivity in, 7
Electric pumpsets, 81
Elite cultivating labour, emergence of, 117: Emerging pattern, 177
Employers and employees identification of, 116
Entrepreneurial, qualities of, 74
Eradication of poverty, process of, 114
Family and animal labour, cost of, 171
Farm management studies, 172
Farmers association, activist of, 95
Female employment, level of, 133
Fertiliser consumption, 38,54,60
Food crops, 93
Food grains, 54; and market, 229; production of, 68
Forest land, 53, 59
Fuelwood, shortage of, 59
General Scarcity of land context of, 222
Ghataprabha irrigation, 85
Goridindla Village, economy of, 79,80
Gross output, cost and income, 179
Growth in agriculture of drought-prone district, causes of, 42; rates of, 28,38; Composition of, 42 219
Guledgudda, 89
Hand-loom Centre 89; industry, 90; weaving, 99
Harijan 91; association, 95
Highly irrigated, 91
High Yielding Varieties, 59; introduction of, 37; technology of, 54
Household Economy, 104, 108; income of, 197ff; industry, 65
Housing, 133 ff; quality of, 135,136
Idle land fallows, 36; proportion of, 53; magnitude, 222
Ilkal, 89
Illiteracy, impact on, 138; proportion of, 139
Inam villages, proportion of,56
Income, levels of, 198, 200; per-household, impact on, 187; sources of, 108; from cultivation, 198; skewed distribution of, 210
Industrial development, 229
Industrialisation, 66; and rural development, 219
Industry, promotion of, 209
Inequality, 210,211,227,228
Infrastructure, 99; and development benefits of, 131
Input oriented growth strategies, 221
Instability in agriculture, 40
Intensive study, selection of, districts for, 9 ff, 14
Inter locked markets, concept of,109
Introduction of irrigation, 139
Irrigation, 37,55,77,78,85,87,97,102, 130,132,135,138, 154,169,174,177, 184, 200, 222,230; animal husbandry and industry, introduction of, 103,104; Indirect cost of, 174; rural industry, 130; commission of (1972), 24,25; impact of, 42, 68,102, 170 ff, 179,220; importance of, 1 ff; potential of, 222; under utilisation of, 69; in private investments, proportion of, 34; in public sector, 5
Jirayat Land, 63
Kalamgal village, 96
Kombagi village, 87
Kambli weaving,82,83,96
Karnataka, 29,132
Khadi Board, 90
Khadi Sarvodaya Sanga, 98
Kokkampalayam, 92; village farmer's association, 94
Korrapadu, 78; Electrification in, 79
Labour transformation of, 225
Land distribution, 115 ff, 125; hold-

ings, 86, 91; under cultivation, 97; reforms, implimentation of, 176; under utilisation of, 36
Landless Artisans, 125; labour, 118; in rural industry, effect of, 119; immigration of, 212
Large farmers, 34,93,117,182; dominance of, 38
Lease market for land, 35,123
Leguminous crops, 37
Level of development, 211; indicator of, 53
Lightly irrigated crops, 60
Literacy, development of,74; educational level, improvement in, 141; level of development, non-monetary indicators of, 137; rate, 30,66
Livestock economy, 97,99
Low yield crops 36
Madras (Estates Abolition and conversion into Ryotwari) act of 1948,71; Presidency, 146
Marginal Cultivators, 117; farmers, 182; in-migration, 29
Material inputs, 171
Medical facilities, 97; infrastructure in DP districts, 31
Metroplitan region, advantage of, 4
Migration, 88,92,95
Mixed character district of, 25
Modern industry, development of, 131; inputs, 230
Mughalkhod village, 84
Mulsavalgi village, 86
Mysore Law Reforms Act, 1961, 63 ff
Nandyal village, 85
Natural environment, 220
Net sown area, 53,67; irrigated proportion of, 55
Non Drought-prone areas, 28,37,38; talukas, 24
Occupational distribution, 106; structure, 103 ff
Oil extraction industry, 99
Operational holdings, 35
Out-migration, 29
Palalyam systems, 71
Paradoxical trend, 225
Parambikulam-Aliyar Project, 69, 92
Pastrures and grazing lands, 53
Peasant community, 78
Periyar, 74
Poor households, 203; proportion of, 204; categories of, 206
Population census ,139
Positivist theory, 3-4
Poverty and inequality, 197 ff, 206; magnitude of, 199; level of development, 197
Private buffer stocks, practice of, 221
Productivity, 7, 88; in relation to land, 171
Programmes, 77, 140
Proletarian cultivators, role of, 118
Proletarianisation, 34; process, 226
Proportions illiterates and Semiliterates, 138
Proxy indicator, level of, 28
Pucca storage facilities, 93
Pumpsets, 83
Quality of housing, 135; life, elitist concern for, 129,130,131,223,224
Rentiers, 206
Rivers: Amaravathi, 69; Bhavani, 66, 69,99; Kaveri, 69; Nayyal, 69
Rural economy, caste structure of, 109; diversification of, 30-31
Rural industry, impact of, 123,180; structure and changes environment, 224
School going children in rural industry, sheep hasbandry, 80
Sirukinar village, 97
Structure of Rural economy, indicators of, 101
Technocratic strategy,230
Technological advance, 147
Tenancy, 62,73; incidence of, 61; reforms, 72
Tenure system, 71
Thread-reeling, 82
Tiller's Day (1.4.1957), 63
Tisupur, 94

Tobacco cultivation, 93
Toddy-tappers-cum-agricultural labourers, 94
Tractors, 38; and drought animals, 70
Traditionally, 96
Traditional bondage relationships loosening of, 124; combination of medern practices, 40; disaster survival practices, 221; patron client relations, 226; patronage, absence of, 124; peasant castes, role of, 109
Tumkur district, 132
Tungabhadra high level canal, 55
Uncultivated land, impact on, 172
Urbanisation, 30; extent of, 30
Vadakalur village, 98
Vaddars community, 82
Vijayanagara, 76
Village economy, infrastructure of, 87, 141; rural industry, 13; types of, 11 ff, 101; viability of, 131; analysis of, 204 ff
Water potential 69; inter basin transfer of, 2; weavers conference in 1957, 89; Co-operative society, 83,90
Weaving and dyeing, 89,96
Wells, irrigation, 60,78,97
Wet and dry regions, 147
While collar class, 133
Women's and Children Welfare Assciation, 83
Workforce in allied agricultural activities, proportion of, 30
Working and breedable, 61
Zamindari system, 5,219